Richard Shaw
Instructor's Resource Manual with Transparency Masters and Video Guide

Consumer Behavior
THIRD EDITION

Michael R. Solomon

PRENTICE HALL Englewood Cliffs, N.J, 07632

Production manager: Lisa Friedrichs
Acquisitions editor: David Borkowsky
Associate editor: Melissa Steffens
Manufacturing buyer: Ken Clinton

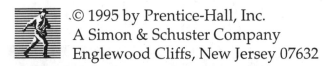

© 1995 by Prentice-Hall, Inc.
A Simon & Schuster Company
Englewood Cliffs, New Jersey 07632

Printed in the United States of America

10   9   8   7   6   5   4   3   2   1

ISBN 0-13-367269-7

Prentice-Hall International (UK) Limited, *London*
Prentice-Hall of Australia Pty. Limited, *Sydney*
Prentice-Hall Canada Inc., *Toronto*
Prentice-Hall Hispanoamericana, S.A., *Mexico*
Prentice-Hall of India Private Limited, *New Delhi*
Prentice-Hall of Japan, Inc., *Tokyo*
Simon & Schuster Asia Pte. Ltd., *Singapore*
Editora Prentice-Hall do Brasil, Ltda., *Rio de Janeiro*

TABLE OF CONTENTS

ABC Video User's Guide

Commentaries on Simmons Connection Exercises

Transparency Masters

PREFACE

This manual accompanies Michael R. Solomon's *Consumer Behavior: Buying, Having, and Being,* Third Edition. It is designed to help you teach core concepts and generate class discussion about consumer behavior.

Your manual is divided into six major parts:
- Lecture Notes
- Field Project Ideas
- Consumer Behavior Challenge
- ABC News Video Guide
- Commentaries on Simmons Connection Exercises
- Transparency Masters

The Lecture Notes portion of the manual contains the following information for each chapter: (1) a chapter summary and (2) lecture/discussion ideas. Included in the Lecture/Discussion Ideas section, you will find:

(a) an outline of the text material in bold print,

(b) brief explanations or examples of the concepts in the outline in standard print,

(c) reference to the proper color transparency and/or transparency master that corresponds to the text material in bold, italicized print,

(d) Real World Applications that consist of additional pertinent examples from the literature not included in the text are separated in boxes with the icon (☯), and

(e) Discussion Topics that suggest possible questions that will help your students personalize the concepts are provided in italics.

Second, a number of Field Project Ideas are presented. In order to enliven the class and to get some students specifically involved in the material to be covered during a particular class period, you could assign field projects to be presented in class by a few students either individually or as a group. Some of these field projects work best as individual projects, some make good group projects and others can be used either way.

Third, possible solutions are provided to the Consumer Behavior Challenge questions that are included in the text. These solutions are by no means complete but are designed to give instructors a starting point during class discussions. In covering these questions, you might want the students to form teams consisting of three to five students and assign each team one question to prepare. Each team could be given two or three minutes of class time to prepare an answer to a Consumer Behavior Challenge question and then share their ideas with the class. This technique tends to make for better discussions and students learn the value of team work. Many of the Consumer Behavior Challenge teaching notes were prepared by Pamela Kiecker of Texas Tech University.

Fourth, the ABC News Connection Video User's Guide was prepared by author Michael R. Solomon. It contains a brief summary of each chapter video, the running time of the video, and suggested discussion questions. All of the information in the ABC News Video Guide is intended to help you use the ABC videotapes to maximum effectiveness.

Fifth, possible solutions to the problems posed in the Simmons Connection Exercises are included. This feature allows the student to analyze the same data used by marketing professionals while studying the actual consumption patterns of different consumer segments. Data files have been specifically selected to accompany end of the chapter exercises for 10 chapters. These exercises were created by Basil Englis of Rutgers University.

Lastly, a series of transparency masters are included that correspond with the material covered in the text. In most chapters you have between 6 to 12 possible transparency masters available for your use. These transparency masters which feature an all graphic format and are designed for increased visibility and ease of use were created by Lewis Hershey, Hershey Consulting Services. He also created the color transparencies.

Preceding the lecture portion of the manual you will find a sample syllabus for both a 15 week semester and a 10 week quarter course. The syllabus contains a course overview, statement of course objectives, and a class schedule. Following the syllabus is a description of optional term projects for either individual or team work. These active learning exercises are designed to get the student to think about how course concepts are implemented in marketing strategies in the real world. Two possible evaluation forms for a student's oral or written work are also included.

I am grateful to Michael Solomon for giving me the opportunity to assemble this Instructor's Manual. Thanks also to Karen Misler for her ideas and guidance throughout the entire project, to Karen Anderson for a great job of copyediting, to Fredric Kropp of the University of Oregon and Dana Lascu of the University of Richmond for reading and offering suggestions on the manuscript, to my Dean, Bob Clark, for his encouragement and prodding. A special thanks to all my students over the past thirty-three years who helped me learn by letting me try out new techniques and ideas on them. Most of all, thanks to my wife, Daffy, (who earned that name when she married me), and my kids, Richard, John and Shannon, who teach me more about consumer behavior daily.

If you have ideas or suggestions that you would be willing to share, you can reach me by mail at Rockhurst College, 1100 Rockhurst Road, Kansas City, MO 64110, by e-mail at IN%"rshaw@vax1.rockhurst.edu" or by FAX at (816) 926-4650.

Richard D. Shaw
Rockhurst College

SAMPLE COURSE SYLLABUS, SEMESTER SYSTEM

Consumer Behavior

Required Text: Michael R. Solomon, *Consumer Behavior: Buying, Having, and Being,* 3rd Edition. Englewood Cliffs, NJ: Prentice-Hall, 1996.

Course Overview: Consumer behavior is one of the most exciting areas in the study of marketing. Every day, all around us, the use of various media to inform, persuade, and influence our purchase decisions compete with other stimuli for our attention--and our hard-earned money! In studying consumer behavior, you will learn how marketers identify and exploit these sources of influence--from learning how we think and process information to how our relationships with others, even our dreams and aspirations, help shape our product choices and purchase decisions.

Course Objectives: The study of consumer behavior is intended to acquaint you with both what it means to be a consumer in a market-oriented society and what, as a marketer, you need to know to understand the role of meeting the consumer's needs in the development of marketing strategy. Accordingly, you will be asked to:

Learn the key terms, definitions, and concepts used in the field.

Identify and discuss the major ideas and processes that characterize the consumer behavior field.

Prepare field projects that personalize the material in the text.

Complete a term-length project that demonstrates both your working knowledge and analytical skills in assessing the consumer behavior process.

Engage in your own consumer behavior with an increased self-consciousness of the forces at work, both internally and externally, whenever you make a purchase.

Class Schedule

Date	Topic	Reading
Date	**Topic**	**Reading**
Week 1	Introduction to Consumer Behavior	Chapter 1
Week 2	Perception Learning and Memory **Field Project Assignments**	Chapter 2 Chapter 3
Week 3	Motivation and Involvement Attitudes **Term Project Assignments: Sign-up**	Chapter 4 Chapter 5
Week 4	Attitude Change and Persuasive Communication **Test #1**	Chapter 6 **Chapters 1-6**
Week 5	The Self	Chapter 7
Week 6	Individual Decision Making	Chapter 8
Week 7	The Purchase Situation, Postpurchase Evaluation, and Product Disposal **Hand in Progress Report on Term Project**	Chapter 9
Week 8	Group Influence, Opinion Leadership, and Diffusion of Innovations **Test #2**	Chapter 10 **Chapters 7-11**
Week 9	Organizational and Household Decision Making	Chapter 11
Week 10	Income and Social Class **Hand in Progress Report on Term Project**	Chapter 12
Week 11	Ethnic, Racial, and Religious Subcultures	Chapter 13
Week 12	Age Subculture **Test #3**	Chapter 14 **Chapters 12-14**

| Week 13 | Cultural Influences on Consumer Behavior | Chapter 15 |

| Week 14 | Lifestyles and Global Culture | Chapter 16 |
| | **Term Projects Due** | |

Week 15	Sacred and Profane Consumption: Cultural Trends	Chapter 17
	and Ethical Issues in Consumer Behavior	
	Test #4	**Chapters 15-17**

SAMPLE COURSE SYLLABUS, QUARTER SYSTEM

Class Schedule

Date	**Topic**	**Reading**
Week 1	Introduction to Consumer Behavior	Chapter 1
	Perception	Chapter 2
	Field Project Assignments	
Week 2	Learning and Memory	Chapter 3
	Motivation and Involvement	Chapter 4
	Attitudes	Chapter 5
	Term Project Assignments: Sign-up	
Week 3	Attitude Change and Persuasive Communication	Chapter 6
	Test #1	**Chapters 1-6**
Week 4	The Self	Chapter 7
	Individual Decision Making	Chapter 8
Week 5	The Purchase Situation, Postpurchase Evaluation,	Chapter 9
	and Product Disposal	
	Group Influence, Opinion Leadership, and Diffusion	Chapter 10
	of Innovations	
	Hand in Progress Report on Term Project	
	Test #2	**Chapters 7-10**
Week 6	Organizational and Household Decision Making	Chapter 11
	Income and Social Class	Chapter 12
Week 7	Ethnic, Racial and Religious Subcultures	Chapter 13
	Hand in Progress Report on Term Project	

| Week 8 | Age Subculture | Chapter 14 |
| | **Test #3** | **Chapters 11-14** |

Week 9	Cultural Influences on Consumer Behavior	Chapter 15
	Lifestyles and Global Culture	Chapter 16
	Term Projects Due	

Week 10	Sacred and Profane Consumption: Cultural Trends	Chapter 17
	and Ethical Issues in Consumer Behavior	
	Test #4	**Chapters 15-17**

TERM PROJECTS

The following sample term projects for individuals and groups are designed to provide some active learning experiences to accompany in-class lectures and discussion and out-of class readings. You may wish to choose one or more projects to assign, allow students to choose a project from the ideas below, or replace these samples with ideas of your own. If you have used projects before, you know that in this course students respond very positively to these kinds of exercises. If you have not used projects before or are new to teaching the course, you will find that consumer behavior projects animate the course content substantially by linking it in the students' minds in a heuristic process of active learning. They are also a lot of fun.

The sample course syllabus provides suggested due dates for deadlines on student projects to ensure term-length work by all students. The deadlines assume that you are either using individual or group projects as the single required project or that you are piggy-backing the deadlines for both individual and group projects.

Individual Projects

1. **John Smith: Consumer Advocate**

Each student picks a product or product category to research for the semester. During the semester, the students investigate the product, the competition, the manufacturer, and the retail/service outlet on the way to becoming an "expert shopper" capable of providing advice as a consumer advocate. Students should be encouraged to shop and research products of high personal relevance: cars, VCRs, stereos--and use *Consumer Reports* as a start for their research. Presentation format and grade option include: research paper 5-10 pages; in class presentations w/paper; video "report from the field" presenting on-site or in-store where possible.

2.   Images of Women in Advertising

How women are depicted in advertisements says a lot about how society, advertisers, and various target markets think about women. Even ads for *Ms* magazine sometimes show women as sex objects. As a term project, have students select examples of women in advertisements shown in the following roles: Sex object, "dumb blonde," submissive, housewife, mother, helpless, professional, powerful, self-actualized, hedonic consumer (or substitute your own categories). For the project, the students should write a brief description of what defines each category of ad and what those categories imply about women in general and the target markets at whom they are aimed. Finally, the project should conclude with a section on the ethics of each category which explores the social impact of each category of women in advertising selected in the project. All written work should include references of both marketing sources and to other scholarly work to support both the definitions of the categories and the critical evaluations of their social impact.

3.   Class Report: Article from the Academic Literature

Undergraduate version:

Have students pick an article from a list provided by the instructor and approved for each student. The student should prepare an abstract to hand-in, and a short in-class presentation for the main points of the article prior to discussion. Depending on the size of the class, you may wish to group thematic articles together to be discussed in class on the same day. Division for thematic discussion, depending again on class size and time limitations can either be by textbook section or by chapter. Planning a discussion/student presentation day into the syllabus is an option provided in the instructor's manual for this exercise. You may wish to use the citations in the Endnotes in this Instructor's Manual as a starting point for selecting a list of articles to read, or simply have students choose from the text citation an article to report on.

Graduate version:

Using the same format as above, the abstract should be made available to the entire class as part of an exam study guide. In addition to the abstract, students should prepare a single page summary critiquing the article and place it into the research context by providing a 5 item (minimum) bibliography of related articles. Encourage students to maintain the abstracts to all articles as part of their study materials for comprehensive or general exams.

4.   The Consumer Behavior Notebook

The project builds on the concept of the anthropologist's fieldwork diary and is particularly useful if you want your students to get a feeling for emic approaches to interpretive consumer behavior study. The notebook should consist of dated entries describing promotional campaigns that use strategies discussed in the text such as subcultural segmentation, psychographic segmentation, appeals to aspirational groups, and is especially well suited for examining appeals to symbolic dimensions of consumer behavior. Each entry should describe the ad or campaign in detail, analyze it according to pre-stated criteria, and draw some conclusions based upon the analysis. Conclusions should specifically address the analytical criteria. For example, subcultural segmentation can be analyzed both in terms of media usage appropriate for the target market and the ethical issues involved in the segmentation process (such as the Philip Morris controversy surrounding the targeting of black urban males for their Uptown brand of menthol cigarettes). Whenever possible, affordable, or feasible, students should include a copy of the ad or campaign. For print media this will be relatively easy but videotaping of television ads or audiotaping of radio spots should also be encouraged whenever possible. You should stagger sections of the project deadlines at about 1/3 intervals for your semester or quarter to ensure that students will work on the notebook throughout the term.

Group Projects

The potential group term projects described below are designed for groups of 3-5 students. Although varying group size may be desirable, depending upon the make-up of your student body and particular class, having more than 5 students per group can become something of a logistical problem.

1.   Measuring Means-Ends Chains

Groups that choose this option (or are assigned to it) should divide the roles and responsibilities for moderating a focus group discussion aimed at getting a groups means-end chain measure for a particular product category. The trick is determining how to combine the information into a means-end chain. You can either assign figuring out how to do this as part of the task or provide hints. For example, the group can keep a running chain or develop one from the group answers and then ask the focus group as a whole to verify and approve the chain. Roles for group members include diagramming, moderating the focus group, and recording verbatim. For this exercise, it is useful as a term project to have the group select more than one focus group of a convenience sample from 3 different subcultural market segments and develop means-end chains for each segment for the same product category. If your university does not have a sufficiently diverse student body for subcultural segmentation, consider using lifestyle segments for drawing focus groups. This exercise should follow a format much like the following:

Beginning:

As a focus group, we want you to share with us your answers to how you go about making a decision for a given product category. Please answer how you as an individual consumer make decisions on the questions we pose to you. Later, as a group, you will have a chance to verify a diagram of your decision-making processes.

Then ask:

Assume that you were in the market for _____ (fill in product category).

What factors do you consider when you are deciding what brand of _____ to buy for yourself?

Then . . .

What two factors are the most important to you in making your decision?

Then, do a laddering for each of the factors mentioned by the consumer. Either of the following formats should work:

Why is _____ important to you?

OR

What does _____ give you?

Continue this process until the focus group cannot go on. Be sure to ask a separate series of laddering questions for each of the two factors elicited. You may want to limit the number of combinations of factors to a manageable number that the focus group as a whole agrees are most relevant. After identifying a rough laddering process, sketch the main steps in the ladder and ask the focus group to verify it for you. Adjust the sketch accordingly.

Turn in the following:

The schematic diagrams of the means-ends chains for each subcultural group.

A perceptual map of the factors of importance as identified by each group.

2. **Modeling and Consumer Behavior**

The purpose of this group project is to have the students generate storyboards on a number of ads that utilize modeling or vicarious learning. During the course of the semester, the groups should videotape at least 5 commercials for different products and product categories that use some form of modeling in the commercial. (A variation might involve having students choose different products in the same product category.) Also modeling of unrealistic lifestyles associated with product usage may be especially interesting (e.g., almost any beer ad). Items the student should turn in include:

- Story boards for each ad in the project. The storyboards should include identification of the following elements:

  - Sound effects
  - Characters
  - Dialogue
  - Description of the action
  - Theme

- Videotape with all the ads used in the project on it.

- A short critical analysis of any ethical dimensions and issues that are raised in the ad.

3.   Reference Group Influences and Campus Consumer Behavior

This project is designed to make the students aware of the use of marketing strategies utilizing reference group influences on your campus. The student group will become something of a "reference group expert" for marketers seeking access to your university's student market. The group must first identify three existing marketing strategies that use different reference group appeals (i.e., informational, utilitarian, and value expressive) in on-campus advertising. The project then involves identifying how the marketing strategy is implemented to reach the target markets on campus. The completed project that is turned in for class credit should consist of:

A description of the marketing strategies your group has selected for review.

An explanation of how these strategies use informational, utilitarian, or value-expressive reference group influence to promote their products.

An analysis (which may include primary research undertaken by the group) of the effectiveness of each strategy.

An assessment of the strategic needs for each product supported by the selected campaigns. In other words, over the next one to five years, do these companies need to do anything different? Will their strategic choices need to be changed? Why or why not?

5. Ask an energetic student to collect a few icons such as Betty Crocker, Charley the Tuna, the Jolly Green Giant, the Morton Salt Girl, Aunt Jemima, or Frito Bandito (you'll have to search the archives to find this one). The student should show how the icons changed over time. If the icons have been modified, was this the result of the social environment or that it was just time for a change?

6. Here's a chance for a student to start some networking. Have the individual interview a business person and ask this person to define consumer behavior. Encourage the student to ask how the business person believes greater knowledge of consumer behavior could help in job performance. See if the student can relate the responses given to the marketing concept and/or relationship marketing. If so, how?

7. Have someone tell the class about a buying experience where post-purchase outcomes had a significant influence on his or her future purchase behavior. The purchase experience can either be in the purchase of a good or service or the experience with a particular organization.

8. Ask a student to interview a peer about the variables thought to be important influences on consumer behavior in the purchase of a specific product (e.g. car, stereo, house, vacation, camera, etc.).   Ask them to do the same for an older person and compare and contrast the responses.

Group Assignments

9. Select a product of interest to your students (e.g., a car, entertainment center, vacation spot, movie, sporting event) and have them make a list of what they consider to be the product's determinant attributes (see chapter or glossary for definition). Compare and contrast the attributes listed by the women and by the men to see how they vary. (See Consumer Challenge Question # 9)

Individual or Group Assignments

10. Many student organizations and activities even varsity teams seem to have a hard time attracting interest in or support for their activity. Have a student or a group select an organization and explain to the class how it could achieve its goals with an understanding of consumer behavior. Ask for specific recommendations.

11. Have a student or group of students obtain political campaign literature, particularly samples that were professionally prepared, for discussion it in the context of consumer behavior. Encourage students to look at all of the aspects of marketing mix and to discuss the appeal that the literature has to specific target markets.

12. Ask two or three students to bring several product or service advertisements and comment on how the advertiser is appealing to wants and needs. See if other students can identify additional wants and needs that could be of interest to the advertiser.

13. Ask a couple of students to bring in a number of consumer goods or pictures of them to class and discuss the different roles that are played by family members in the purchase process of these goods. Suggest that students discuss whether the components of the marketing mix are directed at the individuals playing these roles.

14. Have a student or group of students collect ads for three different brands in an identical product category (e.g. detergent, cars, toothpaste, etc.). Then have them report on the segmentation variables, target markets, and product attributes emphasized in each ad.

15. Have a group of students write down a list of products or services that are purchased frequently by their friends or colleagues. See if they think that the use of these products helps to create bonding.   Discuss whether the rest of the class agrees with the conclusions of the presenters.

16. Assign a student or a group to find an example of a recent product, service, or program that was a failure. *Business Week, U.S.A. Today, The Wall Street Journal, Fortune, Forbes* or some other marketing publications are excellent sources. Have students explain to the class how knowledge of consumer behavior, or the lack of it, could have contributed to the success or failure of the effort.

17. Instead, you could have the students take the positive approach and have them identify an example of a recent product, service, or program which has been successful. The same marketing publications are great sources.   Ask students to suggest how knowledge of consumer behavior more than likely contributed to the successful effort.

18. Send students to collect advertisements for five different brands of the same product. Ask them to report on the likely segmentation variables, target markets, and positioning strategies that emphasize product attributes in their ads. (See Consumer Challenge Question # 10)

CONSUMER BEHAVIOR CHALLENGE

1. This chapter states that people play different roles and that their consumption behaviors may differ depending on the particular role they are playing. State whether you agree or disagree with this perspective, giving examples from your personal life.

Most students will be able to identify the different roles that individuals play at different times, so agreement should be almost universal. After agreeing with this notion, the student will be more likely to accept the idea that consumption behavior is intimately tied with the role itself. The goal of this exercise is to make the student aware that consumption helps to define the roles consumers play and is a central part of those roles. For example, many family social occasions are accompanied by food and drink, and the consumption of these goods act as a shared bond that the group uses to define membership in that group. Another example is the styles of clothing worn by young people to define their group membership.

2. Some researchers believe that the field of consumer behavior should be a pure, rather than an applied, science. That is, research issues should be framed in terms of their scientific interest rather than their applicability to immediate marketing problems. Give your views on this issue.

Instead of viewing research in an either-or framework, i.e., that consumer behavior research must be either pure scientific research or applied knowledge, the student should be encouraged to view it as both. Much research is done on a "knowledge for knowledge sake" basis, but the field of consumer behavior has the potential to make a significant contribution to how the makers of goods and services can best reach the consumer. For example, business firms are able to take the knowledge developed in a pure science research setting and apply it to their marketing efforts by utilizing the results of studies that investigate how consumers process advertising messages. Areas such as space exploration have been able to use pure science research and apply their finding to immediate problems. Consumer behavior knowledge has this same quality.

3. Name some products or services that are widely used by your social group. State whether you agree or disagree with the notion that these products help to form the group bonds, supporting your argument with examples from your list of products used by the group.

Discussion of this question is similar to that pertaining to the first question. In both cases, the focus is on whether consumption behavior has a wider meaning--that of group bonding or identification. The actual products used are not the most important aspect of this discussion. Instead, the focus should be on consumption behavior as more than the satisfying of primary (basic/physiological) needs. It is assumed that most students will agree that consumption has meaning beyond satisfying primary needs. However, differences will be found in (1) the situations in which consumption takes on this additional meaning, (2) the products that do so, and (3) the form of the broadened meaning. Encourage students to examine the products that bring forth meaning, as well as their consideration as to why this phenomenon occurs.

4. Although demographic information on large numbers of consumers is used in many marketing contexts, some people believe that the sale of data on customers' incomes, buying habits, and so on, constitutes an invasion of privacy and should be stopped. Comment on the issue from both a consumer's and a marketer's point of view.

As with many questions of this type there are few objectively right or wrong answers. The goal is, of course, to make the student think about the issues and to be able to critically examine the arguments on both sides. Regardless of the student's specific comments on this issue, the discussion should acknowledge the legitimate interest of both parties and the possibility of a compromise suitable to both groups. This discussion could draw upon the student's personal experiences with receiving mail that obviously came as a result of information about the student being sold to a company that compiles lists. Ask the student about his or her reactions to it and encourage the student to make a special attempt to discuss the advantages and disadvantages to both the direct marketer and potential buyer.

5. List the three stages in the consumption process. Describe the issues that you consider in each of these stages when you made a recent important purchase.

Students can use the material presented in Figure 1-1. The three stages in the consumption process shown are (1) prepurchase, (2) purchase, and (3) post purchase. The student selected should develop fairly unique sets of issues related to each of these phases based on the different products and purchases situation. Figure 1-1 provides a list of issues for each stage from both the consumer's and marketer's perspectives.

6. State the differences between the positivist and interpretivist approaches to consumer research. For each type of inquiry, give examples of product dimensions that would be more usefully explored using that type of research over the other.

The differences between positivism and interpretivism, according to the text, are in their views on (1) the utility of reason towards solving problems, (2) the proper role of technology, and (3) the form of reality. Allowing for these differences, positivism would be more useful than interpretivism in exploring utilitarian product functions, i.e. what the product does and how well it does it. Alternately, interpretivism, with its inclusion of subjective aspects of products, would be more appropriate than positivism when examining the meaning of product dimensions to consumers, the role played by products in individuals' self-definition, and/or cultural and social factors that influence purchase and use. Note that the appropriate areas of research for the two views have considerable overlap.

7. What aspects of consumer behavior are likely to be of interest to a financial planner? To a university administrator? To a graphic arts designer? To a social worker in a government agency? To a nursing instructor?

The listing of the aspects of consumer behavior corresponding to these positions should reflect the particular aspects of each position. For example, a financial planner depends on

14

consumers' willingness to postpone consumption in order to save and invest money to have more later. A social worker must be concerned about people's attitudes towards government, social work in general, the role of government in people's lives. What each of these positions share, and what should underlie the discussion, is their connection to the consumption process, and the fact that consumers will themselves have different needs and wants associated with their consumption. Each of the listed parties would attempt to influence consumers by using a different aspect of consumption, and these differences need to be discussed and analyzed.

8. Critics of targeted marketing strategies argue that this practice is discriminatory and unfair, especially if such a strategy encourages a group of people to buy a product that may be injurious to them or that they cannot afford. On the other hand, the Association of National Advertisers argues that banning targeted marketing constitutes censorship and is thus a violation of the First Amendment. What are your views regarding both sides of this issue?

Discussion of this question closely parallels discussion of Question 4. It is important to guide discussion to the legitimate interests on both sides. However, in this situation the discussion should also examine the legitimacy of each side's basic point. For what groups should target marketing not be allowed? Or under what specific circumstances should target marketing be allowed? Is the argument that target marketing unduly influences those who cannot resist its appeal reasonable? Is the counter-argument that banishing target marketing amounts to censorship and is unconstitutional equally specious? Discussion should initially focus on the validity of each argument, and then evolve toward a compromise that will protect target marketing efforts while recognizing the needs of society..

9. Select a product and brand that you use frequently, and make a list of what you consider to be the brand's determinant attributes. Without revealing your list, ask a friend who is approximately the same age but of the opposite sex to make a similar list for the same product (although the brand may be different). Compare and contrast the identified attributes and report your findings.

Listing a brand's or product's determinant attributes will necessarily be a personal exercise. For example, why someone buys a particular brand toothpaste could depend on their age, family situation, dentist, history of oral hygiene, what their parents bought, packaging tooth paste, where they shop, what they have coupons for, advertising themes, etc. Of the greatest interest in this exercise would be differences between the sexes as to their determinant attributes. (There is a considerable body of research suggesting that males and females differ in their choice behavior). Depending on the brand/product, male and female student will make choices based on different criteria. It could be expected that many students have not thought about the bases they use to make a purchase decision. Making students consciously think about the choices they make should prove enlightening. As an extension, you may want to assign particular products for this exercise in order to highlight the differences between males and females. For example, the attributes of products such as a car, stereo equipment, vacation spot, or a movie are likely to produce significant differences in the weighing of determinant attributes. (Possible Field Project)

10. Collect ads for five different brands of the same product. Report on the likely segmentation variable, target markets, and emphasized product attributes involved in each ad.

Students should enjoy reviewing newspaper and magazine advertisements for this exercise. They likely will report that they are beginning to look at and listen to all types of advertising differently. (Possible Field Project)

ENDNOTES

1 Jonathan Berry, "Database Marketing," *Business Week* (September 5, 1994): 56 (7).

2 Cyndee Miller, "Privacy Vs. Direct Marketing," *Marketing News*, March 1, 1993: 1 (3).

3 John McCormick and Marc Levinson, "The Supply Police," *Newsweek*, February 15, 1993: 48 (2).

4 Andrew Pollack, "Japan Debates Broader Power for Consumers," *The New York Times*, March 8, 1993: A1 (2).

5 Laurel A. Hudson and Julie L. Ozanne, "Alternative Ways of Seeking Knowledge in Consumer Research," *Journal of Consumer Research* 14 (March 1988): 508 21, for a more complete discussion of these approaches.

6 For a more complete description, see Yvonna S. Lincoln and Egon G. Guba, *Naturalistic Inquiry* (Beverly Hills, Calif.: Sage, 1985).

7 For an excellent overview of critical theory, see Jeff B. Murray and Julie L. Ozanne, "The Critical Imagination: Emancipatory Interests in Consumer Research," *Journal of Consumer Research* 18 (September 1991): 192-94.

8 Cyndee Miller, "Sometimes a Researcher Has No Choice But to Hang Out in a Bar," *Marketing News*, January 3, 1994: 16 (2).

9 Harold H. Kassarjian, "Personality and Consumer Behavior: A Review," *Journal of Marketing Research* 8 (November 1971): 409-18.

10 Wendy Gordon and Roy Langmaid, *Qualitative Market Research* (Hants, England: Gower, 1988).

11 Harold Kassarjian, "Personality and Consumer Behavior: A Review," *Journal of Marketing Research* 8 (November 1971): 409-18.

12 For a discussion of these techniques, see Ruth Ann Smith and David S. Lux, "Historical Method in Consumer Research: Developing Causal Explanations of Change," *Journal of Consumer Research* 19 (March 1993): 595-610.

13 "The Dynamics of Scanner Marketing," A Supplement to *Promo* and *Progressive Grocer* Magazines, 1994.

14 William M. Bulkeley, "If Clinton Orders Double Cheese and All the Toppings, It's a Crisis," *The Wall Street Journal*, December 7, 1993, B1.

[15] David A. Aaker and George S. Day, *Marketing Research*, 4th ed. (New York: John Wiley & Sons, 1990).

[16] J. Eugene Webb, Donald T. Campbell, Richard D. Schwartz, and Lee Sechrest, Unobtrusive Measures: Nonreactive Research in the Social Sciences (Chicago: Rand McNally, 1966); R.A. Gould and P.B. Potter, "Use-Lives of Automobiles in America: A Preliminary Archaeological View," in Toward an Ethnoarchaeology of Modern America, ed. R.A. Gould (Providence, R.I.: Brown University, Department of Anthropology, Research Papers in Anthropology, 1984), 4.

Instructor's Notes:

18

FIELD PROJECT IDEAS

Individual Assignments

*1. Some people find scent strips inserted in magazines to be annoying. Have a student find examples of these strips in magazines and then interview a few people to determine their reactions to scent strips. Are they positive or negative? Do the people who were interviewed think that this type of advertising will have any effect on what products a person will buy? Record their remarks.

2. Ask a student to find three ads that contain symbolism. examine the symbols, and discuss the meaning they convey. Then encourage the student to identify the different types of signs used in the ads and the product qualities being communicated by each.

3. Here is a field project that students always like. Have a student photocopy a collection of brand/product symbols and then have this student quiz fellow classmates to see if they can recognize the product or company. This will show students how effective symbols are and how much involuntary learning has taken place in their life. You might give a reward to the student who had the **most** correct responses and the **least** correct.

4. Have a student bring to class several brands of well-known products and their "look-a-like" counterparts. (The slick ads in the Sunday paper are often a good source of pictures of these products if the student can't physically bring in the real thing.) Then have the student compare the shared physical attributes of these products. What are some of the psychological attributes of pricing and packaging?   Are there any legal or ethical implications for the producers of these products?

5. Ask a student to visit a toy store and take note of the various types of toys that are displayed. Then have the student categorize these toys on the basis of age, sex, socioeconomic class, and educational level. Have them discuss how manufacturers and retailers use these attributes to appeal to potential customers.

6. Here is a tough assignment for an undergraduate. Ask a student to spend an afternoon watching a popular soap opera or an evening watching a favorite television show. Ask them to be particularly observant of the various products and services that are used as props during the show. Do these products or services have any symbolic value? Are they used to help develop the plot? How?

7. Have a student visit two different types of restaurants and make a note of how each establishment appeals to the five senses. How are they the same? How are they different?

8. Ask a student to bring in three ads from a favorite magazine. Have the student identify examples of the stimulus factors that the advertiser used to capture attention. What are some of the other stimuli that could have been chosen to accomplish the same thing?

9. Have a student interview 3-5 male and 3-5 female friends regarding their perceptions of both men's and women's fragrances. Then ask the student to construct a perceptual map for each set of products.   Based on the map of perfumes, are there any areas that are not adequately served by current offerings? What (if any) gender differences surfaced regarding both the relevant dimensions used by raters and the placement of specific brands along these dimensions? (See Consumer Challenge Question #2)

10. Instruct a student to find one ad that is rich in symbolism and perform a semiotic analysis of it. Have the student identify each type of sign used in the ad and the product qualities being communicated by it. Then have him or her comment on the effectiveness of the signs that are used to communicate the intended message. (See Consumer Challenge Question #6)

11. Ask the student to use magazines archived in the library to track the packaging of a specific brand over time. Find an example of gradual changes in package design that may have been below the JND. (See Consumer Challenge Question #7)

12. Have a student look through a current magazine, select one ad that captures their attention over the others, and identify the reasons why. (See Consumer Challenge Question #9)

13. Have a student find ads that utilize the techniques of contrast and novelty. Let the student give an opinion of the effectiveness of each ad and whether the technique is likely to be appropriate for the consumers targeted by the ad.   (See Consumer Challenge Question #10)

Group Assignments

14. Have three or four students develop ten brand names for a new (a) hamburger, (b) hair care center, (c) car, or (d) a product of their choice. Then test these names on the class to capture their reaction. Have the project leaders describe the process they went through to choose the names.

15. Either you or a group of students could collect a set of current ads for one type of product (e.g., personal computers, perfumes, laundry detergents or athletic shoes) from magazines. Bring these ads to class and have the students analyze the colors used in them. Students should describe the images conveyed by different colors, and try to identify any consistency across brands in terms of the colors used in product packaging or other aspects of the ads. (See Consumer Challenge Question #8)

Individual or Group Assignments

16. Have the students bring in three food products ads which present the products in a particular scene or setting. Ask them to report on the symbols used in the setting and how they believe the marketers intended them to be interpreted relative to the food product. Do they think the ads are effective?

17. Ask students to bring in a collection of sexually-oriented ads to stimulate discussion of the different techniques and types of products that use sexual themes in their ads. Did they find more nudity magazines targeted toward men or women? See if they think these ads are effective. What are the ethical issues?

18. Have your students look for several examples of magazine advertisements that use sexual themes or illustrations which seem to capture the reader's attention or in some way influence their perceptual process. Are these methods appropriate for the target market the advertiser is trying to reach?

19. Ask students to choose any two restaurants or pubs that are frequented by friends. Have them measure their image profiles by asking ten fellow students or friends to write a list of descriptive words that apply to each restaurant or pub. It will be easier for the subjects if the students provided the subjects with a list of potential descriptions. What conclusions can be drawn from this data?

CONSUMER BEHAVIOR CHALLENGE

1. Many studies have shown that our sensory detection abilities decline as we grow older. Discuss the implications of the absolute threshold for marketers attempting to appeal to the elderly.

It would be wise to begin this exercise by identifying the particular senses and the ways in which they decline the consumer gets older. Once this has been done, students should brainstorm to develop a list of the ways that a message may not be received or interpreted correctly. Students might be encouraged to develop a matrix, placing the senses down the left-hand side and forms of communication across the top. The matrix then should be filled in with descriptions of how communications may fail and how these failures could be avoided. For example, print advertisements aimed at an older audience could use larger type, or radio and television ads could decrease the pace of information presented and slightly increase the volume to allow older recipients to more fully process the information. Retail store and restaurants can increase lighting.

2. Interview 3-5 male and 3-5 female friends regarding their perceptions of both men's and women's fragrances. Construct a perceptual map for each set of products. Based on your map of perfumes, do you see any areas that are not adequately served by current offerings? What (if any) gender differences did you obtain regarding both the relevant dimensions used by raters and the placement of specific brands along these dimensions?

Have the students start this project by listing a number of descriptive words that are or could be used when positioning perfumes in the market place. Have them ask the respondents to position various perfumes on the map according their impressions of the perfumes selected. (Possible Field Project)

3. Assuming that some forms of subliminal persuasion may have the desired effect of influencing consumers, do you think the use of these techniques is ethical?

Many students will consider the use of subliminal persuasion to be unethical. Accordingly, a discussion could focus on why subliminal messages are undesirable. An interesting issue to raise may be how, or even if, subliminal persuasion differs from other advertising consumers are exposed to everyday. Once these differences have been noted, the discussion could turn toward analyzing the reasons why individuals react negatively to subliminal persuasion. Students who believe the use of these techniques is ethical should be encouraged to develop their arguments so that those representing each side of the argument might see the opposing view. Regardless of the position adopted by the majority of student, be prepared to stimulate discussion by developing an argument in favor of the use of subliminal messages. This argument could center on the idea that subliminal persuasion might result in less "clutter." Arguing for its effectiveness, the amount of advertising could decrease overall.

4. Assume that you are a consultant for a marketer who wants to design a package for a new premium chocolate bar targeted to an affluent market. What recommendations would you provide in terms of such package elements as color, symbolism, and graphic design? Give the reasons for your suggestions.

Most students will recognize that the label (package), the weight of the product and the brand name of the product are all combined to communicate the image of the product. In this exercise the students are examining premium product targeted to an affluent market. Obviously, the suggestions developed by students are likely to reflect their own experiences. What needs to be added to the discussion of product labels and names is (1) the colors that will augment the desire premium image, (2) the smell that is associated with candy, (3) the sound of the candy wrapper in your hand, and (4) and the symbolism that may be used to position the product in the consumer's mind. The issue of symbolism may provide the best avenue for discussion, and a broader discussion of how symbols can be used in advertising and promotion would be helpful.

5. Do you believe that marketers have the right to use any or all public spaces to deliver product messages? Where would you draw the line in terms of places and products that should be restricted?

This question needs to split into two parts: (1) whether marketers have the right to use any public spaces, and (2) whether they have the right to use all public spaces. These are the two extremes on the issue, and the students will most likely find themselves somewhere between complete and unlimited access for marketers on one hand, and complete and total ban on the other. A key concept in this discussion is the definition of "public spaces" and, therefore, a common definition should be adopted early in the discussion. To develop their position on this issue, students should be encouraged to list both appropriate and inappropriate places for product messages and offer reasons why each place should be categorized in a particular way. See if they think signs on the highway should be eliminated. If they agree, ask them how they would ever find McDonald's!

6. Find one ad that is rich in symbolism and perform a semiotic analysis of it. Identify each type of sign used in the ad and the product qualities being communicated by each. Comment on the effectiveness of the signs that are used to communicate the intended message.

These types of ads are often found in magazines specifically directed toward women, men, teens, and groups of enthusiasts. Have the students analyze the ad from both the consumer's and the marketer's point of view. (Possible Field Project)

7. Using magazines archived in the library, track the packaging of a specific brand over time. Find an example of gradual changes in package design that may have been below the JND.

You might give a few hints here. For example, Aunt Jemima, the Morton Salt Girl, and Betty Crocker are trademarks that have changed over time and can be found in ads. Package changes include Ivory Soap, Kellogg's Rice Krispies, and Campbell Soup. Students can simply exam automobile ads to see how styles of a particular car has changed over the years; the body is the car's package. (Possible Field Project)

8. Collect a set of current ads for one type of product (e.g., personal computers, perfumes, laundry detergents or athletic shoes) from magazines, and analyze the colors employed. Describe the images conveyed by different colors, and try to identify any consistency across brands in terms of the colors used in product packaging or other aspects of the ads.

See if the students will notice how similar many of the products and brands are in terms of shape, weight, color, and size. (Possible Field Project)

9. Look through a current magazine and select one ad that captures your attention over the others. Give the reasons why.

After students have indicated what the ad caught their attention, probe to see if there are any other reasons. Ask the class if it was struck by any other aspects of the ad. (Possible Field Project)

10. Find ads that utilize the techniques of contrast and novelty. Give your opinion of the effectiveness of each ad and whether the technique is likely to be appropriate for the consumers targeted by the ad.

Opinions will vary here. Some people like novelty in most everything while other want people to be more serious. (Possible Field Project)

ENDNOTES

1 "The Lemon Juice that Wasn't," *Newsweek* (August 2, 1982): 53; Gail Tom, Teresa Barnett, William Lew and odean Selmants, "Cueing the Consumer: The Role of Salient Cues in Consumer Perception." *Journal of Consumer Marketing* 4 (1987) 2: 23-27.

2 Bernice Kanner, *Color Schemes*, New York (April 3, 1989)2: 22.

3 Helen Mundell, "How the Color Mafia Chooses Your Clothes." *American Demographics* (November, 1993) 21 (2).

4 Barnaby J. Feder, "Demographics of the Color Spectrum," *The New York Times* (September 1, 1993): D3.

5 Gerald J. Gorn, Amitava Chattopadhyay and Tracey Yi, "Effects of Color as an Executional Cue in an Ad: It's in the Shade" (February, 1994) Unpublished manuscript, University of British Columbia.

6 Ronald Alsop. "Color Grows more Important in Catching Consumers' Eyes." *Wall Street Journal* (November 29, 1984): 37.

7 Suzanne Oliver, "New Personality." *Forbes* (August 15, 1994).

8 See Marion Tysoe, "What's Wrong with Blue Potatoes?" *Psychology Today* (December, 1985) 6.

9 For one recent example, see Alvin C. Burns, Abhijit Biswas, and Laurie A. Babin, "The Operation of Visual Imagery as a Mediator of Advertising Effects." *Journal of Advertising* XXII (June, 1993)2:71-85.

10 "Ready for Purple Cars?" *Adweek* (January 20, 1992): 20: "Going to the Green." *Advertising Age* (April 11, 1994): 3.

11 Jacqueline Mitchell, "When Mark Mol Makes His Matches, Clients Often Swoon." *The Wall Street Journal* (September 23, 1993): 1 (2).

12 Maroon Tysoe, "What's Wrong with Blue Potatoes?" *Psychology Today* (December 1985)2: 6.

13 Deborah L. Jacobs, "The Titans of Tint make their Picks." *The New York Times* (May 29, 1994) F7.

14 Cynthia Morris, "The Mystery of Fragrance," *Essence* (May 1988) 3:71.

15 James LaRossa. Jr., "Home Fragrances Bloom in Wide Open Field," *Home Textiles* (May 8, 1989) 4: 54.

16 "Memory: It Seems a Whiff of Chocolate Helps." *New York Times* (July 10, 1990).

17 "Environmental Fragrancing: The Muzak of the 90s." *Fragrance Forum* (Fall, 1988); Deborah Toth, "To Relax or Stay Alert: New Mood-Altering Scents," *New York Times* (September 24, 1989): F15.

18 Cyndee Miller. "Interactive Marketing Hits Surrealistic High," *Marketing News* (November 25, 1991): 6.

19 Tim Davis, "Taste Tests: Are the Blind Leading the Blind?" *Beverage World* (April, 1987) 6:42.

20 Quoted by Glenn Collin, "Everything's Coming Up Vanilla" *The New York Times* (June 10, 1994): D1: (2).

21 "Campbell Soups Up Its Old Label." *Sacramento Bee* (April 22, 1994): F1 (2)

22 Timothy E. Moore, "Subliminal Advertising: What You See is What You Get." *Journal of Marketing* 46 (Spring, 1982)" 38-47: Patricia Winters "S-E-X or Pepsi?" *Advertising Age* (August 20, 1990).

23 Wilson Bryan Key, *Subliminal Seduction* (New York: New American Library, Inc.,   1973: Wilson Bryan Key, Media *Sexploitation* (Englewood Cliffs, NJ: Prentice-Hall,   1976); Wilson Bryan Key, *The Clam-Plate Orgy* (Englewood Cliffs, NJ: Prentice-Hall,   1980).

24 See "Blaming Death's Hidden Messages," *Newsweek* (July 30, 1990); 58.

25 L.H. Silverman. "Psychoanalytic Theory: the Reports of My Death Are Greatly Exaggerated." *American Psychologist* 31 (September, 1976); Joel Saegert, "Why Marketing Should Quit Giving Subliminal Advertising the Benefit of the Doubt," *Psychology and Marketing* 4 (Summer, 1987); 107:20.

26 Steven W. Colford, "Feds Set Fund to Ax Outdoor Boards." *Advertising Age* (March 16, 1992) 2: 1.

27 Michael H. Erdelyi, "A New Look at the New Look: Perceptual Defense and Vigilance." *Psychological Review* 81 (1974) 1: 1-25.

28 Robert F. Gilmore and Eugene Secunda, "Zipped TV Commercials Boost Prior Learning." *Journal of Advertising Research* (November/December, 1993): 28-38.

29 Quoted in Stuart Elliott, "When Up is Down. Does it Sell?" *New York Times* (February 21, 1992).

30 T. Alper, "The Interrupted Task Method in Studies of Selective Recall: A Reevaluation of Some Recent Experiments." *Psychological Review* 59 (1952): 71-88.

31 Gail Tom, Teresa Barnett, William Lew, and Jodean Selmants, "Cueing the Consumer: The Role of Salient Cues of Consumer Perception" *Journal of Consumer Marketing* 4 (1987) 2: 23-27; H. White, "Name Change to Rusty Jones Helps Polish Product's Identity," *Advertising Age* 2 (1980) 18: 47-50.

32 David A Ricks, "Products that Crashed the Language Barrier." *Business and Society Review* (Spring, 1983): 46-50.

Instructor's Notes:

36

Chapter 3

Learning and Memory

SUMMARY BULLETS

♦ Learning is a change in behavior that is caused by experience. Learning can occur through simple associations between a stimulus and a response or via a complex series of cognitive activities.

♦ Behavioral learning theories assume that learning occurs as a result of responses to external events. Classical conditioning occurs when a stimulus that naturally elicits a response (an unconditioned stimulus) is paired with another stimulus that does not initially elicit this response. Over time, the second stimulus (the conditioned stimulus) comes to elicit the response as well.

♦ A conditioned response can also extend to other, similar stimuli in a process known as stimulus generalization. This process is the basis for such marketing strategies as licensing and family branding, where a consumer's positive associations with a product are transferred to other contexts.

♦ Operant or instrumental conditioning occurs as the person learns to perform behaviors that produce positive outcomes and avoid those that result in negative outcomes.

♦ While classical conditioning involves the pairing of two stimuli, instrumental learning occurs when reinforcement is delivered following a response to a stimulus.

♦ Reinforcement is positive if a reward is delivered following a response. It is negative if a negative outcome is avoided by not performing a response. Punishment occurs when a response is followed by unpleasant events. Extinction of the behavior will occur if reinforcement is no longer received.

♦ Cognitive learning occurs as the result of mental processes. For example, observational learning takes place when the consumer performs a behavior as a result of seeing someone else performing it and being rewarded for it.

♦ Memory refers to the storage of learned information. The way information is encoded when it is perceived determines how it will be stored in memory.

♦ The memory systems known as sensory memory, short-term memory, and long-term memory each play a role in retaining and processing information from the outside world.

♦ Information is not stored in isolation; it is incorporated into knowledge structures, where it is associated with other related data. The location of product information in associative networks, and the level of abstraction at which it is coded, help to determine when and how this information will be activated at a later time. Some factors that influence the likelihood of retrieval include the level of familiarity with an item, its salience (or prominence) in memory, and whether the information was presented in pictorial or written form.

♦ Products also play a role as memory markers; they are used by consumers to retrieve memories about past experiences (autobiographical memories) and are often valued for their ability to do this. This function also contributes to the use of nostalgia in marketing strategies.

♦ Memory for product information can be measured through either recognition or recall techniques. Consumers are more likely to recognize an advertisement if it is presented to them than to recall one without being given any cues.

LECTURE/DISCUSSION IDEAS

I.   **The Learning Process** -- relatively permanent change in behavior
          incidental learning (unintentional acquisition of knowledge)

(Use TM 3-1 Here)

   A. **Behavioral Learning Theories** -- e.g. black box (stimulus and response)

          1. **Classical Conditioning** -- e.g. Pavlov's dog (ring bell and get food)
(Use Color Transparency 8 Here)
(Use Color Transparency 9 Here)
(Use TM 3-2 Here)

             a. **Repetition** -- repeated exposure to stimulus increases its strength
                e.g. advertising jingles "Coke is it!"

Real World Application
☻ For a recent study that examined the specific effects of different conditioning procedures on subsequent attention to a stimulus, see the Chris Janiszewski and Luk Warlop article.[1]

             b. **Stimulus Generalization** -- similar stimuli evoke similar responses
                   e.g. to consumers "look alike products are really the same"

             c. **Stimulus Discrimination** -- similar stimuli do not evoke similar
                   responses e.g. "Don't be fooled by imitations! Get 'The Club'!"

Discussion Topic: Can you think of some products that have similar packaging? Similar shapes? Similar names?

2. **Operant Conditioning** -- (also instrumental conditioning) people learn to perform behaviors that produce positive outcomes and vice-versa. positive reinforcement; negative reinforcement; punishment e.g. deodorant ad "Raise your hand if you're Sure!"

Real World Application

☯ A recent study showed that when the verbal information in an ad was presented on the right and pictorial aspects appeared on the left, the format was preferred to others, even though the actual information in the ad did not change. This study showed support for the position that classical conditioning can occur without awareness.[2]

Discussion Topic: What are some products that promise "good things will happen" if you buy their products? Can you think of some products who tell you that you will be "punished" if you don't buy them?

B. **Cognitive Learning Theory** -- stresses importance of internal mental process

1. **Issue of Consciousness** -- do we develop conscious hypotheses and then act? or do we process information in an automatic, passive way?

2. **Observational Learning** -- we notice reinforcements received from behavior modeling: we imitate the behavior of others e.g. Michael Jordan

Discussion Topic: Who are some of the "models" chosen to sell products? Can you think of some "models" that companies probably won't hire again?

C. **Behavioral Learning Applications** -- how they apply to marketing

1. **How Marketers Take Advantage of Classical Conditioning Principles** -- e.g. the Marlboro Man; Busch's "Mountain Man"

a. **Repetition** -- e.g. person must be exposed to an ad many times before it registers; however, ads do 'wear out' (people get tired of them.)

b. **Conditioning Product Associations** -- music, humor, imagery, jingles affect the credibility of the message

c. **Applications of Stimulus Generalization** -- brand names that
capitalize on people's positive associations with an existing name
-- e.g. "The Unvarnished Truth". . . an unfinished furniture store
-- e.g. family branding, product line extensions, and licensing.

Discussion Topic: What are some of the clever company or product names that you've heard of?

Real World Application

☙ (1) Jordache, maker of designer jeans that were very popular in the early 1980s, licensed its name to a diaper manufacturer, hoping that the name would bring back fond memories to baby boomer parents. (2) Filmmaker Spike Lee sold nearly $2 million worth of baseball caps bearing the "X" logo from his movie "Malcolm X." (3) To accompany the relaunch of the humor magazine National Lampoon, the name has been licensed to a cruise line (for Laugh Boat Comedy Cruises featuring toga parties), trading cards, and a computer game. (4) Even imprisoned cult leader Charles Manson has gotten in on the act -- T-shirts bearing his likeness were popular among California surfers, and he received ten cents for every shirt sold.[3]

☙ Other services employing stimulus generalization include (1) a hot dog stand called Mustard's Last Stand, (2) a Chicago septic-tank cleaner known as The Wizard of Ooze, and (3) such hair stylist as The Last Hairhouse and From Hair to Eternity. The capitalization on well known names can result in a law suit if the association is too close. For example, McDonand's field suit against McSleep Hotels to prevent infringement of company name.[4]

☙ (1) General Foods gives discount points to repeat buyers of its products, which can be applied toward the purchase of Sears merchandise. (2) Baskin-Robbins offers free ice cream or frozen yogurt for every 10-12 purchases, and (3) Polaroid and Pan Am are collaborating on a Frequent Smileage Program, where dollars accumulated for buying Polaroid products can be used toward tickets on Pan Am.[5]

☙ A debate is raging over the trademark rights to a popular school yard game called Pogs that originated on the West Coast.. Players stack disks and hit them with another piece called a slammer, trying to flip over as many as possible. The cardboard disks have become an advertising medium, and companies like Walt Disney Co. and Knott's Berry Farm print logos and promotions on them. The World POG Federation bought the trademark rights from an Hawaiian juice maker (the name comes from a passion fruit, orange and guava drink known as POG, which comes with a cardboard cap used in the game). A competing company is now arguing that the word is generic.

☙ Similar disputes in the toy industry have included battles over the rights to names like Rollerblades and Frisbees (both companies won the right to retain their trademarks).[6]

☙ An unethical application occurs in the field of direct marketing, where a few mailers try to increase responsiveness (especially among unsuspecting elderly consumers) to offers by putting them in envelopes that closely resemble official U.S. mailings.

---

2. **How Marketers Take Advantage of Instrumental Conditioning Principles**
-- person is rewarded or punish for purchase decision, e.g. Crest "Look, Ma, no cavities!"; also frequent flyer mileage

FIELD PROJECT IDEAS

Individual Assignments

1. Assign a student to visit a popular mall or supermarket. From observations, have the student cite specific examples of how retail stores made use of behavioral learning principles. Which behavioral learning principles did the student notice?   Ask for an oral report.

2. Send a student to the supermarket to identify a package where the marketer's knowledge of stimulus generalization and/or discrimination was obvious in the packaging. If possible, have the student bring the item to class and explain his or her observations.

3. Encourage a student to find three advertisements--one each based on (1) cognitive learning, (2) classical conditioning, and (3) instrumental conditioning. Allow the student to discuss with the class the nature of each advertisement and how it utilizes a specific type of learning.

4. Have a student ask two friends to look through the same magazine. After a few minutes, ask them to list the ads that they remember. Then ask them if any of these ads are for products they use. To what extent do they use the products advertised in the ads they didn't list? How would learning theory apply?

Group Assignments

5. Ask a group of students to develop a number of environmental or ecological design suggestions for a department store manager to use to encourage people to shop at that store.

6. Recite for the class something you have memorized (poem, limerick, spoonerism, an old jingle, a song, Pledge of Allegiance, Boy or Girl Scout Oath, etc.) Encourage someone to recite something they have memorized. Then ask someone to repeat something you said at the beginning of this class and something you said last week. (Long-term and short term memory exercise.)

Individual or Group Assignments

7. Demonstrate the extent to which consumer learning is often unintentional by asking students to identify the corporate sponsors of five slogans. (For example, Diet Coke says "Just for the taste of it. . .") You could ask a student to do this as an individual project.

8. Have students search for pictures of products that have high nostalgia value for people in their age group. Tell them to show these pictures to their peers and ask them to reminisce. Then have the students analyze these memories and prepare a television ad that would incorporate what they learned in their research. For extra credit, have them make a video of their ad. (See Consumeer Behavior Challenge #6)

9. Break the class into groups and have each group make a list of commercials that have used popular songs in the ad. Ask them why they think the advertiser chose these songs to be placed in the ad and have them describe the target markets.

10. Here is another exercise where you can break the class down into groups. Have each group review Figure 3-3 on the Components of Observational Learning and then tell the class about some product they have purchased based on this model.

11. This can either be an in-class project or a student project. Select a product brand that is familiar to those participating (e.g. Honda Accord, Jiffy Peanut Butter, Absolut Vodka.) Use word-association (i.e., mention key words and have subject write down the first comes to mind) and sentence completion (i.e. give half of a sentence and have the respondent complete it) to discover the "semantic network" for the brand.

12. Have a student or a team identify a convenience product such as toothpaste or bath soap and then suggest ideas on how this product might be promoted using both positive and negative reinforcement theories.

CONSUMER BEHAVIOR CHALLENGE

1. Identify three patterns of reinforcement and provide an example of how each is used in a marketing context.

The three patterns of reinforcement noted in the text are discussed in the section on operant conditioning. They are (1) positive reinforcement, (2) negative reinforcement, and (3) punishment. After reviewing the examples of each type of reinforcement provided by the students, the instructor may ask students to examine the relative frequency with which each is used in various marketing contexts. Additional discussion might focus on the advantages and disadvantages of each type of reinforcement and situational factors that may influence the effectiveness of each.

2. Describe the functions of short-term and long-term memory. What is the apparent relationship between the two?

The functions of both short- and long-term memory, and the relationship between the two are discussed in the chapter. The concept of associative networks also was introduced. In discussing the relationship between short-term and long-term memory, special emphasis should be placed on the transfer on information from short-term to long-term memory, and its implications for marketing. Marketing stimuli from the environment must be transferred, retained, and withdrawn in order to be effective. Efforts to increase the effectiveness of marketing activities, therefore, depends on an understanding of memory functions. The instructor might ask students to analyze a variety of marketing stimuli to assess why some stimuli are more memorable than others and the relationship between memory (or recall) of a particular item and actual purchase of that item.

3. Devise a "product jingle memory test." Compile a list of brands that are or have been associated with memorable jingles, such as Chiquita Banana or Alka-Seltzer. Read this list to friends, and see how many jingles are remembered. You may be surprised at the level of recall.

Students should be able to generate a large number of product jingles for the "memory test." Most of these will be highly advertised products that students have been exposed to recently (e.g., Diet Pepsi with Ray Charles: "You've got the right one baby, uh-huh"; Zest soap: "Zestfully clean. You're not fully clean until you're Zestfully clean;" Energizer Bunny: "Keep on going and going and going.") It might be surprising to note that many of the advertised products are not targeted at the student/consumer, and yet students will have high levels of recall for the jingles. As the instructor you may want to develop your own list of older jingles (many of which the students will not remember) that students will find interesting and fun. (Possible Field Project)

4. Identify some important characteristics for a product with a well-known brand name. Based on these attributes, generate a list of possible brand extension or licensing opportunities, as well as some others that would most likely not be accepted by consumers.

The list of characteristics will, of course, depend on the product chosen. Generally it will include distinctive aspects of products. For example, BIC has been a successful brand extension each time a new product promoted. Also the existing brand name benefited from the characteristics consumers associate with the name BIC--namely, cheap, plastic, and disposable. However, t;heri attempt in the perfume category was a disaster. Because brand extension is based on the transfer of some positive product characteristics(s), either physical or emotional, to the new product, the list students generate should lend itself to identification of that "something" that would enable an extension to be successful.

5. One troubling aspect of product licensing is when movies targeted to an adult audience spawn tie-ins intended for kids. This resulted in a public relations problem for McDonald's Corporation, which was strongly criticized for its cross-promotional deal with the Warner Bros. movie **Batman Returns.** *The movie was rated PG-13, so (in theory at least) it couldn't be seen by the kids who were stockpiling Batman collectors' cups and Happy Meals. Similarly, Mattel sells a line of* **Beverly Hills, 90210** *dolls. An executive explains that these are suitable for little girls because "there is some kind of moral to every story." Do you agree with this reasoning? What, if any, guidelines should be placed on product licensing?*

This question could generate some lively discussion. Legally the companies do not have a problem because they have the freedom to promote legally produced products and shouldn't be prohibited from doing so. However, from both a social responsibility and an ethical point of view, a company should not be promoting products that might be detrimental to the mental or spiritual health and welfare of a group that is not yet mature enough to make an informed judgment. Some will legitimately argue that it is the parents' responsibility to supervise what their children see and do not see, not the public's. In still another vein, one can argue that if parents wants their children to have these products, why should they be hindered? Others will say that the companies are actually responsible for family confrontations that need not even take place. See if the class can develop a list of product licensing guidelines.

6. Collect some pictures of "classic" products that have high nostalgia value. Show these pictures to consumers, and allow them to free associate. Analyze the types of memories that are evoked, and think about how these associations might be employed in a product's promotional strategy.

Consumers' responses to "classic" product pictures should prove interesting to students. They should be encouraged to evaluate the types of meaning associated with products and asked to determine the relative effectiveness of various messages for different target consumer groups. The real emphasis, however, should be placed on students' recommendations for translating the special meaning of these products for consumers into effective promotional messages. (Possible Field Project)

ENDNOTES

[1] Chris Janiszewski and Luk Warlop, "The Influence of Classical Conditioning Procedures on Subsequent Attention to the Conditioned Brand," *Journal of Consumer Research* 20 (September 1993): 171-189.

[2] Chris Janiszewski, "Preconscious Processing Effects: The Independence of Attitude Formation and Conscious Thought," *Journal of Consumer Research* 15 (September 1988): 199 209.

[3] Yumiko Ono, "To Complete This Jordache Look, Just Add a Bib and Teething Ring," *The Wall Street Journal* (August 9, 1994): B1; R. Lee Sullivan, "Spike Strikes Again," *Forbes* (April 11, 1994); Marcy Magiera, "Lampoon Returns with Bevy of Tie-Ins," *Advertising Age* (February 22, 1993): 46; "Charles Manson Gets Royalties on T-Shirts," *The New York Times* (November 25, 1993): A21.

[4] Diane Schneidman, "Use of 'Mc' in Front of Travel Firms' Names Leads to Lawsuits," *Marketing News* (November 20 1987): 17.

[5] Monica Gonzales, "Rewards for Regulars." *American Demographics* (May 21, 1988); Tammie Wright, "Frequent-Flier Programs Spawn Host of Imitators," *Marketing News* (May 8, 1989)2: 2.

[6] Junda Woo, "Schoolyard Game Sets Off Trademark-Generic Battle," *The Wall Street Journal* (August 29, 1994): B5.

[7] Bernd H. Schmitt, Nader T. Tavasolli, and Robert T. Millard, "Memory for Print Ads: Understanding Relations Among Brand Name, Copy, and Picture," *Journal of Consumer Psychology* 2 (1993) 1: 55-81.

[8] For an overview of the approach, see Thomas J. Reynolds and Jonathan Gutman, "Laddering Theory, Method, Analysis, and Interpretation," *Journal of Advertising Research* 28 (February/March 1988): 11-34.

[9] Jacob Jacoby and Wayne D. Hoyer. "The Comprehension Miscomprehension of Print Communication: Selected Findings," *Journal of Consumer Research* 15 (March 1989): 434-44.

[10] Richard D. Johnson and Irwin P. Levin, "More Than Meets the Eye: The Effect of Missing Information on Purchase Evaluations," *Journal of Consumer Research* 12 (September 1985): 169-78.

[11] Jolita Kiselius and Brian Sternthal, "Examining the Vividness Controversy: An Availability-Valence Interpretation," *Journal of Consumer Research* 12 (March 1986), 418-31; Howard Ehrlichman and Jack N. Halpern, "Affect and Memory: Effects of Pleasant and Unpleasant Odors on Retrieval of Happy and Unhappy Memories," *Journal of Personality and Social Psychology* 55 (1988)5: 769-79.

[12] Charles E. Young and Michael Robinson, "Video Rhythms and Recall," *Journal of Advertising Research* (June/July 1989): 22-25.

[13] Julie A. Edell and Richard Staelin, "The Information Processing of Pictures in Print Advertisements," *Journal of Consumer Research* 10 (June): 45 61; Michael Houston, Terry Childers, and Susan Heckler, "Picture-Word Consistency and the Elaborative Processing of Attributes," *Journal of Marketing Research* 24 (November 1987): 359-69.

[14] Bruce Bower, "Fading Remembrances of Television Past," *Science News* 135 (March 18, 1989): 167.

[15] Raymond Serafin, "Roadmaster Re-Enters Buick Fleet," *Advertising Age* (September 10, 1990): 28.

[16] Adam Finn, "Print Ad Recognition Readership Scores: An Information Processing Perspective," *Journal of Marketing Research* 25 (May 1988): 168 77; Myron Glassman and John B. Ford, "An Empirical Investigation of Bogus Recall," *Journal of the Academy of Marketing Science* 16 (Fall 1988): 38-42.

[17] For a recent study that provides contradictory evidence on this issue, see Tom J. Brown and Michael L. Rothschild, "Reassessing the Impact of Television Advertising Clutter," *Journal of Consumer Research* 20 (June 1993): 138ff.

[18] Adam Finn, "Print Ad Recognition Readership Scores: An Information Processing Perspective," *Journal of Marketing Research* 25 (May 1988): 168-77.

[19] Surendra N. Singh, and Gilbert A. Churchill, Jr., "Response-Bias-Free Recognition Tests to Measure Advertising Effects," *Journal of Advertising Research* (June/July 1987): 23-36; Armen Tashchian, J. Dennis White, and Sukgoo Pak, "Signal Detection Analysis and Advertising Recognition: An Introduction to Measurement and Interpretation Issues," *Journal of Marketing* 25 (November 1988): 397-405.

[20] For a study that examined the impact of encoding instructions on recall, see Marian Friestad and Esther Thorson, "Remembering Ads: The Effects of Encoding Strategies, Retrieval Cues, and Emotional Response," *Journal of Consumer Psychology* 2 (1993) 1: 1-23.

Instructor's Notes:

12. Ask five students to each find a print ad that appeals to each level of Maslow's hierarchy. (Make sure they coordinate their activities so you'll have all five levels.) Have each student explain why their ad appeals to this level.   Ask why they think the firm selected this particular appeal.

13. Either collect a sample of ads or have your students do so that appear to appeal to consumers' values. Ask them what value is being communicated in each and how this is done. See if they think this is an effective approach to designing a marketing communication. (See Consumer Behavior Challenge #5)

CONSUMER BEHAVIOR CHALLENGE

1. Describe three types of motivational conflicts, citing an example of each from current marketing campaigns.

The text lists the three types of motivational conflicts as : (1) approach-approach (choosing between two desirable alternative, e.g. new car or new entertainment center), (2) approach-avoidance (referring to the negative and positive aspects of many products that the consumer must consider, e.g. I want a new car but I would have to pay higher insurance and I couldn't take a vacation), and (3) avoidance-avoidance (having to choose between two undesirable alternatives, e.g. do I have the mechanic overhaul my motor or do I buy a motor out of a wrecked car.) In citing examples, students should identify the particular characteristics of the marketing campaign that define it as one type of conflict or another. Additional discussion could be centered on the effectiveness of using each type of conflict for particular product types.

2. Should consumer researchers have the right to probe into the consumer's unconscious? Is this a violation of privacy, or just another way to gather deep knowledge of purchase motivations?

It is important to recognize that student perceptions of the ethics in this issue will undoubtedly depend on their perceptions of the method's intrusiveness. For example, asking consumer about their likes and dislikes and using an interpretation of their responses to infer unconscious motives will probably not strike students as an invasion of their privacy. However, more intrusive (and secretive or deceptive) means likely will draw a more negative reaction. [A related question for discussion would be the ethics of attempting to influence people's consumption. Advertising often is attacked for manipulating consumers so this point is likely to be raised in the discussion of probing the consumer's unconscious.]

3. Devise separate promotional strategies for an article of clothing, each of which stresses one of the levels of Maslow's hierarchy of needs.

Students should be encouraged to review Maslow's hierarchy of needs, including physiological, safety, belongingness, esteem, and self-actualization. While their selection of clothing articles for this exercise maybe diverse, there is likely to be some consistency within need categories. Examples include (1) the promotion of name brand/designer label clothing stressing consumers' need to belong to a particular social group; (2) the promotion of warm and durable jackets or boots stressing consumer physiological need; (3) the promotion of protective equipment of amateur athletes (e.g., knee and elbow guards, helmets, and goggles) stressing consumer's safety needs; (4) the promotion of elegant dress or a tux for esteem, (5) anything you want to wear (like Sam Walton did) because clothes don't matter than much to you.

4. What is the difference between a want and a need? Do marketers have the power to create needs?

A **need** is a basic physiological or emotional requirement while a **want** is a form of consumption used to satisfy a need. For example, the basic hunger need may be satisfied by a variety of products (wants), such as a cheeseburger or a piece of raw seaweed. If students view needs and wants in this manner, they will likely determine that marketers do not have the ability to create needs. However, marketers can, if successful in their efforts, influence how needs are satisfied (in terms of specific wants.) I need something to eat, and I want ground beef--not ground Collie!!

5. Collect a sample of ads that appear to appeal to consumers' values. What value is being communicated in each, and how is this done? Is this an effective approach to designing a marketing communication?

Encourage students to look at the types of values in either the Rokeach Value Survey or List of Values (LOV) to determine which consumer values they would like to share with the class. (Possible Field Project)

6. Construct a hypothetical means-end chain model for the purchase of a bouquet of roses. How might a florist use this approach to construct a promotional strategy?

Students should be encouraged to review the text discussion of the means-end change model and incorporate the laddering technique of probing for more and more abstract associations between products and desired outcomes in completing this exercise. Attributes of a bouquet of roses are beauty, pleasant scent, deep and vivid colors. If you kept probing you could probably find feelings of being loved, a sense of respect and admiration, sympathy, or romance. In discussing how florists might use this approach to construct a promotional strategy, students should include the Means-End Conceptualization of the Components of Advertising Strategy (MECCAs).

7. Describe how a man's level of involvement with his car would affect how he is influenced by different marketing stimuli. How might you design a strategy for a line of car batteries for a segment of low-involvement consumers, and how would this strategy differ from your attempts to reach a segment of men who are very involved in working on their cars?

Different levels of involvement with a product influence the amount of attention paid to marketing stimuli, affecting the amount of cognitive processing capacity directed toward stimuli (e.g., the product related information in an ad). In discussing the development of advertising targeted at low involvement consumers, students should recognize that peripheral cues are used in place of product-related information. Behaviors resulting from such cues do not last long and are likely to change over time. (Bobby Unser uses a Die-Hard battery!) Conversely, developing advertising directed toward high involvement consumers will rely less on peripheral cues and more on substantial product-related information (i.e., the central route to persuasion). Behaviors resulting from this emphasis will be more resistant to change. (How many amps? How many minutes of reserve capacity? What are the cold cranking amps? What are the marine cranking amps?)

8. Interview members of a celebrity fan club. Describe their level of involvement with the "product," and devise some marketing opportunities to reach this group.

Student responses to this exercise might consider a variety of celebrities--movie stars, musician, politicians--living and dead. They might be asked to consider the Elvis Presley fan club phenomenon in terms of the tremendous marketing opportunities that have derived from tours of his home in Memphis (Graceland), his personal property displayed in "museums" (guitars, clothing, music awards, etc.), his "signature" hairstyle and sideburns, other actors' and musicians' remakes of his movies and songs, television programs, Elvis parades, books, postage stamps, etc. (Possible Field Project)

9. High involvement is just a fancy term for expensive." Do you agree?

If students have an inadequate understanding of involvement, it is likely that they will agree with this statement. What needs to be made clear is that the price of a product is only one potential determinant of product involvement. The instructor should stress the role that personal relevance of the product has for an individual, and point out that it is influenced by the person, the product, and the unique purchase/consumption situation. A good exercise would be for students to develop a list of items that they would classify as high involvement. Along with the list, they should provide price estimates for each item (or simply note them as "expensive" or "not expensive"). This type of display would illustrate the lack of association between involvement and price.

ENDNOTES

[1] For an interesting ethnographic account of sky-diving as voluntary high-risk consumption activity, see Richard L. Celsi, Randall L. Rose, and Thomas W. Leigh, "An Exploration of High-Risk Leisure Consumption Through Skydiving," *Journal of Consumer Research* 20 (June 1993): 1-23. See also Jerry Adler, "Been There, Done That," *Newsweek* (July 19, 1993): 43 (7). For an empirical treatment of river rafting as a "high involvement" activity, see Eric J. Arnould and Linda L. Price, "River Magic: Extraordinary Experience and the Extended Service Encounter," *Journal of Consumer Research* 20 (June 1993) 1: 24-45.

[2] Stuart Elliott, "Brochure on AIDS Is the Latest Departure from Benetton," *New York Times* (April 29, 1992): D19.

[3] Jerry Mander, *Four Arguments for the Elimination of Television* (New York: William Morrow, 1977).

[4] Jagdish N. Sheth, Bruce I. Newman, and Barbara L. Gross, *Consumption Values and Market Choices: Theory and Applications* (Cincinnati, South-Western Publishing Co.: 1991).

[5] Wagner A. Kamakura and Jose Afonso Mazzon, "Value Segmentation: A Model for the Measurement of Values and Value Systems," *Journal of Consumer Research* 18 (September 1991) 2: 208-218.

[6] For a recent study that equates the learning of marketing information with the processing of trivia, see Scott A. Hawkins and Stephen J. Hoch, "Low-Involvement Learning: Memory Without Evaluation," *Journal of Consumer Research* 19 (September 1992): 212-25.

[7] Judann Dagnoli and Alison Fahey, "What's Behind the Mystery Ad?" *Advertising Age* (September 16, 1991): 17.

[8] Ronald C. Goodstein, "Category-Based Applications and Extensions in Advertising: Motivating More Extensive Ad Processing," *Journal of Consumer Research* 20 (June 1993): 87-99. Joan Meyers-Levy and Alice M. Tybout, "Schema Congruity As a Basis for Product Evaluation," *Journal of Consumer Research* 16 (June 1989): 39 54; Douglas M. Stayman, Dana L. Alden, and Karen H. Smith, "Some Effects of Schematic Processing on Consumer Expectations and Disconfirmation Judgments," *Journal of Consumer Research* 19 (September 1992): 240-55.

[9] Leisa Reinecke Flynn and Ronald E. Goldsmith, "Models of Enduring Product Involvement and Opinion Leadership," *Association of Marketing Theory and Practice* (Spring 1993): 378-386.

[10] David R. Eppright, "Involvement and Party Affiliation Effects on Campaign Television Exposure," Proceedings of the Annual Meeting of the Southern Marketing Association, ed. Robert L. King, Richmond, Va., 1991, 94-97.

Instructor's Notes:

a. **Reconciling Cognitive Elements** -- conflict causes discomfort so we are motivated to reduce a negative state (e.g. "I smoke." "Smoking causes health problems")

b. **Postpurchase Dissonance** -- evaluations of a product tend to increase after it is purchase (e.g. I don't want to appear stupid.)

Discussion Topic: Why do people read the ads for products they already own?

Real World Application
- One common way to build positive attitudes is to stress the security provided by product warranties and guarantees, as well as follow-up mailings soliciting feedback about product performance. While it is generally assumed that product warranties have a positive effect on attitudes, one recent study questions this assumption.[11]

---

2. **Self-Perception Theory** -- we observe our own behavior to determine our attitudes (e.g. I eat chocolates . . . I must have a sweet tooth.)

a. **The Foot-in-the-Door Technique** -- a salesperson is more likely to make a sale if he can get the prospect to talk. . .and agree

Discussion Topic: What is a technique that salespeople use to help you to agree with whatever they are saying? (e.g. "you would rather have a matched set than a bunch of odds and ends, wouldn't you?")

- The opposite of the foot-in-the-door technique is the door-in-the-face technique, a strategy often used by car salespeople who quote shoppers an unrealistically high price. When the second, more reasonable quote is offered, the customer may accept it because it appears that a big concession is being made.[12]

---

3. **Social Judgment Theory** -- our attitude affects how we categorize new information (e.g. If someone we don't like donates to Jerry's Kids, it's just a tax write-off)

(Use Color Transparency 14 Here)
(Use TM 5-3 Here)

a. **Latitudes of Acceptance and Rejections** -- ideas that fit our present attitudes are favorably receive and those that don't are not

b. **Assimilation and Contrast** -- e.g. the more I get involved with a product, the less likely I am to accept ideas different from mine

Discussion Topic: Why do you suppose some people tend to keep buying cars from the same manufacturer every time they get a new car? Why do you suppose some people go out of their way not to??

4. **Balance Theory** -- consists of three elements: a person's perceptions, an attitude object, and some other person or object
   - perceptions are either positive or negative
   - perceptions are altered to make them consistent

Real World Application
- ☯ The easy way to determine if a triad is balanced is to use the multiplicative rule: a positive times a positive is positive, a positive times a negative is negative, and a negative times a negative is positive. Simply multiply all three signs in a triad to determine if it is stable.

a. **Marketing Applications of Balance Theory** -- if a likable personality is in a new product ad, we assume it must be all righ

5. **Congruity Theory** -- also addresses how attitudes are affected when a person is linked to an object
   - how much positive boost will a product get from an endorser?
   - how will the endorsement negatively affect the endorser?

Discussion Topic: Who are some celebrity endorsers who have fallen in disfavor with the public? How do you suppose this has affected the sales of the product they endorsed? Did any of the companies stop using these endorsers?

- ☯ The theory specifically addresses the linking of two attitude objects by an assertion (usually a person with a positive attitude tends to make positive statements about an object and a person with a negative attitude makes negative statements). One of the advantages of the theory compared to balance theory is that it allows the analyst to consider degrees of positivity or negativity instead of global good bad judgments.

- ☯ *Conde Nast Traveler* magazine rejected ads for Keebler Chips Deluxe Cookies, and *Architectural Digest* and *Bon Appetit* will not accept pet food ads.[13]

IV. **Attitude Models** -- developed to specify the different elements that affect attitudes

A. **Multi-Attribute Attitude Models** -- consumers attitude affected by object's attributes

(Use TM 5-4 Here)

- attributes: are characteristics of the attitude object
- beliefs: are cognitions about the specific attitude object
- importance of weight: reflects the priority consumers place on the object

the length of time the respondent has owned the product and then have the respondent evaluate the product according to some criteria determined by the class. See if the people who more recently purchased the product have a more positive attitude toward it than those who have owned it for a longer period of time.

11. Ask a group of students to have three people write down the names of the best and worst provider of an identical service--e.g. a bank, a dentist, a dry cleaners, a hair dresser, an airline, a fast food restaurant. Have the respondents give five descriptive words for each providers--ask them to use negative words that can be used in polite society. How could both service providers use this information?

Individual or Group Assignments

12. Ask a group of students to think about restaurants they like and don't like to patronize. Have them design a multi-attribute model for three of these restaurants, making sure both spectrums are included. Have students make suggestions how the managers could improve the restaurant's images by following the strategies and tactics found in this chapter.

13. You can either facilitate this project yourself or have a group of students do it. Bring to class a number of products (or pictures of products) and ask those assembled about their attitude toward the products. This is a good way to start a conversation about the characteristics of attitudes.

14. Have a group of students search various types of magazines that appeal to different target markets, and then ask them to lead a discussion on how these ads were designed to appeal the the specific target market.

CONSUMER BEHAVIOR CHALLENGE

1. Contrast the hierarchies of effects outlined in the chapter. How will strategic decisions related to the marketing mix be influenced by which hierarchy is operative among target consumers?

The "standard learning" hierarchy assumes a purposeful and involved process in attitude formation leading to a decision that may lead to brand loyalty. On the other hand, the "low-involvement" hierarchy assumes a minimal amount of knowledge and sees the attitude formed "after-the-fact." The chapter specifically notes that the use of marketing stimuli would be more effective in the low-involvement situation because the consumer uses these inputs as a basis for selection and attitude formation, instead of product-related characteristics. However, students should note that the product is the key ingredient in the marketing mix and consequently, long-term success is less likely to result from simple low-involvement attitude formation.

2. List three functions played by attitudes, giving an example of how each function is employed in a marketing situation.

<u>Utilitarian Function</u>--related to the principles of reward and punishment.

> Example: Pleasure of owning a Lexus/pain of paying for it;
> Example: Some people enjoy drinking alcohol. If they drink too much, however, the result is a headache.

<u>Value-Expressive Function</u>--expresses the consumer's central values or self-concept.

> Example: People who wear Diesel Jeans feel that they are in fashion; they feel different from everyone else.

<u>Ego-Defensive Function</u>--protects the person from external threats or internal feelings.

> Example: People may use mouthwash in order to feel confident about their breath and their overall attractiveness to members of the opposite sex.

<u>Knowledge Function</u>-- the result of a need for order, structure, or meaning.

> Example: "Have you driven a Ford lately?" Consumers may want to explore why they should test drive a Ford. What does the product offer the consumer?

[When providing examples of these functions, students should also be able to describe the types of marketing activities that most often are associated with each function. Discussion could include students' reasons for pairing a particular function with a specific marketing activity, or the type of consumption situation in which each function would lead to an "optimal" decision.]

3. Think of a behavior someone does that is inconsistent with their attitudes (e.g., attitudes toward cholesterol, drug use, or even buying things to make them stand out or attain status). Ask the person to elaborate on why he or she does the behavior, and try to identify the way the person has resolved dissonant elements.

Students should be able to generate many diverse examples of this type of consumer behavior. Assume you are a high school student who is health conscious but who may smoke occasionally because your friends smoke. The reason you smoke may be to "fit in" with a group, or the behavior may serve as some type of initiation into the group. You may resolve dissonant elements by telling yourself that an occasional cigarette won't hurt you as long as you keep exercising and eating right.

4. Using a series of semantic-differential scales, devise an attitude survey for a set of competing automobiles. Identify areas of competitive advantage or disadvantage for each model you incorporate.

The semantic-differential scale often is used to describe a consumer's beliefs about product, brands, and /or companies. Students are likely to develop scale items reflecting a variety of beliefs about individual products, where a set of product attributes are rated on a series of scales. For example:

My travel agent is:

very efficient	1--2--3--4--5--6--7	very inefficient
very accessible	1--2--3--4--5--6--7	very inaccessible
very friendly	1--2--3--4--5--6--7	very unfriendly

Semantic-differential scales also may be used to compare the images of competing brands, as in the following example:

Honda Accords have good interior features.
            Agree 1--2--3--4--5--6--7   Disagree

Ford Probes have good interior features.
            Agree 1--2--3--4--5--6--7   Disagree

Chevrolet Storms have good interior features.
            Agree 1--2--3--4--5--6--7   Disagree

(Possible Individual or Group Field Project)

5. Construct a multi-attribute model for a set of local restaurants. Based on your findings, suggest how restaurant managers can improve their establishment's images via the strategies described in the chapter.

The multi-attribute models that students develop for a set of local restaurants should include:
  (1) a number of product attributes--characteristics of the restaurants, such as price, type of foods, number of menu items, location, etc.
  (2) beliefs regarding specific restaurants (in terms of attributes)
  (3) important weights reflecting the relative priority of specific attributes for them individually

While there likely will be some common elements in the models developed, students should be encouraged to think about how each model is reflective of the individual responsible for the product evaluation. The instructor should point out to students the complexity of consumer attitudes, as demonstrated by the diversity of attitudinal statements, product attributes, beliefs and importance weights that might be chosen. (Possible Individual or Group Field Project)

ENDNOTES

[1] Steve Lohr, "Major British Advertiser: Government," *New York Times* (May 23, 1989): D1.

[2] Stuart Elliott, "When Products Are Tied to Causes," *New York Times* (April 18, 1992)2: 33.

[3] Julie Michaels, "Sex Symbols Animating Interest in Vasectomies," *Advertising Age* (July 17, 1989): 30; Christi Phelps, "Drive for Safer Sex Launches New Caped Crusader's Career," *San Diego Business Journal* (October 23, 1988): 1.

[4] Michael R. Solomon and Susan P. Douglas, "Diversity in Product Symbolism: The Case of Female Executive Clothing," *Psychology & Marketing* (Fall, 1987): 189-212.

[5] Dolf Zillman, "Mood Management Through Communication Choices," *American Behavioral Scientist* 31 1988)3: 327-40.

[6] Amitava Chattopadhyay and Prakash Nedungadi, "Does Attitude Toward the Ad Endure? The Moderating Effects of Attention and Delay," *Journal of Consumer Research* 19 (June 1992): 26-33.

[7] Karen A. Machleit and Arti Sahni, "The Impact of Measurement Context on the Relationship Between Attitude Toward the Ad and Brand Attitude for Familiar Brands," *Advances in Consumer Research* 19, eds. John F. Sherry, Jr., and Brian Sternthal (Provo, Utah: Association for Consumer Research, 1992), 279-83.

[8] Srinivas Durvasula, J. Craig Andrews, Steven Lysonki, and Richard G. Netemeyer, "Assessing the Cross-National Applicability of Consumer Behavior Models: A Model of Attitude Toward Advertising in General," *Journal of Consumer Research* 19 (March 1993): 626-636.

[9] Michael S. LaTour and Tony L. Henthorne, "Female Nudity: Attitudes Toward the Ad and the Brand, and Implications for Advertising Strategy" 10 (1993) 3: 25-32.

[10] Amitava Chattopadhyay and Prakash Negungadi, "Does Attitude Toward the Ad Endure? The Moderating Effects of Attention and Delay," *Journal of Consumer Research* 19 (June 1992): 26-33.

[11] Sunil Erevelles, "Do Warranties Really Affect Product Attitudes?" in Proceedings of the Southern Marketing Association, ed. Robert L. King, Richmond, Va., 1991, 36-41.

[12] Ian Brennan and Kenneth D. Bahn, "Door-in-the-Face, That's-not-all, and Legitimizing a Paltry Contribution: Reciprocity, Contrast Effect and Social Judgment Theory Explanations," in Advances in Consumer Research 18, eds. Rebecca H. Holman and Michael R. Solomon (Provo, Utah: Association for Consumer Research, 1991), 586-90; John C. Mowen and Robert B. Cialdini, "On Implementing the Door-in-the-Face Compliance Technique in a Business Context," *Journal of Marketing Research* 17 (May 1980): 253-58.

[13] Karen Springen and Annetta Miller, "When Ads Don't Fit the 'Image'," *Newsweek* (January 22, 1990): 48.

[14] Richard P. Bagozzi, Hans Baumgartner, and Youjae Yi, "State Versus Action Orientation and the Theory of Reasoned Action: An Application to Coupon Usage," *Journal of Consumer Research* 18 (March 1992): 505-18.

[15] For a study that examined this problem, see Vicki G. Morwitz, Eric Johnson, and David Schmittlein, "Does Measuring Intent Change Behavior,?" *Journal of Consumer Research* 20 (June 1993) 1: 46-61.

[16] Ida E. Berger, Brian T. Ratchford, and George H. Haines, Jr., "Subjective Product Knowledge as a Moderator of the Relationship Between Attitudes and Purchase Intentions for a Durable Product," *Journal of Economic Psychology* 15 (1994): 301-314.

[17] Paul W. Miniard and Joel B. Cohen, "Modeling Personal and Normative Influences on Behavior," *Journal of Consumer Research* 10 (September 1983): 169-80.

[18] Chris T. Allen, Karen A. Machleit, and Susan Schultz Kleine, "A Comparison of Attitudes and Emotions as Predictors of Behavior at Diverse Levels of Behavioral Experience," *Journal of Consumer Research* 18 (March 1992): 493-504.

[19] Russell H. Fazio, Martha C. Powell, and Paul M. Herr, "Toward a Process Model of the Attitude Behavior Relation: Accessing One's Attitude Upon Mere Observation of the Attitude Object," *Journal of Personality and Social Psychology* 44 (1983): 723-35.

Instructor's Notes:

CHAPTER 6
Attitude Change and Persuasive Communications

SUMMARY BULLETS

♦ Persuasion refers to an attempt to change consumers' attitudes.

♦ The communications model specifies the elements needed to transmit meaning. These include a source, message, medium, receiver, and feedback.

♦ Two important characteristics that determine the effectiveness of a source are its attractiveness and credibility. While celebrities often serve this purpose, their credibility is not always as strong as marketers hope.

♦ Some elements of a message that help to determine its effectiveness are whether it is conveyed in words or pictures, whether an emotional or a rational appeal is employed, the frequency with which it is repeated, whether a conclusion is drawn, whether both sides of the argument are presented, and whether the message includes fear, humor, or sexual references.

♦ Advertising messages often incorporate such elements from art or literature as dramas, lectures, metaphors, allegories, and resonance.

♦ The relative influence of the source versus the message depends upon the receiver's level of involvement with the communication. The elaboration likelihood model specifies that a less-involved consumer will more likely be swayed by source effects, while a more-involved consumer will more likely attend to and process components of the actual message.

LECTURE/DISCUSSION IDEAS

I. **Changing Attitudes Through Communication** -- to wear or not to wear fur?
    (Use TM 6-1 Here)

    A. **Strategic Issues in Persuasion Attempts** -- active attempts to change attitudes

        • models, messages, media, and markets

B. **Communications Model** -- source, encoding, message, medium, decoding, receivers, and feedback

(Use Color Transparency 15 Here)
(Use TM 6-2 Here)

II. **Communications Model: The Source** -- credibility and attractiveness (likable and trustworthy)

A. **Choosing a Source Dimension** -- which dimensions do we want to stress?

Discussion Topic: What categories of products would want to make sure their source is credible? . . . is attractive?

Real World Application
☻ In a controversial campaign for Maxwell House coffee, TV newscasters Linda Ellerbee and Willard Scott plugged the product in a setting resembling a news show. This format attempted to capitalize on their backgrounds to produce the inference that their reports were news rather than commercials.[1]

B. **Risk Reduction** -- which source do we select to reduce risk?
- experts are used to reduce performance risk
- celebrities are used to reduce social risk
- typical consumer are used with products that are low risk

C. **Source Credibility** -- source is perceived as an expert, objective and trustworthy

---

☻ In one study, the brand attitudes of subjects whose level of physiological arousal was elevated through physical exertion (which decreases one's ability to process cognitive information) were more influenced by the status of a product endorser, while those who were not aroused were more influenced by argument strength.[2]

D. **Building Source Credibility** -- link sources qualifications to the product (e.g. ball players and athletic shoes)

E. **Source Biases** -- source is perceived as "uninformed" or a "hired gun"

Discussion Topic: Can you think of some company spokespersons who do not seem to fit the image of the company?

F. **Source Attractiveness** -- source is perceived as having "social value"

1. **Physical Attractiveness and Attitude Change**
- "What is beautiful is good"
- "Beautiful people are smarter"

a. **Beauty as an Attention Getter** -- e.g. Cindy Crawford

Discussion Topic: Can you name some spokespersons who are "attention getters"?

b. **Beauty as a Source of Information** -- e.g. George Brett

Discussion Topic: Can you name some spokespersons who are "sources of information"?

G. **Celebrities as Communications Sources** -- well-known and admired
    (e.g. Shaquille O'Neal and Bill Cosby)

1. **The Strategic Value of Celebrities** -- can differentiate among similar
    products

a. **Soldiers in the Cola War** -- "Bring in the troops!"

Discussion Topic: Which is your favorite: Pepsi or Coke? Who has endorsed Pepsi in the last few years? Who has endorsed Coke? Whom do you like best?

2. **Why are Stars so Persuasive?** -- they can be both credible and
    attractive

Real World Application

☙ Marketers who appropriate the images of celebrities are vulnerable to lawsuits.

   (1) Vanna White of *Wheel of Fortune* fame sued Samsung Electronics over an ad that spoofed the show. The ad, which was making the point that the company's products would be around for a long time, showed a robot wearing a blond wig and an evening gown turning letters on a video board, and he caption said "Longest-running game show. 2012 A.D." White argued that Samsung had misappropriated her "identity," even though it did not use her exact likeness.

   (2) Another lawsuit was filed against Host International on behalf of the actors who played Norm and Cliff on the popular TV show *Cheers*. The company operates a chain of airport bars called *Cheers*, which feature talking robots that are replicas of Cliff and Norm.[3]

☙ (1) Former football quarterback Johnny Unitas was sued by a group of investors for endorsing a mortgage firm. The founder subsequently went to jail for fraud. (2) Actress Jamie Lee Curtis jeopardized her relationship with Hertz by going topless in the movie *Trading Places*. (3) Ringo Starr went into treatment for alcohol abuse after plugging Sun Country wine coolers, and (4) Eric Clapton did spots for Michelob despite being a recovering drug addict.[4]

☙ One exception to the rule that highly credible sources are more persuasive is when speakers with low credibility advocate a position incongruous with their own interests. For example, a drug dealer, while not well-regarded by many, might be very effective in an anti-drug campaign.[5]

81

a. **Wanted: Believable Celebrities** -- we may distrust motives

b. **Testing Celebrity Images** -- must have clear and popular image

3. **The Sleeper Effect** -- an effective source can be obnoxious or disliked
(e.g. Mr. Whipple "Please don't squeeze the Charmin!")

III. **Communications Model: The Message** -- should stress uniqueness or customer benefit

A. **Message Elements** -- some of the variables to consider are listed below:
(Use TM 6-3 Here)

1. **Words Versus Pictures**
(Use Color Transparency 16 Here)

- use words to stress facts and reason (high involvement)
- use pictures to achieve emotional responses (low involvement)
- visual images help us "chunk" and remember
- verbal materials decay more rapidly in memory

Discussion Topic: When would you use words to carry your advertising message? When would you use pictures to carry your advertising message?

Real World Application
- ☯ Both the size and color of illustrations can have a strong impact on responses to an ad and in causing attitude change. The use of one-color newspaper ads in a field study resulted in 41 percent more sales volume than when the same ads were run in black-and-white.[6]

---

2. **Vividness** -- powerful descriptions and graphics help us remember

---

- ☯ Attempts to influence attitudes by highlighting the behavior of other people in the same situation are more successful when put into concrete terms. For example, a commercial that features five people explaining their product choice is more vivid than the abstract claim that four out of five consumers chose Brand X.[7]

---

3. **Message Repetition** -- repetition helps us remember but ads 'wear out'

Discussion Topics: Can you think of some ad you are tired of hearing? Why?

4. **Two-Factor Theory** -- fine line between familiarity and boredom

B. **Constructing the Argument** -- what is the best way to persuade?

1. **One- Versus Two-Sided Arguments --**
   - supportive argument is one-sided and most often used
   - two-sided messages give positive and negative information and are seldom used
   - refutation arguments raise a negative issue and dismiss it

---

Real World Application

☯ Quaker Rice Cakes reacted to their consumer research that told them people felt rice cakes tasted like styrofoam or cardboard. In ads for a new line of flavored cakes, the company showed a picture of a foam cup with a piece bitten off. The copy read: If this is what you think of rice cakes, wait till you taste 'em now.[8]

☯ Another factor that may influence the persuasive potential of a message is syntactic complexity. For example, the statement, "Trident gum is sugarless" is less complex than the statement, "Trident gum does not contain sugar." These alternatives can make a difference, especially when motivation to process the statement is relatively low.[9]

---

2. **Drawing Conclusions** -- should the advertiser draw conclusions or leave it to the consumer to decide

(Use Color Transparency 17 Here)

Discussion Topic: Do you think it is smarter to draw conclusions in an ad for your customers or to let them do it themselves?

3. **Comparative Advertising** -- compares two specifically named products and seems to be effective for new products

---

☯ Direct comparative ads are most effective when they encourage differentiation between the two brands, especially when they lower consumer's perceptions of the comparison brand. This effect is particularly robust when the attribute in question is typical of the product category.[10]

C. **Types of Message Appeals --**

(Use TM 6-4 Here)

1. **Emotional Versus Rational Appeals** -- emotional appeal tries to bond the consumer with the product (e.g. Hallmark); ads that made you think are easier to recall

2. **Sex Appeals** -- ranges from subtle hints to blatant displays of skin

   a. **Does Sex Work?** -- it draws attention and can be ineffective if the consumer perceives it as a trick. It seems to be effective if the product itself is sexually related (e.g. perfume)

Discussion Topic: Do you find more nudity in ads in men's or women's magazines?

3. **Humorous Appeals** -- what is funny to one may be offensive to another

---

Real World Application
- One reason for the mixed findings regarding humor is that humorous appeals increase in persuasiveness. Over time humor creates generalized arousal that results in a more active memory trace process and an enhancement of cognitive processing in the long term. (This effect would not show up on conventional measures of ad effectiveness that are taken immediately following exposure to the humorous ad.)[11]

---

   a. **Does Humor Work?** -- it gets attention but the humor can cause distraction. Subtle appropriate humor is usually better

Discussion Topic: What are some of your favorite ads that use humor? Do you buy those products or products from their competition?

- A recent attempt by Subaru to satirize the typical commercial for sports cars backfired. In one TV commercial for the SVX, the announcer claims the car can reach speeds of 140 miles an hour. This statement is followed by the question: "How important is that, with extended urban gridlock, gas at $1.38 a gallon, and highways full of patrolmen?" Unfortunately, auto safety groups didn't seem to get the joke; focusing on the mph claim, they called the ads "offensive and totally inappropriate."[12]

---

4. **Fear Appeals** -- used in over 15% of television ads

- A print ad for *Fortune* magazine capitalizes on widespread job anxiety to emphasize the business intelligence that can be attained in its pages. A picture of a bewildered looking yuppie asks, "What's worse, getting laid off on Friday or being told to pick up the slack on Monday?"[13]

- Some evidence indicates that downscale, more traditional consumers are more susceptible to fear appeals.[14]

---

   a. **Slice-of-Death** -- appeals to anxieties about careers and love lives

Discussion Topic: Who can think of an ad in which the models fear losing their jobs?

b. **Does Fear Work?** -- usually in moderate amounts
(Mechanic says, "Pay me now or pay me later.")

Discussion Topic: What are some of the products that you can think of that seem to use
fear to attract customers?

> ☮ Research on the effectiveness of fear appeals has yielded mixed results. One reason may be due to thassumption that a specific type of message will uniformly generate a high level of fear among all consumers.[15]

D. **The Message as Art Form: Metaphors Be with You** -- Mr. Goodwrench, California Raisins, Tony the Tiger (cereal equated with strength), Merrill Lynch bull "a breed apart"

- metaphor involved an explicit comparison (A is B)
- resonance combines a play on words with a relevant picture (unfinished furniture store is called "The Unvarnished Truth"

1. **Forms of Story Presentation** -- can be told in words or pictures

> Real World Application
> ☮ In one study on transformational advertising, projective measures were used to determine if subjects' exposure to prior advertising would affect product usage experiences. A hiking scene was rated as more enjoyable when Coors was present relative to Lowenbrau, while the reverse was found when a barbecue scene was substituted. Coors' advertising has relied on an outdoor theme, while Lowenbrau concentrates on more social settings.[16]

IV. **The Source Versus the Message: Sell the Steak or the Sizzle** -- highly involved consumers look for the "steak" and less involved consumers are more affected by the "sizzle"

> ☮ When a consumer is more motivated to process an ad because it is relevant to his or her goals, the impact of central processing on brand attitudes is increased and that of peripheral cues is decreased.[17]

A. **The Elaboration Likelihood Model** -- assumes that once customers receive a message they begin to process it

(Use Color Transparency 18 Here)
(Use TM 6-5 Here)

1. **The Central Route to Persuasion** -- if the message is relevant, it either generates cognitive responses or counterarguments in the mind of the receive

---

Real World Application

☯ During a persuasive message, advertisers may attempt to provide distractions to reduce the amount of counterarguing a person is able to do. This strategy is effective when the argument for choosing the product is fairly weak. A similar result can sometimes be obtained by embedding the message in an involving program. The viewer is distracted as he or she processes the show's contents, so the commercial message is more easily accepted.[18]

---

2. **The Peripheral Route to Persuasion** -- if receivers are not motivated to think about the argument, they analyze the source and the message and decide if they should consider the argument

3. **Support for the ELM** (Elaboration Likelihood Model) -- a thought-listing technique using three independent variables
   - message-processing involvement: high or low involvement
   - argument strength: use strong or weak arguments in ads
   - source characteristics: viewed as positive or negative by receivers

FIELD PROJECT IDEAS

Individual Assignments

1. Have a student visit an ad agency and interview an advertising executive. Ask the executive about one of the advertising campaigns he/she has developed and how (or whether) it was designed to change consumers' attitudes toward the product, service, or company. Have the student summarize the interview with the class.

2. Ask one of your students to interview three people and have each respondent identify an advertisement that they have a positive attitude toward and an ad that they have a negative attitude toward. Be sure to inquire to find out how their attitudes toward the ads influence their attitudes toward the products.

3. Here is a project for someone who likes to be creative. Have this person select an existing product or service and design a couple of ads (print or electronic media) which make use of the principles discussed in this chapter. The student should explain why he or she thought these particular ads would be effective.

4. Find someone who is nostalgic or likes history to select a product brand and look up advertisements for it over the past 20 years or so. [Good library sources include *National Geographic*, *Ladies Home Journal*, *Reader's Digest*, and *Time*. Coke, Pepsi, Miller Beer, Hallmark and others have excellent videos of their old ads and the students tend to enjoy watching these.] Are these ads reflect your perceptions of changes in consumer attitudes?

5. Ask a student to read some ads from a print media or view or listen to ads on the broadcast media. Find out to what extent the following message appeals appear to be used: (a) emotional, (b) rational, (c) sex, (d) humorous, (e) fear. Which does he or she feel is most powerful? Which is most persuasive? Which is most credible?

6. Here is an activity for the class comedian. Have a student bring in three television ads that employ humor. Then ask the student to analyze the ads and explain what makes the ads funny and what causes them to wear out. What types of products can change your attitude by using humor in the message?

7. Negative attitudes are often difficult to change. Ask a student to think of a company that has had some bad press. How has the company handled the news? Have they been successful in turning the situation around? What techniques did they employ (or are they employing)? What suggestions do you have for the company?

8. Ask a student to identify several spokespeople in recent TV ads. Speculate on the ages of the spokesperson and the age of the target audience. Do companies seem to let a spokesperson age along with the target audience or do they seem to find a new spokesperson? Why you suppose certain spokespersons were selected for these roles?

Group Assignments

9. Bring in a number of print or television ads that use celebrity endorsers or have students do it). Ask the class how effective they think the ads are. By evaluating the spokesperson as either "good" or "poor", determine whether the class likes the celebrity. Do they find the ads believable or contrived? Probe to find out why they feel this way.

10. Bring in a number of print or television ads that rely on the use of metaphors or resonance (or have your students do it.) What are your student's initial reaction to the ads? How effective do they think they are? Do they think some other approach would be more convincing? Why?

Individual or Group Assignments

11. Ask a group of students to interview several of their friends to find out what non-aerosol products they use. Did they formerly use an aerosol product? If so, see if you can determine why they changed their buying decision. Have them explain their attitude toward the environment in general. Find out what other measures they take to protect the environment.

12. Have students make a list of all the commercials shown on evening or late news on each of the major television channels.   Then ask them to categorize each ad according to product category, and whether it used drama or argument to persuade the viewer. Also have them record the number of minutes during the 30-minute news programs allotted for ads.

13. Encourage two or three students to compare and contrast high-involvement processing and low-involvement processing as is found in the Elaboration Likelihood Model of Persuasion in (Figure 6-5). Have the students relate these stages to the processes they followed on a recent purchase. See if any of the stages were reversed in the mind of the student.

14. There is probably a pub near campus that many students avoid because of its lack of cleanliness. Ask one of your students or a team to take charge of this establishment and develop a promotional campaign that would change consumers attitude toward this pub. What is the difference between atmosphere and cleanliness? Could a manager clean the place up "too much"? Explain.

CONSUMER BEHAVIOR CHALLENGE

1. A government agency wants to encourage the use of designated drivers by people who have been drinking. What advice could you give the organization about constructing persuasive communications? Discuss some factors that might be important, including the structure of the communications, where they should appear, and who should deliver them. Should fear appeals be used, and if so, how?

Steps the government agency should take:
> The target market(s) should be established. (teenage drivers)
> Both the source and the message must be considered.
> The source must be both credible and attractive to the target audience.
> Make a list of possible sources for the message.

One of the largest target markets would be teenage drivers, thus making it necessary for the source to be aligned with that group. Such a person, or organization, would also have to be perceived as having social value, or having source attractiveness, in order to have the greatest persuasive impact. Likewise, the structure of the communication would need to be tailored to meet the processing needs and likes of the target market. Recall that uninvolved consumers will respond to peripheral cues best, and therefore the use of celebrity endorsers and other non-product-related aspects will have a greater effect. Fear appeals should be used judiciously and only with moderate emphasis on the negative aspects.

[The instructor may elect to provide samples of public issue advertisements, or encourage students to collect some advertisements that can be used to stimulate discussion of issues relevant to the design of this form of advertising. Possible Field Project Idea.]

2. Are infomercials ethical? Should marketers be allowed to use any format they want to present product-related information?

The instructor may initiate a discussion on this topic by simply stating that infomercials are unethical because they are longer and therefore, more persuasive than commercials. Their greater persuasive power, the argument would follow, encourages consumption that would otherwise not occur. Presenting a position to the students, and having them debate it among themselves, will stimulate students' examination of both sides of the issue. The second issue is a related one. Should marketers be allowed to use any format they wish? The recent dispute over the possibility that an ad agency would put advertising in outer space illustrates the type of public resistance to some advertising formats. This discussion should attempt to outline where and how marketing communication might occur, including descriptions of venues that would be acceptable and unacceptable.

3. Discuss some conditions where it would be advisable to use a comparative advertising strategy.

Comparative advertising may be effective for low-involvement products, like convenience goods, new brands that have advantages over existing brands, and for brands that are experiencing decreased sales using noncomparative advertising. For new product introductions, comparative ads benefit from the association they form between established products and new, unknown products. Students should recognize that repositioning an older established brand also would be a viable situation for comparative advertising. The discussion also might include an analysis of conditions when it would not be advisable to use comparative ads. Students should be encouraged to list ads they have seen or heard and to describe the aspects of each ad that would make the use of comparative advertising advisable or inadvisable.

4. Why would a marketer consider saying negative things about his or her product? When is this strategy feasible? Can you find examples of it?

The use of two-sided arguments is effective when the audience is well educated and not loyal to the product. These conditions exist for many new product introductions and brand extensions. When the advertised product is complex, something negative can be said about the minor attribute without producing an overall negative affect, as long as positive descriptions of major attributes of the product also are included. For example, Curtis Mathis has advertised that its televisions are very expensive (a negative attribute) while countering with information about the superb quality, workmanship, and service provided.

5. A marketer must decide whether to incorporate rational or emotional appeals in its communications strategy. What factors would favor choosing one approach over the other?

Students' responses should include the issues of product involvement and complexity. Emotional appeals can be used with low involvement products to increase the level of consumer's involvement with the products. Emotional appeals also are appropriate for homogeneous or commodity-type products. Alternatively, rational appeals are recommended when there are significant differences between product alternatives.

6. Collect ads that rely on sex appeal to sell products. How often are benefits of the actual product communicated to the reader?

Students will be able to find examples of products that use sex appeals in almost any magazine, but magazines targeted toward either men or women are the best sources. (Possible Field Project Idea)

7. To observe the process of counterargumentation, ask a friend to talk out loud while watching a commercial. Ask him or her to respond to each point in the ad or to write down reactions to the claims made. How much skepticism regarding the claims can you detect?

Students will enjoy this project. You might encourage a student to video tape a few ads and show the tape to a friend. This will give the student an opportunity to choose a few ads that make a number of claims that can be analyzed. (Possible Field Project Idea)

8. Make a log of all the commercials shown on one network television channel over a six-hour period. Categorize each according to product category and whether they are presented as drama or argument. Describe the types of messages used (e.g., two-sided arguments), and keep track of the types of spokespeople (e.g., television actors, famous people, animated characters). What can you conclude about the dominant forms of persuasive tactics currently employed by marketers?

The instructor might want to encourage students to work in pairs in order to better manage the recording of 10 and 15 second commercials. One person could write about one commercial while the other person is listening to the next commercial--this is especially important because of the number of 10 and 15 second ads. (Possible Field Project Idea)

9. Collect examples of ads that rely on the use of metaphors or resonance. Do you feel these ads are effective? If you were working with the products, would you feel more comfortable with ads that use a more straightforward, "hard-sell" approach? Why or why not?

Make sure students review the section of the text that describes how metaphors and resonance are used in advertising before they go in search of ads. Encourage the students to discuss both the positive and the negative aspects of metaphors or resonance. (Possible Field Project)

ENDNOTES

1 James Cox, "Star-Stuck Advertisers Lean on Celebs," *USA Today* (June 20, 1990): 80.

2 David M. Sanbonmatsu and Frank R. Kardes, "The Effects of Physiological Arousal on Information Processing and Persuasion," *Journal of Consumer Research* 15 (December 1988): 379-85.

3 David A. Kaplan, "I'd Like to Buy a Dollar," *Newsweek* (April 5, 1993): 54.

4 "A Celebrity Malpractice? Hurt Investors Try to Sack a Quarterback," *Newsweek* (December 23, 1985): 65; James Cox, "Star-Struck Advertisers Lean on Celebs," *USA Today* (June 20, 1990): 80.

5 Brian Sternthal, Ruby Dholakia, and Clark Leavitt, "The Persuasive Effects of Source Credibility: Tests of Cognitive Response," *Journal of Consumer Research* 4 (1978)4: 252-60.

6 Andrew A. Mitchell and Jerry C. Olson (1981), "Are Product Attribute Beliefs the Only Mediator of Advertising Effects on Brand Attitude?" *Journal of Marketing Research* 18 (1981)3: 318-32; R. Sparkman and L.M. Austin, "The Effect on Sales of Color in Newspaper Advertisements," *Journal of Advertising* 9 (1980): 39-42.

7 Michael R. Solomon, Sarah Drenan, and Chester A. Insko, "Popular Induction: When is Consensus Information Informative?" *Journal of Personality* 49 (1981)2: 212-24.

8 Stuart Elliott, "Resorting to Blandishments to Fight Image of Blandness," *New York Times* (August 10, 1992): D7.

9 Tina M. Lowrey, "The Relation Between Syntactic Complexity and Advertising Persuasiveness," in Advances in Consumer Research 19, eds. John F. Sherry, Jr. and Brian Sternthal, (Provo, Utah: Association for Consumer Research, 1992), 270-74.

10 Cornelia Pechmann and S. Ratneshwar, "The Use of Comparative Advertising for Brand Positioning: Association Versus Differentiation," *Journal of Consumer Research* 18 (September 1991): 145-60.

11 H. Bruce Lammers, Laura Leibowitz, George E. Seymour, and Judith E. Hennessey, "Humor and Cognitive Responses to Advertising Stimuli: A Trace Consolidation Approach," *Journal of Business Research* 11 (1983): 173-85.

12 Randall Rothenberg, "When Jokes Backfire, Campaigns Explode," *New York Times* (August 26, 1991): D6.

13 Kevin Goldman, "Everybody's Afraid of the Big Bad Boss," *The New York Times* (January 12, 1994): B1 (2).

14 J..L. Burnett and R.L. Oliver, "Fear Appeal Effects in the Field: A Segmentation Approach," *Journal of Marketing Research* 16 (1976): 181-90.

15 Herbert J. Rotfeld, "Fear Appeals and Persuasion: Assumptions and Errors in Advertising Research," *Current Issues and Research in Advertising* 11 (1988)1: 21-40.

16 David A. Aaker and Douglas M. Stayman, "Implementing the Concept of Transformational Advertising," *Psychology & Marketing* 9 (May/June 1992): 237-53.

[17] Scott B. MacKenzie and Richard A. Spreng, "How Does Motivation Moderate the Impact of Central and Peripheral Processing on Brand Attitudes and Intentions?" *Journal of Consumer Research* 18 (March 1992): 519-29.

[18] Punam Anand and Brian Sternthal, "The Effects of Program Involvement and Ease of Message Counterarguing on Advertising Persuasiveness," *Journal of Consumer Psychology* 1 (1992)3: 225-38.

Instructor's Notes:

CHAPTER 7

The Self

SUMMARY BULLETS

♦ Consumers' self-concepts are reflections of their attitudes toward themselves. Whether these attitudes are positive or negative, they will help to guide many purchase decisions; products can be used to bolster self-esteem or to "reward" the self.

♦ Many product choices are dictated by the consumer's perceived similarity between his or her personality and attributes of the product. The symbolic interactionist perspective on the self implies that each of us actually has many selves, and a different set of products is required as props to play each. Many things other than the body can also be viewed as part of the self. Valued objects, car, homes, and even attachments to sports teams or national monuments are used to define the self when these are incorporated into the extended self.

♦ A person's sex-role identity is a major component of self-definition. Conceptions about masculinity and femininity, largely shaped by society, guide the acquisition of "sex-typed" products and services.

♦ Advertising and other media play an important role in socializing consumers to be male and female. While traditional women's roles have often been perpetuated in advertising depictions, this situation is changing somewhat. The media do not always portray men accurately either.

♦ A person's conception of his or her body also provides feedback to self-image. A culture communicates certain ideals of beauty, and consumers go to great lengths to attain these. Many consumer activities involve manipulating the body, whether through dieting, cosmetic surgery, tattooing, and the like.

♦ Sometimes these activities are carried to an extreme, as people try too hard to live up to cultural ideals. One example is found in eating disorders, where women in particular become obsessed with thinness.

LECTURE/DISCUSSION IDEAS

I.   **Perspectives on the Self** -- judged by our physical appearance and possessions

---

Real World Application

☙ The value placed on individuality and a distinction between an inner and an outer self developed with the self-consciousness wrought by Puritanism between 1500 and 1800. The notion of secular fulfillment (and the conflict between an individual's needs and those of society) that drives much of modern-day hedonistic marketing was a dominant issue in the Romantic period (the late eighteenth and early nineteenth century).[1]

☙ According to objective self-awareness (OSA) theory, our conscious attention flips back and forth between the self and the external world. When a person is in an OSA state, he or she sees the self as others do, which usually arouses negative feelings, because we are often critical of the image we see. A somewhat similar perspective regards self-awareness as a feedback loop, much like the regulatory mechanism in a thermostat. We check our current self against our goals, altering our behavior if necessary to get back on track.[2]

    A. **Self-Concept** -- attitude a person holds toward oneself

(Use TM 7-1 Here)

        1. **Components of the Self-Concept**
- content: facial attractiveness and mental aptitude
- positivity or negativity (self-esteem)
- intensity, stability, and accuracy (assessment and reality)

        2. **Self-Esteem** -- attitude toward oneself

            a. **Self-Esteem Advertising** -- Marines "If you have what it takes"

Discussion Topic: What are some examples of ads that promote self-esteem?

        3. **Real and Ideal Selves**
- real self: realistic appraisal of qualities we have and don't have
- ideal self: what we would like to be

☙ Recent evidence indicates that self-assessment may also occur when consumers compare themselves to their most negative self-images, the undesired self.[3]

---

            a. **Fantasy: Bridging the Gap Between Selves** -- daydreams
(Use Color Transparency 20 Here)

    B. **Multiple Selves** -- based on roles, we are a number of different people (husband, father, boss)

(Use TM 7-2 Here)

Discussion Topic: How many multiple selves do you have?

        1. **Symbolic Interactionism** -- many social selves (self-fulfilling prophesy)

            a. **The Looking-Glass Self**--imagining other's reactions toward us

    C. **Self-Consciousness** -- feeling painfully aware of ourselves at times
- (e.g. one notices a spot on clothes, yet people may pick their nose a stoplight.)

Discussion Topic: What was one of your most embarrassing moments? If the circumstances were different would you have been less self-conscious?

        1. **Chronic Self-Consciousness** -- some people are more sensitive than others

II.   **Personality** -- unique psychological makeup

    A. **Classic Personality Theories** -- psychological and psychoanalytic theorists

        1. **Neo-Freudian Theories** -- Karen Horney's theory
- compliant: moving toward others
- detached: moving away from others
- aggressive: moving against others

        2. **Jungian Theory** -- Carl Jung rejected the sexual aspects of personality and developed analytical psychology based on a person's past and future

            a. **Archetypes** -- universally shared ideas and behavior patterns

Discussion Topic: Why are little kids scared of the dark? How do you get over this . . . or do you?

    B. **Trait Theory** --extrovert, introvert, innovative, materialistic, self-conscious

---

Real World Application

☯ Materialism has been conceptualized as a personality trait, though later work has regarded the construct as a value: this perspective will be discussed later in the book.[6]

☯ The trait of innovativeness is particularly relevant to many marketing applications, insofar as its measurement can aid researchers in assigning consumers to adopter categories. Differences in the adoption of product innovations will be discussed Chapter 17.[7]

☯ Trait theory is helpful in understanding the dynamics involved in breast reconstruction and the use of prostheses by mastectomy patients whose female identity is threatened by the loss of one or both breasts.[8]

---

    1. **Problems with Trait Theory in Consumer Research** -- mixed results

III.   **Consumption and Self-Concept** -- "props" are important in the roles we play
(Use Color Transparency 19 Here)
(Use TM 7-3 Here)

    A. **Products That Shape the Self: You Are What You Consume**
(Use Color Transparency 21 Here)
- food (e.g. vegetarian or meat and potatoes)
- leisure activities (e.g. racquetball or bowling)
- car (Porsche or Yugo)

    1. **Loss of Self** -- reaction when treasured objects are lost or stolen

Discussion Topic: Have you ever had your home burglarized? What did they take? How did this make you feel?

    B. **Self/Product Congruence** -- consistency between our self-image and purchases

---

☯ A common way to assess these matches is to use a technique known as the Q-sort. Consumers sort various products into categories according to the extent each is associated or not associated with the self.[9]

☯ People are more likely to rate more socially desirable products as similar to themselves; person/product congruence also increases with ownership.[10]

---

1. **Problems with the Congruence Concept**--not all products fit
   description e.g., theory may work with perfume but not toasters

C. **The Extended Self** -- in some cultures, possessions are buried with the dead

---

Real World Application
☯ Pets are often an integral part of the extended self. Many consumers are devoted to their pets and regard them as family members. This link is so strong that people often infer the features of owners from their pets.[11]

---

1. **Levels of the Extended Self** -- four levels
   - individual level: "You are what you wear" (car, jewelry)
   - family level: includes your house and furniture
   - community level: includes your neighborhood and home town
   - group level: your religion, flag, sports team

Discussion Topic: Do you think people should be allowed to burn the flag to protest a government action they disagree with?

☯ The degree to which people incorporate their communities into their selves helps to predict how cohesive and safe a neighborhood will be. One study that examined suburban areas found a relationship between the use of "territorial markers," such as shrubs, to indicate one's property and willingness to defend one's neighborhood. Another group of researchers also found that residents who personalized their homes by displaying property markers and holiday decorations were more attached to their communities and that these actions also deterred property crimes.[12]

IV. **Sex Roles** -- we tend to conform with culture's expectations but guidelines change

A. **Gender Differences in Socialization**

(Use TM 7-4 Here)

   - men stress self-assertion and mastery
   - women stress affiliation and harmony

Discussion Topic: Do you think that men and women react differently to the same stimulus such as a baby picture?

1. **Macho Marketers** -- stress competition, language of warfare, penetration, power, control, manipulation, etc.

B. **Gender Versus Sexual Identity** -- masculinity and femininity are not biological

1. **Sex-Typed Products** -- car is masculine product; boys' and girls' toys; pink phones

Discussion Topic: Why do you suppose we have boys' and girls' toys? Is society or marketing responsible for this?

2. **Androgyny** -- possession of both masculine and feminine traits

---

Real World Application

☯ The decision about how to portray a man or a woman (for example, whether a woman's family, sexuality, or professional life be emphasized) should take into consideration the intended function of the product. Consumers are most comfortable with role portrayals that are consistent with the product in question; a family role should be emphasized for family products, and so on.[13]

C. **Female Sex Roles** -- play a greater role in decisions on traditionally male goods

---

☯ To protest the sex role stereotypes perpetrated by children's dolls, a group of performance artists bought at least 300 talking G.I. Joe and Barbie dolls, switched voice boxes, and replaced the altered dolls on store shelves. The Barbies utter macho phrases like "Eat lead, Cobra,!" while the G.I. Joe dolls wonder, "Will we ever have enough clothes?"[14]

---

1. **Segmenting Working Women** -- professional women, managers, etc.

☯ The traditional demarcation between men and women is perpetuated in Japanese comic books, which are widely read by children and adults (they comprise over 25 percent of Japan's publishing industry). Female characters in these books tend to have lives centered around their husbands and children. Negative consequences occur when they try to pursue professional careers.[15]

---

a. **Subsegments of Working Women** -- four groups
- Housewives who do not plan to work outside of home
- Housewives who plan to work at some point
- Career-oriented working women seeking professional success
- "Just-a-job" women who work because they need the money

Discussion Topic: Of these four subsegments of working women, which do you think most women would prefer? Which would most men prefer?

Real World Application

- Some countries are redefining the role of women at a faster pace than others. This process tends to reflect the rate at which women are working outside of the home. For example, the percentage of active women (defined as those not in school, retired, or disabled) who are in the workforce is approximately 65 percent in the United States, while 50 percent of Italian women are employed, and only 37 percent work in Venezuela. Many cultures appear to be undecided about accepting an updated version of the female sex role. For example, while it is not unusual for Russian women to work as physicians, pilots, or scientists, the ideal of women as anchor of the family is still dominant in that culture. When a female cosmonaut landed at the Salyut-7 space station, the flight engineer greeted her by saying: "We've got an apron ready for you, Sveta." It's as if you've come home. Of course, we have a kitchen for you; that'll be where you work.[16]

- A growing number of women are deciding to isolate themselves from men when they vacation; one guidebook lists over 400 women-only tours. While some are targeted to lesbians, others are designed to teach traditionally male skills or to encouraging bonding with other women.

b. **Appealing to Independence and Mobility**--women buying more cars

- Initially, manufacturers tried to sell slower electric cars to women. When women said they preferred internal-combustion engines, the manufacturers replaced hand cranks with electric starters and enclosed the vehicles to appease them.[17]

- Over 70 percent of the buyers of Chevrolet's Storm and Prizm models are women. Women are more sensitive to the aesthetics of the car showroom. They are more likely to notice and be turned off if the selling floor is dirty, and they are more likely to shop at more dealers before buying. Hyundai has responded to this difference by designing car dealerships to resemble shopping malls, emphasizing a light and airy atmosphere.[18]

- Prompted by concerns about how advertising portrayed women, the National Advertising Review Board in 1975 issued a checklist for advertisers to consider when creating or approving an ad. These guidelines caution against perpetuating sexual stereotypes, such as portraying women as weak, over-emotional, or subservient to men. Marketers, by and large, have responded to this challenge, though with mixed success. Note that even Virginia Slims, which bases it campaign on women's progress, still says, "You've come a long way, baby!"[19]

2. **The Depiction of Women in Advertising** -- still depicted in traditional roles: submissive, stupid, tempermental, sex objects

(Use Color Transparency 22 Here)

   ❧ For a study that examined how relationships between men and women are portrayed in ads, see Klassen, Jasper and Schwartz article.[20]

   ❧ The degree to which men and women are presented in traditional roles varies across cultures, as might be expected. For example, compared to advertising in the United States, Australian commercials do not emphasize sex-role differences, while Mexican commercials emphasize them a bit more.[21]

a. **Updated Images** -- women are now the central characters in TV ads;role-reversal

Discussion Topic: Can you think of any ads where they have females performing acts that were predominately male roles in the past?

D. **Male Sex Roles** -- tough, aggressive, muscular but also compassionate

   ❧ In a commercial for Cascade dishwasher powder, two men have anxiety attacks because their dates are due for a dinner party and their glasses are spotted.[22]

1. **The Joys of Fatherhood** -- clothes, choices, cooking, parenting

   ❧ Men are taking on more domestic duties to compensate for the increasing numbers of working women. For example, over three-quarters of American men go on a major shopping trip in a four-week period, and men account for about 40 percent of food shopping dollars. Most men expect their sons to shop as much as their daughters do, and these attitudes do not seem to be affected by income or education. Many who shop are more likely to view themselves as considerate, contemporary people than those who don't.[23]

2. **What's Good for the Goose** . . . men are now portrayed as helpless, bumbling, dumb

3. **From Cheesecake to Beefcake** -- becoming sex objects

Discussion Topic: Can you think of an ad in which the male is a sex object?

   ❧ Men's vulnerability was the centerpiece of an ad campaign for Champion Athletic Apparel. In one execution, four soccer players hold their crotches with pained expressions and the ad reads, "There's no such thing as a free kick. It's just a question of who pays."[24]

E. **Gay and Lesbian Consumers** -- interested in graduate school, physical fitness, self-improvement, more stress in daily lives, self-employed

V.   **Body Image** -- subjective evaluation of one's physical self

(Use Color Transparency 23 Here)
(Use TM 7-5 Here)

Real World Application
☙ For a recent discussion of the body from a postmodern, feminist perspective see the Joy and Venkatesh article.[25]

A. **Body Cathexis** -- emotional significance of some object or idea to a person

B. **Ideals of Beauty** -- physical features, clothing styles, cosmetics, hair styles skin tone, youthfulness, muscular tone, etc.

(Use TM 7-6 Here)

Discussion Topic: Women: Write down on a piece of paper what your ideal man looks like. Men: Write down a on piece of paper what your ideal woman looks like.
[This will lead to a wild discussion.]

☙ Attractiveness is such an integral part of our culture that it has spawned many terms to describe good-looking people. These include such words as majestic, haunting, fetching, fair, drop-dead, knockout, classic, ravishing, swell, bitchin', foxy, and more recently fly, Ca-junga!, robo-babe, and babia majora. Students should be able to generate their own list, and can examine these terms for their connotations (e.g., many terms to describe women are animal metaphors, such as chick and fox). What do these terms say about our cultural assumptions regarding beauty?

---

1. **Ideals of Beauty Over Time** -- bound feet, skinny waists, inserted plates in lips, long necks, tan, white, breast reduction/enlargement

---

☙ Psychologists estimate that between 2-10 percent of people are so unhappy with some aspect of their appearance that it constricts their daily activities. Body dysmorphic disorder, or imagined ugliness, is now a formal psychiatric diagnosis.[26]

C. **Working on the Body** -- diet food/drinks, tanning salons

---

☙ The market for thinness is a segmented one. Generally, the people who are serious about dieting are those who do not need to be. Despite the abundance of diet-related products on the market, the right message is reaching the wrong people. Obesity is considered by many to be a more severe health problem than smoking. It is more prevalent among lower socioeconomic groups, rural residents, and African-Americans.[27]

---

1. **Fattism** -- "you can never be too thin or too rich"

Discussion Topic: Do you think that the concept "thin is in" will change somewhat because people will not want others to think they are anorexic, bulimic, or have AIDS?

Real World Application
☯ Recent studies have provided more evidence for fattism. They have shown that obese women encounter a significant earnings disadvantage in the workplace. Ongoing litigation is being carried out to determine if overweight people are covered by the American Disabilities Act of 1990.[28]

---

a. **Diet and Exercise** -- dieting, low-fat, low-cal, Weight Watchers

---

☯ In researching the diet market, Diet-Rite Cola found that dieters feel vulnerable and tend to have a poor body image. Instead of devising a typical campaign featuring thin women in skimpy bathing suits drinking soda, the commany decided to focus on people who were having trouble keeping their weight down--the typical consumers of diet drinks. In one commercial, actor Lee Majors is goaded by fit women while struggling to lift weights.[29]

☯ Although many consumers continue to play the diet game, a grassroots anti-diet rebellion is afoot. Support groups are encouraging women to free themselves from dieting obsessions. These groups claim that women are comparing themselves to an impossible standard, and they instead stress self-acceptance and realistic goals. Some analysts espouse the idea that society is punishing women for their achievements by forcing them to live a daily regimen of semistarvation. This topic an be used to generate a lively class discussion about the role of marketing in distorting and perpetuating appearance ideals.[30]

☯ Bulimic women perceive their bodies to be very large and their ideal body size, extremely thin. Female bulimics in college are often obsessed with weight, appearance, and academic performance, and they have severely negative self-concepts.[31]

---

b. **Unrealistic Standards?** -- Barbie is unnaturally long and thin

2. **Eating Disorders** -- anorexia and bulimia

a. **Exercise Addiction** -- compulsive runners

☯ Many male executives apparently feel threatened by younger rivals and are flocking to plastic surgeons, hair replacement centers, tanning salons and so on, to improve their appearance. The proportion of male plastic surgery patients jumped from about 5 percent to 20 percent in one decade. This practice is also beginning to trickle down to adolescents. Some doctors estimate that the number of cosmetic operations performed on teens has doubled or even tripled in the past few years.[32]

---

3. **Cosmetic Surgery** -- silicon implants, liposuction, face lifts

a. **Body Decoration and Mutilation** -- why?

- to separate group members from nonmembers
- to place the individual in the social organization
- to place the person in a gender category
- to enhance sex-role identification
- to indicate desired social conduct
- to indicate high status or rank
- to provide a sense of security

b. **Tattoos** -- body art traditionally associated with social outcasts

FIELD PROJECT IDEAS

Individual Assignments

1. Ask a student to bring to class two brands within the same product category that project different images to the consumer. Have the student discuss the projected images that is being projected by comparing and contrasting the two different brands. What techniques did the marketer use to project these images? Is the self-concept of the buyer important?

2. Have a student develop a set of scales to measure consumers' self-images and their image have of a car such as the Honda Accord. The student should administer the scales to 5 people who drive the selected car. Do the images appear to be compatible?

3. Ask a student to look through a number of magazines to find at least three examples of promotions that appear to be using Freudian concepts. Then have him/her explain the specific concepts to the class noting whether they are effective. Does the student like the way the concepts are used? Are there any objections?

Group Assignments

4. Have each student interview four people (one each in their 20's, 30's, 40's, 50's) to determine how important appearance is on the job. Ask your students if they feel that an employee's appearance should be considered in performance evaluations. See if their attitudes change when the employee must deal directly with customers. This activity is also interesting when you ask the subjects about the proper appearance in church or at an important social function.

5. Ask your students to compile a list of ten household chores. Then have each student interview two couples (one newlywed and the other seasoned) to determine who usually performs that chore--the husband or the wife. If possible have the students ask the subject when their spouse is not around. Do they agree? This can be fun to analyze during class.

6. Bring to class a sample of a personality inventory. (A good example can be found in a book by David Keirsey and Marilyn Bates, *Please Understand Me*, Prometheus Nemesis Book Company, Box 2748, Del Mar, CA 92014, 1984.) If possible, let the students take some form of the Myers-Briggs or another inventory so they can discover their own personality traits. Use the personality inventory to begin a discussion on the measurement of personality.

Individual or Group Assignments

7.   Ask a couple of students to go out and interview the managers of two retail clothing stores of their choice. See if they can discover the degree to which the managers believe that consumers' personalities and self-images are important to the marketing and promotional activities of their store. Ask the students if they are in agreement with the managers.

8. Have a male student and a female student separately interview three women and three men whom they think are just about the right weight for their height and bone structure. The students should ask the respondents if they think of themselves as overweight, underweight, or about right. Then, see if they can determine how the subjects reached their conclusions. And, ask the subjects if they are doing anything to keep their weight under control.

9. As mentioned in the Real World Applications, research shows that as people incorporate their communities into their "selves", the community tends to be safer. Ask a group of students to drive around in three neighborhoods (poor, average and rich) and observe some of the visible signs of safety or lack of safety. They could make a short video tape of what they observed.

10. If it is a holiday season when you cover this chapter, have a group of students drive through a few different neighborhoods to see how many visible signs of the holiday are displayed. Ask them about their observations. Once again, they could video tape what they see and show this to the class.

11. Send the students out in pairs to visit a store that they like. Ask the students to observe and describe personalities of the sales force. Now send them to visit a store they dislike. Did they notice any difference in the personalities of the sales force? Do they think that poor or unexciting personalities will have an affect on salesmanship?

12. Have a student or the entire class, write an obituary for two products (e.g. Osh-kosh overalls, Calvin Klein purse). The obituary should talk about the individual personality of the products and should show the differences.

CONSUMER BEHAVIOR CHALLENGE

1. How might the creation of a self-conscious state be related to consumers who are trying on clothing in dressing rooms? Does the act of preening in front of a mirror change the dynamics by which people evaluate their product choices? Why?

When women try on clothing in a dressing room the presence of other women and mirrors might create a self-conscious state. By "checking themselves out" in a mirror asking other people how something looks, or hearing someone tell them that they look good. In an outfit, women's self-consciousness is likely to be heightened. These acts and interactions will determine whether a potential customer feels confident about wearing the outfit and, therefore, is willing to buy it.

2. Is it ethical for marketers to encourage infatuation with the self?

Students will have their own opinions. Encourage them to think about self-infatuation and the related concepts of self-consciousness and self-esteem.

3. List three dimensions by which the self-concept can be described.

1. content -- facial attractiveness versus mental aptitude
2. positivity or negativity -- self-esteem
3. intensity, stability over time, and accuracy -- the degree to which one's self assessment corresponds to reality.

4. Compare and contrast the real versus the ideal self. List three products for which each type of self is likely to be used as a reference point when a purchase is considered.

The real self is the perception of oneself as one believes he actually is while the ideal self is the perception of oneself as one would like to be.
The products student choose will differ. For example, a person might buy a PaperMate ball-point pen for use around the house, but will carry a Cross Pen (which was probably a gift) when out in public.

5. Watch a set of ads featuring men and women on television. Try to imagine the characters with reversed roles (i.e., the male parts played by women and vice versa). Can you see any differences in assumptions about sex-typed behavior?

Student will have fun with this challenge though it will be an eye-opener to some. An example of an ad that has women and men playing their traditional roles is a Duncan Hines cake mix commercial. The commercial shows the wife/mother making a cake. When the care is ready, the father/husband and children are smiling and happy. The ad then says, "Nothin' says lovin' like a cake from the oven." If one switches the roles of the man and woman, the ad somehow would not correspond to our image of having a cake baked by someone who loves us. Most of the time we will want to see ads that reflect a reality as we normally perceive it. (Possible Field Project Idea)

6. To date, the bulk of advertising targeted to gay consumers has been placed in exclusively gay media. If it was your decision to make, would you consider using mainstream media as well to reach gays, who constitute a significant proportion of the general population? Or, remembering that members of some targeted segments have serious objections about this practice, especially when the product (e.g., liquor, cigarettes) may be viewed as harmful in some way, do you think gays should be singled out at all by marketers?

Students should consider the text discussion of gay and lesbian consumers. There more likely will be a difference of opinion on this issue. The instructor might encourage different groups of students to take each side of the argument, irrespective of their personal opinions on the matter. Due to the potential sensitivity of the topic, the instructor might ask the students to think about segmentation and target marketing efforts, in general, and consider why this case is or is not different from targeting any other consumer group. (Possible Class Activity -- Debate)

7. Do you agree that marketing strategies tend to have a male-oriented bias? If so, what are some possible consequences for specific marketing activities?

Students should consider the discussion of "macho marketers" in the text. Ask them to generate examples of marketing activities that reflect the presence and absence of male bias. In general, the instructor should encourage students to think about the consequences of male-oriented bias across disciplines, not just in the contest of marketing activities. (You might ask the men if they see any evidence of female-oriented bias in advertising and marketing.)

8. In the past, some marketers have been reluctant to use disabled people in advertising out of fear they would be seen as patronizing or that their ads would be depressing. Should the disabled be viewed as a distinct market segment, or should marketers continue to assume that their wants and needs are the same as those of the rest of the mainstream market?

The issues raised in this question are similar to those for question #6. That is, should marketers apply the basic marketing principles of segmentation, target marketing and product positioning, based on the assessment of consumers as distinctive groups--whether rich or poor, male or female, homosexual or heterosexual, handicapped or not? Students should be challenged to express their individual views. While disucssing this specific question, the instructor may want to refer to a commercial for Spray-n-Wash that pictured a mother and a daughter with Downs-Syndrome. The commercial said that this mother and daughter had enough to worry about without thinking about stains in their clothes. Critics opposed the advertiser's use of the handicapped in the ad.

9. Construct a "consumption biography" of a friend or family member. Make a list and/or photograph his or her most favorite possessions, and see if you or others can describe this person's personality just from the information provided by this catalogue.

Students might like to bring in a short video tape of the types of products the subject owns. This is usually a fun exercise as students love to guess who the subject is. Usually, of course, they can pinpoint who the person is and can come close to describing the person's personality. (Possible Individual Field Project)

10. Some consumer advocates have protested the use of superthin models in advertising, claiming that these women encourage others to starve themselves in order to attain the "waif" look. Other critics respond that the media's power to shape behavior has been overestimated, and that it is insulting to people to assume that they are unable to separate fantasy from reality. What do you think?

This is a good topic for a debate. An instructor might want to seek volunteers or to simply select two teams each consisting of one male and one female student. Give each team an opportunity to present their side of the argument and then allow time for rebuttal. (Possible In-Class Activity)

ENDNOTES

[1] Roy F. Baumeister, Dianne M. Tice and Debra G. Hutton, "Self-Presentational Motivations and Personality Differences in Self-Esteem," *Journal of Personality* 57 (September 1989): 547-75.

[2] S. Duval and R.A. Wicklund. *A Theory of Objective Self-Awareness* (New York, Academic Press, 1972); Charles S. Carver and Michael F. Schleler, *Attention and Self-Regulation: A Control-Theory Approach to Human Behavior* (New York: Springer-Verlag, 1981); M. Joseph Sirgy, "Self-Cybernetic: Toward an Integrated Model of Self-Concept Processes." *Systems Research* 7 (1990): 1:19-32.

[3] Daniel M. Ogilvie, "The Undesired Self: A Neglected Variable in Personality Research," *Journal of Personality and Social Psychology* 52 (1987) 2: 379-85.

[4] Ira Teinowitz, "Coors Keys on Fantasy," *Advertising Age* (September 11, 1989): 114.

[5] Peter S. Greenberg, "Hotels Play Up Fantasies," *The Asbury Park Press* (May 27, 1990) : B1.

6 Russell W. Belk, "Materialism: Trait Aspects of Living in the Material World," *Journal of Consumer Research* 12 (December 1985); 265-80; Dennis Cole, Newell D. Wright, M. Joseph Sirgy, Rustan Kosenko, Don Rahtz, and H. Lee Meadow, "Testing the Reliability and Validity of Belk's and Richins' Materialism Scales," in *Proceeding of the Academy of Marketing Science* (1992); Seth R. Ellis, "A Factor Analytic Investigation of Belk's Structure of the Materialism Construct," in *Advances in Consumer Research* 19, eds,John F. Sherry, Jr. and Brian Sternthal (Provo, Utah: Association of Consumer Reseaarch, 1992), 688.

7 For recent advances in measurement of this trait, see Ronald E. Goldsmith and Charles F. Hofacker, "Measuring Consumer Innovativeness," *Journal of the Academy of Marketing Science* 19 (1991) 3: 209-21; Gordon R. Faxall and Ronald E. Goldsmith, "Personality and Consumer Research: Another Look," *Journal of the Market Research Society* 30 (1988)2: 111-25.

8 Betty L. Feather, Susan B. Kaiser, and Margaret Rucker, "Breast Reconstruction and Prosthesis Use as Forms of Symbolic Completion of the Physical Self," *Home Economics Research Journal* 17 (March 1989): 216-27.

9 M. Joseph Sirgy, "Self-Concept in Consumer Behavior: A Critical Review," *Journal of Consumer Research* 9 (December 1982): 287-300.

10 George E. Belch and E. Laird Landon, Jr., "Discriminant Validity of a Product-Anchored Self-Concept Measure," *Journal of Marketing Research* 24 (May 1977): 252-56.

11 Marcel Heiman, "Man and His Pet," in *Motivations in Play, Games and Sports*, eds., Ralph Slovenko and James A. Knight (Springfield, IL Charles C. Thomas, 1967), 329-48.

12 Julian J. Edney, "Property, Possession and Performance: A Field Study of Human Territoriality," *Journal or Applied Social Psychology* 2 (1972) 3: 275-82; Barbara B. Brown and Carol M. Werner "Social Cohesiveness, Territoriality, and Holiday Decorations: The Influence of Cul-de-Sacs," *Environment and Behavior* 17 (September 1985): 539-65.

13 Lawrence H. Wortzel and John M. Frisbie, "Women's Role Portrayal Preferences in Advertisements: An Empirical Study," *Journal of Marketing* 38 (October 1974); 41-46.

14 David Firestone, "As Barbie Talks Tough, G.I. Joe Goes Shopping," *The New York Times* (December 31, 1993): A12.

15 Sean Ledden and Fred Fejes, "Female Gender Role Patterns in Japanese Comic Magazines," *Journal of Popular Culture* 21 (Summer 1987): 155-70.

16 John F. Burns, "An Apron For Soviet Woman in Space," *New York Times* (August 28, 1982): D1; Denise Rusoff, "British Women Get the Jobs," *American Demographics* (December 1987): 54; Rena Bartos, "Marketing to Women: The Quiet Revolution," *Marketing Insights* (June 1989): 61.

17 Sandra Salmans, "When an It is Labeled as He or a She," *New York Times* (November 16, 1989) C1.

18 Julie Candler, "Woman Car Buyer: Don't Call Her a Niche Anymore," *Advertising Age* (January 21, 1991): S-8; Frieda Curtindale, "Marketing Cars to Women," *American Demographics* (November 1988).

19 *Advertising and Women: A Report on Advertising Portraying or Directed to Women* (New York: The National Advertising Review Board, 1975).

20 Michael L. Klassen, Cynthia R. Jasper, and Anne M. Schwartz, "Men and Women: Images of Their Relationships in Magazine Advertisements," *Journal of Advertising Research* (March/April 1993): 30-39.

21 Mary C. Gilly, "Sex Roles in Advertising: A Comparison of Television Advertisements in Australia, Mexico, and the United States," *Journal of Marketing* 52 (April 1988) 75-85.

22 Kim Foltz, "In Ads, Men's Image Becomes Softer," *New York Times* (March 26, 1990): D12.

23 "Do Real Men Shop?" *American Demographics* (May 1987): 13.

24 Lena Williams, "Bodies Go Public: It's Men's Turn Now," *New York Times* (October 31, 1990): C1.

25 Annamma Joy and Alladi Venkatesh, "Postmodernism, Feminism, and the Body: The Visible and the Invisible in Consumer Research," *International Journal of Research in Marketing*, in press.

26 Daniel Goleman, "When Ugliness is Only in Patient's Eye, Body Image Can Reflect Mental Disorder," *New York Times* (October 2, 1991) C13.

27 Jeremy Schlossberg, "The Demographics of Dieting," *American Demographics* (July 1987): 35.

28 Peter Passell, "An Ugly Subject: The Prejudice Against Hiring Homely People," *The New York Times* (January 27, 1994): D2.

29 Jeffrey A Trachtenberg, "Beyond the Hidden Persuaders," *Forbes* (March 23, 1987): 131.

30 Jan Seligmann "Let them Eat Cake," *Newsweek* (August 17, 1992) 2:57.

31 Donald A. Williamson, C. J. Davis, Anthony J. Goreczny, and David C. Blovin, "Body-Image Disturbances in Bulimia Nervosa: Influences of Actual Body Size," *Journal of Abnormal Psychology* 98 (1989) 1: 97-99; Mariette Brouwers, "Depressive Thought Content Among Female College Students with Bulimia," *Journal of Counseling and Development* 66 (May 1988): 425-8.

32 Jerry Adler, "New Bodies for Sale," *Newsweek* (May 27, 1985): 64; "Vanity in the Executive Suite," *Dun's Business Month* (September 1985); 72-79; Gary M. Kaplan, "Putting on a Happier Face," *Nation's Business* (August 1986): 40; Anne Taylor Fleming, "Youths Who Look for a '10' in the Mirror," *New York Times* (December 20, 1989): C10.

33 Nicholas D. Kristof, "Changing the Face of China, One Face at a Time," *New York Times* (June 19, 1991): A4.

Instructor's Notes:

Individual or Group Assignments

11. Have a student read several recent product rating reports from *Consumer Reports* and then evaluate the rating system the organization used. (You might want to assign this to a team of students and have each student be responsible for one product rating.) Ask the students what other information they would have found useful.

12. Ask a student or a group of students to bring to class an advertisement that is designed to activate the problem-recognition process. Does the student think that the ad works on the consumer's actual state or desired state? See if the student(s) can improve the problem recognition features of the ad.

13. [Students will have to be warned in advance for this field project.] Over a one-week period, have the students record ten situations which caused them to enter the problem-recognition stage of the decision-making process. Which types of situations occurred most frequently?

14. Ask a student or a team of students to bring to class three advertisements that attempt to change the reader's desired or ideal states. See if the students can identify the techniques the advertisers employed to accomplish their goal.

15. Have a student or a group of students construct the Stages in the Consumer Decision Making (Figure 8-1) process that they went through for a recent large-scale purchase (e.g. expensive clothing, car, stereo system, appliance, furniture, etc.) Ask them if they think they gathered enough information before making their decision. See if they were satisfied with the quantity or quality of the information they had at their disposal.

CONSUMER BEHAVIOR CHALLENGE

1. If people are not always rational decision makers, is it worth the effort to study how these decisions are made? What techniques might be employed to understand experiential consumption and to translate this knowledge into marketing strategy?

In discussing the utility of studying rational decision making (or extended problem solving), the instructor should stress the importance of using different methods in investigating the complex nature of consumer decision making. What also needs to be made clear is that other less purposeful methods also play a role. To understand and apply experiential consumption to marketing strategy will require more knowledge of how consumers develop their overall impression of a product and how they integrate it into their decision-making process. Contributions from other disciplines, such as psychology and sociology, also will be important. The real challenge will be applying this disparate information to marketing strategy.

2. List three product attributes that can be used as quality signals and provide an example of each.

Students should draw from the chapter material that identifies the following product attributes used as quality signals:
1. Price -- "You get what you pay for."
2. Brand Name -- well known name will denote high quality to the consumer and a lesser known name will denote low quality.
3. Country of Origin -- particular countries become known for producing high (low) quality product. Students should recognize that these attributes frequently are used by less knowledgeable and/or less involved consumers.

3. Why is it difficult to place a product in a consumer's evoked set after it has already been rejected? What strategies might a marketer use in an attempt to accomplish this goal?

It is difficult to place a product into an evoked set after it has been rejected because consumers are "cognitive misers." This means that people conserve their mental resources and expend only a minimum effort required to solve a problem. Once a product has been eliminated from consideration on the basis of some evaluation process, consumers are not likely to expend additional cognitive resources to re-evaluate that product.

Promotional strategies can be used to get the consumer to reconsider the product. Price discounts, coupons, special offers, rebates, or free samples. will increase the possibility that a product will re-enter the evoked set. Any other means to get the consumer to try the product will increase the possibility of consideration of the product, and successful trial will increase the chances of a product being included in the consumer's evoked set.

4. Define the three levels of product categorization described in the chapter. Diagram these levels for a health club.

The text discussed the following levels of product categorization:
1. Superordinate -- the broadest and most abstract level (e.g. health clubs)
2. Basic Level -- the most useful category to classify products because these
    items have much in common with each other (e.g. weight/powerlifting clubs)
3. Subordinate Level -- the most specific category (e.g. Nautilus Fitness Clubs)

5. Discuss two different noncompensatory decision rules, and highlight the difference(s) between them. How might the use of one rule versus another result in a different product choice?

The use of a particular noncompensatory rule will influence the product chosen: (1) the lexicographic rule will result in a choice based on a particularly important attribute; (2) the elimination-by-aspects rule will result in a choice based on the particular cut-off points established, and (3) the conjunctive rule will result in a choice based on the particular brands being considered and the cut-off points.

[The choice of particular noncompensatory decision rules is not the crucial aspect of this exercise. It is important, however, that students appreciate the differences between the rules they choose to discuss. In addition, students should understand the more basic difference between noncompensatory and compensatory rules and how each uses different information to arrive a a decision. The instructor should encourage students to think about why particular choice rules are used and ways that marketers could appeal to consumer using each of these rules.]

6. Choose a friend or parent who grocery shops on a regular basis, and keep a log of their purchases of common consumer products over the semester. Can you detect any evidence of brand loyalty in any categories based upon consistency of purchases? If so, talk to the person about these purchases. Try to determine if his or her choices are based upon true brand loyalty or based on inertia. What techniques might you use to differentiate between the two?

To begin with, the instructor should ask the students to differentiate between brand loyalty and inertia. Brand loyalty is represented by a pattern of repeat product purchases, accompanied by an underlying positive attitude toward the brand. Inertia describes consumption at the low end of involvement, where decisions are made out of habit because the consumer lacks the motivation to consider alternatives.

For example a student said that her mother buys the same cereal every week. In discussing the reason for buying the cereal, her mother said she bought it because it was what the student's father liked. She considered him to be brand loyal. Techniques the student could use to find out if the father is truly brand loyal would be to ask him to try other cereals. After trying these alternative, if he insisted that his was the best, he could be considered to be brand loyal. (Possible Field Project)

7. Form a group of three. Pick a product and develop a marketing plan based upon each of the three approaches to consumer decision making: rational, experiential, and behavioral influence. What are the major differences in emphasis among the three perspectives? Which is the most likely type of problem-solving activity for the product you have selected? What characteristics of the product make this so?

The three approaches to consumer decision making discussed in the book are:
1. Rational--the consumer is a careful, analytical decision maker who tries to maximize utility in purchase decisions
2. Experiential--stresses the gestalt or totality of the product or service.
3. Behavioral--stresses that consumer decision are learned responses to cues.

To provide an example for individual groups exercises, the instructor could first ask the class as a whole to pick one product and make suggestions for a marketing plan. The class should then be encouraged to form their own groups and devise a marketing plan for their products. It would be interesting to have groups use different approaches to market the same product, and other groups use the same approach to market different products. (Possible Field Project)

8. Locate a person who is about to make a major purchase. Ask that person to make a chronological list of all the information sources consulted prior to making a decision. How would you characterize the types of sources used (i.e., internal versus external, media versus personal, etc.)? Which sources appeared to have the most impact on the person's decision?

The instructor could begin by reviewing the stages in the consumer decision making process: problem recognition, information search, evaluation of alternatives, product choice, and outcomes. The following scenario might be developed in the context of this exercise:

Jane Smith is in the market for a new computer. She looked at store ads first to compare features and prices of many computers. The next step was to ask friends and colleagues what they thought about the brands she was considering. After much research, she finally decided on a brand and made a purchase. [The sources used were external, media, and personal. Sources that had the most impact on where were external and personal.] (Possible Field Project)

9. Perform a survey of country-of-origin stereotypes. Compile a list of five countries and ask people what products they associate with each. What are their evaluations of the products and likely attributes of these different products? The power of a country stereotype can also be demonstrated in another way. Prepare a brief description of a product, including a list of features, and ask people to rate it in terms of quality, likelihood of purchase, and so on. Make several versions of the description, varying only the country from which it comes. Do ratings change as a function of the country of origin?

Students may have strong association for many countries tied to specific products or product categories. Examples might include European import/luxury cars, French wines, Italian leather goods, Swedish crystal, and Japanese electronics. It may be interesting to expand the notion of country of origin, and ask students to talk about areas in the U.S. that are particularly well-known for specific products. Alternatively, for both country and region of origin, students should be challenged to think of examples that represent weak or poor association that marketers would want to avoid. (Possible Field Project)

10. Ask a friend to talk through the process he or she used to choose one brand over others during a recent purchase. Based on this description, can you identify the decision rule that was most likely employed?

The instructor might begin by reviewing the two types of decision rules, namely, compensatory and noncompensatory. Compensatory decision rules involve averaging information about attributes of competing products where a poor rating on one attribute can be offset by a good rating on another. Noncompensatory decision rules, alternately, would find a brand with a low rating on one relevant/important attribute eliminated from the consumer's choices, despite higher ratings on less relevant/important attributes. The specific types of compensatory and noncompensatory rules also should be reviewed.

ENDNOTES

1 Stephen J. Hoch and Young-Won Ha, "Consumer Learning: Advertising and the Ambiguity of Product Experience," *Journal of Consumer Research* 13 (September 1986): 221-33.

2 Gordon C. Bruner, "Problem Recognition Styles and Search Patterns: An Empirical Investigation," Journal of Retailing 62 (Fall 1986): 281-97.

3 Kevin Goldman, "Marketing Female Condom is a Challenge," *The Wall Street Journal* (July 27, 1994): B4.

4 Julie L. Ozanne, Merrie Brucks, and Dhruv Grewal, "A Study of Information Search Behavior During the Categorization of New Products," *Journal of Consumer Research* 18 (March 1992): 452.

5 Catherine A. Cole and Siva K. Balasubramanian, "Age Differences in Consumers' Search for Information: Public Policy Implications," *Journal of Consumer Research* 20 (June 1993): 157-169.

6 "Zen and the Art of Buying a Car," *New York Times* (September 8, 1991): F10.

7 James R. Bettman and C. Whan Park, "Effects of Prior Knowledge and Experience and Phase of the Choice Process on Consumer Decision Processes: A Protocol Analysis," *Journal of Consumer Research* 7 (December 1980): 234-48.

8 Jacob Jacoby, Robert W. Chestnut, Karl C. Weigl, and William Fisher, "Pre-Purchase Information Acquisition: Description of a Process Methodology, Research Paradigm and Pilot Investigation," in Advances in Consumer Research 3, ed. Beverlee B. Anderson (Ann Arbor, Mich.: Association for Consumer Research, 1976), 306-14; Charles M. Schaninger and Donald Sciglimpaglia, "The Influence of Cognitive Personality Traits and Demographics on Consumer Information Acquisition," *Journal of Consumer Research* 8 (September 1981): 208-16; Merrie Brucks, "The Effects of Product Class Knowledge on Information Search Behavior," *Journal of Consumer Research* 12 (June 1985): 1-16; Eloise Coupey, "Restructuring: Constructive Processing of Information Displays in Consumer Choice," *Journal of Consumer Research* 21 (June 1994): 83-99.

9 William Boulding and Amna Kirmani (1992), "An Experimental Examination of Signalling Theory: Do Consumers Perceive Warranties as Signals of Quality?" unpublished manuscript, Duke University, Durham, N.C., 1992.

10 William P. Putsis, Jr. and Narasimhan Srinivasan, "Buying or Just Browsing? The Duration of Purchase Deliberation," *Journal of Marketing Research* 31 (August 1994): 393-402.

11 Joel Huber, John W. Payne, and Christopher Puto, "Adding Asymmetrically Dominated Alternatives: Violations of Regularity and the Similarity Hypothesis," *Journal of Consumer Research* 9 (June 1982): 90-98; Itamar Simonson, "Get Closer to Your Customers By Understanding How They Make Choices," unpublished manuscript, University of California, Berkeley, 1992.

12 Joseph W. Alba and J. Wesley Hutchinson, "Dimensions of Consumer Expertise," *Journal of Consumer Research* 13 (March 1987): 411-54.

13 Deborah Roedder John and Mita Sujan, "Age Differences in Product Categorization," *Journal of Consumer Research* 16 (March 1990): 452-60.

14 Joseph W. Alba and J. Wesley Hutchinson, "Dimensions of Consumer Expertise," *Journal of Consumer Research* 13 (March 1987): 411-54.

[15] James R. Bettman and Mita Sujan, "Effects of Framing on Evaluation of Comparable Alternatives by Expert and No-vice Consumers," *Journal of Consumer Research* 14 (September 1987): 141-54; Paul M. Herr, "Priming Price: Prior Knowledge and Context Effects," *Journal of Consumer Research* 16 (June 1987): 67-75; Christopher P. Puto, "The Framing of Buying Decisions," *Journal of Consumer Research* 14 (December 1987): 301-15.

[16] Stuart Elliott, "What's in a Name? Perhaps Billions," *New York Times* (August 12, 1992): D6; Suein L. Hwang, "New Marlboro Man is a Mere Shadow of His Former Self," *Wall Street Journal*, September 14, 1992)2: B1.

[17] Scott Hume, "Brand Loyalty Steady," *Advertising Age* (March 2, 1992): 19.

[18] Andrew Pollack, "Japan Eases 57 Varieties Marketing," *New York Times* (October 15, 1992)2: D1.

Instructor's Notes:

7. See if someone will interview a complaint handler for a local department store to describe a recent experience with a dissatisfied customer. The complaint handler should explain why the customer was unhappy. Have the student explore whether complainers seem to have any common traits.

8. Ask a student to relate to the class a purchase experience in which dissatisfaction resulted from the product or service purchased. Have the student tell the class how he/she reacted in terms of postpurchase dissonance. How could the seller avoid future similar incidents?

Group Assignments

9. Distribute to the class a list of specific product and the stores that stock those particular products. Then have each student write down the name of the store where he or she would most probably go to buy that product. Have them explain their choices.

10. Once again a popular word in society is "conservation." Many consumers have become more interested in conserving than in "throwing away".   See what ideas the class has for creative recycling.   Can they figure out a way to profitably market these ideas to the public?

Individual or Group Assignments

11. Ask a student or a group to bring to class advertisements which demonstrate a store's effort to cultivate a particular image among consumers. Do they think the ads are effective?

12. Have students bring to class two advertisements that they believe promote a product in a way that is inconsistent with what the product can deliver. The students should explain their reasoning.

13. Ask a team of students to visit a nearby popular malls to observe the activities of customers and employees. What nonretailing activities do they observe (art exhibits, performances, fitness walking, socializing, etc.)? Are these activities beneficial or harmful to retailers?

14. Have a student or a group of students bring several mail-order catalogs to class and discuss with the class the differences between the in-store and non-store purchasing processes. You might have the student(s) draw up a "profile" of a typical purchaser from each of these catalogues..

15. Ask some students bring to class two advertisements that they believe are oriented toward reducing the buyer's cognitive dissonance. Now have them comment on the effectiveness of the specific approaches selected by the advertisers..

CONSUMER BEHAVIOR CHALLENGE

1. Discuss some of the motivations for shopping as described in the chapter. How might a retailer adjust his or her strategy to accommodate these motivations?

Shopping motives listed in the chapter are: 1) functional and tangible needs, 2) pleasurable and intangible reasons, 3) social experiences, 4) sharing of common interests, 5) interpersonal attraction, 6) instant status, and 7) "the thrill of the chase." Shopping is a way of acquiring needed products as well as satisfying some important social need.

Retailers might adjust their strategies to accommodate these motives by creating a theme environment, like that of the Banana Republic. They might offer additional complementary services--for example, a tanning salon might include manicures, massages, makeovers. Encourage your students to think of specific examples appropriate for their favorite stores.

2. A number of court cases in recent years have attempted to prohibit special interest groups from distributing literature in shopping malls. Mall management claims that these centers are private property. On the other hand, these groups argue that the mall is the modern-day version of the town square and as such is a public forum. Find some recent court cases involving this free-speech issue, and examine the arguments pro and con. What is the current status of the mall as a public forum? Do you agree with this concept?

This exercise will challenge the student to conduct primary and secondary research. Encourage exploration of this issue with other students, faculty members, and consumer advocacy groups. A search should be conducted of published sources such as court cases and the *Law Review*. They might call the management office of a local mall for additional information.

3. What are some positive and negative aspects of requiring employees who interact with customers to wear some kind of uniform or to mandate a dress code in the office?

Employee uniforms will impact the overall image and atmospherics of some retail outlets. The positive aspects of requiring employees who interact with customers to wear some kind of uniform or to mandate a dress code in the office include: 1) portraying a professional image, 2) helping employees to feel "equal" in terms of dress, and 3) making it easier for customer to identify employees of the business. The negative aspects include some employees might feel uncomfortable in some uniforms, others may feel their "freedom" of apparel (to look good) is being limited, and employees may also feel their individuality is being restricted.

Students should quite easily identify examples of some jobs or professions that require uniforms (e.g., police, firefighters, nurses, priests, McDonald's staff.)

4. Think about exceptionally good and bad salespeople you have encountered in the past. What qualities seem to differentiate them?

The instructor might ask students to recall the last time they went shopping. In the context of that shopping trip, students should describe the characteristics of the salespeople who assisted them. The instructor, or a member of the class, should generate a list of the most common traits mentioned and use the class discussion to profile both good and bad salespeople. The students also should be encouraged to consider the text discussion of source credibility, including such characteristics as similarity, attractiveness, expertise, trustworthiness, likability, etc.

5. List the five stages of a long-term service relationship. How can a practitioner of relationship marketing incorporate each stage into his or her strategy?

The five stages of a long-term sales relationship are 1) awareness, 2) exploration, 3) expansion, 4) commitment, and 5) dissolution. The instructor might highlight the importance of relationship marketing for the 1990s and encourage students to think of creative ways to incorporate each phase into business strategies.

6. Discuss the concept of "timestyle." Based on your own experiences, how might consumers be segmented in terms of their timestyles?

The concept of "timestyle" reflects how individuals allocate their time to various activities. You might want to discuss your own timestyle with the class and encourage students to do the same. A discussion of how consumers might be segmented on the basis of their timestyles should be included. Products that benefit from different timestyles also could be discussed. For example: how much time do you spend teaching, grading papers, researching, doing college and community service. How much time do you spend with your family, doing household chores, eating, sleeping, exercising, having fun, etc.

7. Compare and contrast different cultures' conceptions of time. What are some implications for marketing strategy within each of these frameworks?

Conceptions of time are not universal; cultural differences with regard to time exist. Examples of such that are mentioned in the text include: 1) linear separable time--events proceed in an orderly sequence and different times are well defined, 2) procedural time--people ignore the clock completely, and 3) circular or cyclic time--people are governed by natural cycles (Latino cultures.

Marketing implications that correspond to the above concepts are: 1) under linear separable time--people sell clocks, watches, timers, have lunch hours specials, happy hours, after dinner drinks, etc. 2) under procedural time--people do things when the "time is right" so from a marketers need to show causal relationships to let the consumer know that "the time is now," and 3) under circular or cyclic time--the future doesn't make sense so we live for now. These consumers will not wait for a better product, they will buy whatever is available now. Don't bother trying to sell them insurance.

8. The movement away from a "disposable consumer society" toward one that emphasizes creative recycling creates many opportunities for marketers. Can you identify some?

Products can be disposed of by storage, temporary disposal, and permanent disposal. Recycling is an important disposal option as well. Student are likely to generate many and diverse examples of marketing opportunities in light of this new consumer emphasis. For example: A company may pick up yard waste for a fee and then turn that into compost to sell back to the homeowner! A company could pick up used oil that could be re-refined. One farmer lets companies dump old tires on his farm for a fee, and he grinds them up and resells them as a road surfacing material.

9. Conduct naturalistic observation at a local mall. Sit in a central location and observe the activities of mall employees and patrons. Keep a log of the nonretailing activity you observe (e.g., special performances, exhibits, socializing, etc.). Does this activity enhance or detract from business conducted at the mall?

Students tend to like this exercise. Now that they have been exposed to a variety of consumer behavior constructs, they are likely to see things in the retail context that the didn't notice before. They will probably notice a wide variety of nonretailing activities in the mall. Encourage your students to think about the advantages and disadvantages of these other activities from *both* the consumers' and retailers' points of view. (Possible Field Project)

10. Select three competing clothing stores in your area, and conduct a store-image study for them. Ask a group of consumers to rate each store on a set of attributes, and plot these ratings on the same graph. Based on your findings, are there any areas of competitive advantage or disadvantage you could bring to the attention of store management? (Note this technique was described in Chapter 5.)

Students should review the section on Store Image (including Store Gestalt and Atmospherics) before beginning this exercise. You might encourage the student to select stores that are very different from each other rather than "direct competitors." Consider using this as an opportunity to discuss the strengths and weakness of this type of market research. (Possible Field Project)

11. Using Table 9-1 as a model, construct a person/situation segmentation matrix for a brand of perfume.

You might want to ask different groups of students to construct a matrix for other very different types of products such as convenience versus specialty goods. Since the text hasn't covered demographic and psychographic characteristics yet (but this was probably covered in a Principles class), tell students to look up these terms in the glossary and index for further information. (Possible Field Project or In Class Group Project)

12. What applications of queuing theory can you find employed among local services? Interview consumers who are waiting on lines to determine how (if at all) this experience affects their satisfaction with the service.

The students should consider the explanation of queuing theory--the mathematical study of waiting in lines--as part of the psychological time construct. As suggested, a consumer's experience of waiting can radically influence his or her perception of service quality. While we assume that something must be pretty good if we have to wait for it, the negative feelings aroused by long waits can quickly discourage consumers. Lines at movie theatres, restaurants, ticket booths, and university class registration, all provide contexts in which students might investigate the psychology of time. (Possible Field Project)

13. The store environment is heating up as more and more companies put their promotional dollars into point-of-purchase efforts. Shoppers are now confronted by videos at the checkout counter, computer monitors attached to their shopping carts, and so on. Place-based media even expose us to ads in nonshopping environments. Recently, a health club in New York was forced to remove TV monitors that showed advertising on the Health Club Media Networks, since it was claimed that they interfered with workouts. Do you feel that these innovations are overly intrusive? At what point might shoppers "rebel" and demand some peace and quiet while shopping? Do you see any market potential in the future for stores that "countermarket" by promising a "hands-off" shopping environment?

Student opinion will vary based on their knowledge/experience and feelings/beliefs about place-based media. You might ask your students if they have encouraged this type of promotion and explore their reaction at the time of exposure. Students might also be asked to consider a more objective opinion, in light of what they have learned from this course. They should be challenged to view the advantages and disadvantages of these practices, from the perspectives of *both* consumers and retailers.

ENDNOTES

[1] Isadore Barmash, "Sending the Very Best, for No Particular Reason," *New York Times* (June 9, 1991): F12.

[2] Joe Schwartz, "Climate-Controlled Customers," *American Demographics* (March 1992): 24-33.

[3] Kenneth C. Gehrt, Thomas N. Ingram, and Vince Howe, "Nonstore Versus Store Retailing: A Situationally Based Market Structure Assessment," *Journal of Direct Marketing* 5 (Spring 1991)2: 44-53.

[4] Molly O'Neill, "Drop the Mop, Bless the Mess: The Decline of Housekeeping," *The New York Times* April 11, 1993): 1 (2).

[5] *A New Partnership: New Values and Attitudes of the New Middle Generation in Japan and the U.S.A.* (Tokyo: Dentsu Institute for Human Studies, 1989).

[6] Michael Lev, "Raising Fast Food's Speed Limit," *New York Times* (August 7, 1991)2: D1.

[7] "Attention Shoppers," *U.S. News & World Report* (July 31, 1989): 66.

8 Marianne Meyer, "Attention Shoppers!" *Marketing and Media Decisions* 23 (May 1988).

9 Cynthia Crossen, "If You Are What You Eat, They've Got Your Number," *Wall Street Journal* (August 31, 1989): B1; Stan Rapp, "Frequent Flyers Move Over, Here Comes the Frequent Shopper," *Direct Marketing* 51 (January 1989): 70.

10 Douglas B. Leeds, "Lifestyle Marketing: Prominent Force in P-O-P (point-of-purchase)," *Potentials in Marketing* (November December 1989): 40.

11 Charles S. Areni and David Kim, "The Influence of In-Store Lighting on Consumers' Examination of Merchandise in a Wine Store," *International Journal of Research in Marketing* 11 (March 1994)2: 117-125.

12 Scott Donaton, "Whittle New Gamble: Mall Showrooms Give Feel of Auto Test Drives," *Advertising Age* (September 9, 1991)2: 1.

13 "Signage Ups Sales at Kids 'R' Us By 20%; Effective Use of Photomurals Stimulates Customers' Imaginations," *Chain Store Age Executive* 63 (July 1987): 46.

14 "Coupons at the Right Price Can Torpedo Brand Loyalty," *Advertising Age* (May 18, 1992): 52.

15 Michael Wahl, "Eye POPping Persuasion," *Marketing Insights* (June 1989): 130.

16 Alison Fahey, "Advertising Media Crowd into Aisles," *Advertising Age* (June 18, 1990): 18; Scott Donaton and Kate Fitzgerald, "New Media Concepts Grow," *Advertising Age* (May 14, 1990): 4.

17 Nigel C.G. Campbell, John L. Graham, Alain Jolibert, and Hans Gunther, "Marketing Negotiations in France, Germany, the United Kingdom, and the United States," *Journal of Marketing* 52 (April 1988): 49-62.

18 Lee Boyan, "Who's More Productive?" *American Salesman* (November 1989): 16.

19 Joseph W. Newman and Richard A. Werbel, "Multivariate Analysis of Brand Loyalty for Major Household Appliances," *Journal of Marketing Research* 10 (November 1973): 404-09.

20 "Nike Finds a Use for Worn-Out Soles," *The New York Times* (August 4, 1993): D3.

21 John Thogersen, "A Model of Recycling Behaviour, with Evidence from Danish Source Separation Programmes," *International Journal of Research in Marketing* 11 (March 1994) 2: 145-163.

22 Carl Frankel, "Blueprint for Green Marketing," *American Demographics* (April 1992)4: 34.

23 David Bejou and Debbie M. Thorne, "Exploring the Differences Between Recyclers and Non-Recyclers: The Roles of Demographics and Personal Factors," in Marketing: Toward the Twenty-First Century, ed. Robert L. King (Richmond, Va.: The Southern Marketing Association, 1991), 110-15; see also Jacob Hornik, Michelle Madansky, Joseph Cherian, and Chem Narayna, "Consumer's Recycling Behavior: A Meta-Analysis," in Marketing Technical Report and Reprint Series (Chicago, Ill.: The University of Chicago, 1992).

24 Lynda W. Warren, Sennae C. Ostrom, and Anne H. Rosenfeld, "Pack Rats: World-Class Savers," *Psychology Today* (February 1988): 58.

25 Ronald Paul Hill, "Criminal Receiving: The 'Fence' as Marketer," *Journal of Public Policy & Marketing* (1992).

CHAPTER 10
Group Influence, Opinion Leadership, and Diffusion of Innovation

SUMMARY BULLETS

♦ Consumers belong to or admire many different groups and are often influenced in their purchase decisions by a desire to be accepted by others.

♦ Individuals have influence in a group to the extent that they possess social power; types of power include: information power, referent power, legitimate power, expert power, reward power, and coercive power.

♦ We conform to the desires of others for one of two basic reasons. People who model their behavior after others because they take others' behavior as evidence of the correct way to act are conforming because of informational social influence. People who conform to satisfy the expectations of others and/or to be accepted by the group are affected by normative social influence.

♦ Group members often do things they would not do as individuals because their identities become merged with the group; they become deindividuated.

♦ Individuals or groups whose opinions or behavior are particularly important to consumers are reference groups. Both formal and informal groups influence the individual's purchase decisions, although the impact of reference group influence is affected by such factors as the conspicuousness of the product and the relevance of the reference group for a particular purchase.

♦ Opinion leaders who are knowledgeable about a product and whose opinions are highly regarded tend to influence others' choices. Specific opinion leaders are somewhat hard to identify, but marketers who know their general characteristics can try to target them in their media and promotional strategies.

♦ Other influencers include market mavens, who have a general interest in marketplace activities, and surrogate consumers, who are compensated for their advice about purchases.

♦ Much of what we know about products comes about through word-of-mouth communication (WOM) rather than formal advertising. Product-related information tends to be exchanged in casual conversations.

♦ While word-of-mouth often is helpful for making consumers aware of products, it can also hurt companies when damaging product rumors or negative word of mouth occurs.

♦ Sociometric methods are used to trace referral patterns. This information can be used to identify opinion leaders and other influential consumers.

♦ The diffusion of innovations refers to the process whereby a new product, service, or idea spreads through a population. A consumer's decision to adopt a new item depends on his or her personal characteristics (i.e., if he or she is inclined to try new things) and on characteristics of the item. Products stand a better chance of being adopted if they demand relatively little change in behavior from consumers and are compatible with current practices. They are also more likely to diffuse if they can be tried prior to purchase, if they are not complex, if their use is visible to others, and, most importantly, if they provide a relative advantage vis-à-vis existing products.

LECTURE/DISCUSSION IDEAS

I. **Reference Groups** -- actual or imaginary group that has significant influence on a person's evaluations, aspirations, or behavior. (e.g., co-workers, family, friends)
(Use TM 10-1 Here)

   A. **Types of Reference Group**s -- some have greater influence than others

      1. **Formal vs. Informal Groups** -- fraternity vs. dorm friends

Discussion Topic: What are some formal and informal groups to which you belong?

      2. **Membership vs. Aspirational Reference Groups** -- people we know, work with, and socialize with vs. people we admire and want to be like

Discussion Topic: Give an example of an aspirational reference group of yours.

      a. **Identificational Reference Groups** -- people just like us
         • propriquity: physical nearness or distance (imitate those closest)
         • mere exposure: we tend to like things we see often
         • group cohesiveness: greatest with small groups (exclusiveness)

b. **Aspirational Reference Groups** -- what you want to be, not who you are

---

Real World Application
☯   Human consumers are not alone: Even cockroaches and rats have been found to prefer familiar stimuli over novel ones![1]

---

3. **Positive vs. Negative Reference Groups** -- we imitate and try to get close to positive groups and we try to avoid negative groups

Discussion Topic: What is an example of a negative reference group for you?

B. **When Reference Groups Are Important** -- most important for publicly consumed goods (e.g., luxuries, socially conspicuous goods not privately consumed)

☯   For a recent study examining reference group effects in both the United States and Thailand that also distinguishes between family and peer groups, see Childers and Rao's article.[2]

C. **The Power of Reference Groups** -- "capacity to alter the actions of others"
(Use TM 10-2 Here)

1. **Referent Power** -- admired groups are copied (e.g., clothes, cars)
2. **Information Power** -- those who know things (e.g., editor of *Vogue*)
3. **Legitimate Power** -- power by social agreement (e.g., police, doctors)
4. **Expert Power** -- specific knowledge or skill (CPAs, prominent economists)

Discussion Topic: Who is someone you view as having expert power?

5. **Reward Power** -- power to provide positive reinforcement (e.g. boss gives raises)
6. **Coercive Power** -- short-term power (e.g. intimidating sales people)

II.   **Conformity** -- real or imagined group pressures (norms: informal rules of behavior)
(Use TM 10-3 Here)

Discussion Topic: Have the class write a list of social norms that they tend to follow on a daily basis. How do these norms get started?

☯   If anything, peer pressure as a factor in adolescent sexual behavior appears to be increasing. A recent major survey of American sexual practices reports that more than a third of younger women reported that peer pressure led them to have sex for the first time. This rate compares with 13% of older respondents in the study.[3]

A. Types of Social Influence

- normative social influence: person conforms to meet group's expectations to gain reward or avoid punishment
- informational social influence: group's behavior is taken as evidence of reality

Discussion Topic: Can you think of some behavior triggered by normative social influence?

1. Reasons for Conformity

- cultural pressures: teenagers tend "to follow the crowd"
- fear of deviance: group applies penalties to "rule violators"
- commitment: the more dedication, the stronger the follower
- group unanimity, size and expertise: "law of large numbers"
- sex differences: those who possess feminine personality traits conform more

Discussion Topic: Can you think of something you bought because of peer pressure that you really didn't want to buy?

B. Social Comparison: "How'm I Doing?" -- the behavior of others is a yardstick of reality (right music, art, clothes, etc.)

(Use TM 10-4 Here)

1. Choosing Comparison Groups -- we like to choose who we want to be compared against: "level the playing field," "birds of a feather"

Discussion Topic: What is an activity (sports, music, art, etc.) at which you are pretty good? Have you ever competed with someone who was much better than you? . . . much worse than you? With whom do you prefer to compete?

C. Compliance and Obedience -- more allegiance shown to people who are confident

1. Tactical Requests

- foot-in-the-door techniques: make a small request first, then a bigger one
- low-ball technique: ask for a small favor that turns out to be costly
- door-in-the-face technique: make extreme request first, then the reasonable one

2. **Group Effect on Individual Behavior** -- your identity is submerged in a group

    a. **Shopping Patterns** -- more unplanned purchases when you're in a group

Discussion Topic: Have you ever gone shopping with a group of people your own age? Do you remember buying something that you probably wouldn't have if you were alone? Did you take it back, give it away, or throw it away?

    b. **Social Loafing** -- don't devote as much time to task when in a large group
        (e.g. people in large groups leave smaller tips)

☯ A recent study examined cross-country differences in norms regarding tipping.[6]

---

    c. **The Risky Shift** -- groups show greater willing to take risks than individuals
        • decision polarization: position becomes more extreme after group discussion

D. **Resistance to Influence** -- we take pride in our individualism and uniqueness

1. **Anticonformity vs. Independence** -- defiance of the group vs. do your own thing

    a. **The Need for Freedom** -- censorship makes us want things more

    b. **The Need for Uniqueness** -- don't want to "seem to be copying" others

Discussion Topic: What are some things that you own that are pretty unique? How do you feel when people talk about this?

III.   **Word-of Mouth Communication** -- this information tend to be more reliable and
        trustworthy than that from formal channels

Real World Application
☯ Word-of-mouth communication has been shown to be a stronger determinant of bank patronage than is advertising.[7]

☯ Over 60 percent of the patrons at Club Med's Western Hemisphere resorts came because of personal recommendations (not counting referrals from travel agents).[8]

A. **The Dominance of WOM** -- both positive and negative WOM extremely powerful
    but negative WOM is more so.

1. **Consumer-Initiated WOM**
   - the person is highly involved with product
   - the person is highly knowledgeable about product
   - the person has genuine concern for someone else
   - the person may be uncertain about the wisdom of his recent purchase

Discussion Topic: When you are planning to go to a movie, what are some of the sources of information you check before you make your decision?

2. **Marketer-Initiated WOM** -- most WOM campaigns happen spontaneously

   a. **Iowaization** -- companies ask us for names of friends who could benefit

---

Real World Application
☻ Music companies apparently pay people, posing as ordinary consumers, to log on to the Internet and type good things about new bands for the benefit of other subscribers.[9]

---

3. **Efficiency of WOM** -- rapid transmission

☻ Ninety percent of the U.S. adult population knew that President Kennedy had been assassinated within forty-five minutes of the first news account, though fifty percent heard the news from another person rather than directly from the mass media.[10]

---

4. **Negative WOM** -- weighted more heavily than positive WOM

Discussion Topic: Suppose you were going out to dinner at a new restaurant and a close friend of yours said, "I went there last week and the food was cold and the service was lousy!" How would you weigh this information in your decision making? Would you seek more information? Do you think you would change your plans?

   a. **Rumors: Distortion in the WOM Process** -- "professional rumor mongers"
      (e.g. rumors started about McDonald's, Procter and Gamble, Nestle', etc.)

   b. **Consumer Boycotts** -- can be effective or not effective

Discussion Topic: Have you ever been involved in a boycott of some product or organization? How did you get involved? Was your goal accomplished?

IV.   **Opinion Leadership** -- important influence on brand popularity in many instances
(Use Color Transparency 28 Here)
(Use TM 10-5 Here)

A. **The Nature of Opinion Leadership**
Opinion leaders:
- are technically competent
- have prescreened, evaluated and synthesized, unbiased product information
- are socially active
- are similar to the consumer in values and beliefs
- are often among the first to buy new products

Discussion Topic: Whom do you know that you would classify as an opinion leader? In what areas is he/she a leader?

☯ While opinion leaders often encourage the adoption of new products, at times they can exert a negative influence on novelty and risk taking, especially if they find the product to be deficient or in violation of the community's expectations or standards. Opinion leaders uphold the dominant norms in a community. If these norms favor conservatism, non-innovativeness may be stressed. For example, religious leaders may be influential in discouraging the use of various product categories such as alcohol and contraceptives.[12]

1. **The Extent of an Opinion Leader's Influence**
- generalized opinion leader: someone sought for all types of products
- monomorphic: experts in a limited field
- polymorphic: experts in several fields (but usually concentrated)

2. **Opinion Leaders vs. Other Consumer Types**

a. **Innovative Communicators** -- may or may not even purchase products they recommend

b. **Opinion Seekers** -- more involved in a product category

c. **Market Mavens** -- transmit marketplace information of all types

Discussion Topic: Do you know someone who seems to have information about almost any product or service you mention? When do you seek their advice? Does this person ever get on your nerves?

      d. **Surrogate Consumers** -- person hired by a consumer to provide input into purchase decision (e.g., stockbrokers, interior designers, wedding consultants, etc.)

Real World Application

☞ Although Nike and Reebok dominate the athletic shoe market, the power of influential publications to stir up consumer interest was seen first-hand by Hyde Athletic Industries. After the company's Saucony Jazz 3000 shoes got the Consumer Reports top rating for good value, sales soared. Since the magazine's core readership prides itself on being product experts, the subscriber is likely to contain a high proportion of influential opinion leaders. This example can propel the class into a discussion of the power of reviewers to make or break a product or service (e.g., restaurants or movies). Should a few individuals possess such power?[13]

B. **Identifying Opinion Leaders** -- many technical ads are designed for the opinion leader not the average consumer

---

☞ The Roper Organization has been tracking a group it calls Influentials since 1945. To qualify as an Influential, a person must have done at least three community activities in one year (e.g., attending a public meeting, holding office in a local organization, etc.). Comprising about 10 percent of the population, Influentials entertain, travel, and spend money on hobbies at a higher rate than the general population.[14]

---

1. **Professional Opinion Leaders** -- (e.g. doctors and scientists who obtain specialized information from technical journals and other practitioners)

☞ Pharmaceutical firms have long recognized the crucial role played by pharmacists in influencing prescriptions. Virtually every major company has a program targeted to pharmacists. For details on Schering's efforts in this area. see reference.[15]

---

2. **Consumer Opinion Leaders** -- (e.g. fashion panels in department stores)

3. **The Self-Designating Method** -- a person is asked, "Are you an opinion leader?"

      a. **Problems with Self-Designation** -- not always reliable since we exaggerate

Discussion Topic: Is there any category of consumer products in which you think that you might be considered an opinion leader?

4. **Sociometry** -- traces communication patterns among group members

    a. **Tracing Referrals** -- usually advice comes from family and friends

V.   **The Diffusion of Innovations** -- process whereby a new product, service, or idea spreads through a population

(Use Color Transparency 29 Here)
(Use TM 10-6 Here)

> ☯ One study has provided a cross-national analysis of diffusion processes.[16]

A. **Adopting Innovations**
- six stages: awareness, information, search, evaluation, trial and adoption
- five levels: innovators, early adopters, early majority, late majority, laggards

1. **Innovators** -- 2.5% of the population; are category specific (clothes *or* food)

2. **Early Adopters vs. Innovators** -- both are similar except for the degree of concern

B. **Types of Innovations** --
- symbolic innovation: new social meaning (e.g. new hairstyle, car design)
- technological innovation: functional change (central air, car airbags)

Discussion Topic: What are some symbolic or technological innovations that have taken place over the past five years? When did you become aware of them? Have you adopted any of them yet? Are there any innovations that you don't intend to adopt?

1. **Behavioral Demands of Innovations**

    a. **Continuous Innovation** -- modification of an existing product (e.g. new colors for kitchen appliances)

    b. **Dynamically Continuous Innovation** -- a more pronounced change in existing product (e.g. automatic ice maker in refrigerator)

    c. **Discontinuous Innovation** -- microwave oven

Discussion Topic: Have groups of students write down examples of (1) continuous innovations, (2) dynamically continuous innovations and (3) discontinuous innovations. Ask the teams to discuss the significance of these innovations.

2. **Prerequisites for Successful Adoption** -- factors necessary for success

   a. **Compatibility** -- must fit consumer's lifestyle

   b. **Trialability** -- reduce risk by letting me try it (e.g. trial size containers)

   c. **Complexity** -- the lower the better

   d. **Observability** -- innovations that are observable spread faster (e.g. fanny pack)

   e. **Relative Advantage** -- must give advantages other products don't

Discussion Topic: What do you think were the three most important innovation in your lifetime? in your parent's lifetime? in your grandparent's lifetime?

Real World Application

☯ It is important to emphasize that relative advantage does not just mean adding a product attribute which may or may not be desired. One company offered a new type of deodorant made with Vitamin D, and touted this addition as a relative advantage over other brands. Unfortunately, the company failed to convince consumers that spraying Vitamin D on their armpits was something to be desired, and the brand failed.

FIELD PROJECT IDEAS

Individual Assignments

1. Have a student do an analysis of a rumor that was started about a product or company (e.g., the "Satanic" connection in Procter and Gamble's moon-and-stars logo, Pop Rocks candy will make your stomach explode, McDonald's puts worms in its hamburgers, there are spider eggs in Bubble Yum, etc.). What effect did these rumors have on sales? How did the company handle this situation?

2. Ask a student to find one magazine advertisement for a consumer product that uses "the expert" as a reference group appeal and another which features a top corporate executive. Have the student discuss the impact of each appeal on consumers.

3. Have a student think about some goods and services that he/she has purchased recently. To what extent did word-of-mouth communication influence purchases?

4. Send a student to interview three friends about a product they recently purchased for the first time. Why did they purchase it? What was the role of "word of mouth" and personal influence (whether real or simulated)? You might encourage the student to make a short video tape of the interview and show it to the class.

5. Encourage a student to think of something he/she recently purchased in which advice was actively sought from others. For what reasons was advice sought. Why was the particular person selected to provide this advice?

6. Ask a student to interview someone who has attended a home party where products were sold (e.g., Amway, cookware, Tupperware, Sarah Coventry jewelry, Mary Kay, lingerie). What types of group power (such as referent, expert, reward, coercive) can be identified?

7. Have a student conduct a sociometric analysis within college or Greek housing or his/her neighborhood or family. Choose five varying product/service categories (e.g., fast food, medical care, hair care, movies, music, clothes, car repair) and ask a few individuals to identify other people with whom they share information. Try to trace the avenues of communication. See if opinion leaders for various categories can be identified.

Group Assignments

8. Ask the class to write down the various groups to which they are members. In which of these groups are conformity pressures the greatest? Why do they think this the case? (In Class Project)

9. Ask each student to think about individual family members, friends, and acquaintances. On paper, have them identify people who act as opinion leaders, product innovators, and market mavens. Describe what each person does. Have a few students share their observations with the class.

Individual or Group Assignments

10. Ask a student or group of students to make a list of aspirational groups that are of interest to many college students. Then ask them to bring to class a few print ads that are targeted to college students with these particular aspirations.

11. Have a student determine who the fashion leaders are at your university (or his/her church, place of employment, social group, neighborhood). See how well they fit the profile discussed in the chapter. This can be adapted to a group activity.

12. Here is a good activity for observant students. Have them look around and identify what special language, clothes, props, and sets are characteristic of various groups present in society.

13. Social norms tend to become obvious only when they are broken. Send a few brave students out to violate one or more social norms. (Tell them to shake hands with their left hand, eat their desserts first, belch during class, wear shoes that don't match, walk with their books on their head, make the narrow end of their ties extend a little below the wide end, sing in the elevator, or ask them to violate a social norm of their own. Note: Remind them to make sure they are only violating norms--not a law--unless you or your university is willing to provide bail money! What do these students observe when they violate the social norm?

14. For your students who are a little more shy have them watch MTV for about 10 minutes and jot down as many violations of social norms as they can identify.

15. Ask a student or a group to collect ads which attempt to incorporate word-or-mouth communications. Have them comment on the credibility of the ads. Is the promoter used in the ad an effective influencer?

16. For students who need some rest, ask them to spend one hour watching a network television channel during prime time. Have them record the total number of commercials that aired. For each commercial using a celebrity endorser, record the celebrity's name, the product or service advertised, and whether the celebrity was used in a testimonial, as an endorser, an actor, as a spokesperson, or as the background voice.

CONSUMER BEHAVIOR CHALLENGE

1. Compare and contrast the five bases of power described in the text. Which are most likely to be relevant for marketing efforts?

1. Referent Power -- admired groups are copied (e.g., clothes, cars)
2. Information Power -- those who know things (e.g., editor of *Vogue*)
3. Legitimate Power -- power by social agreement (e.g., police, doctors)
4. Expert Power -- specific knowledge or skill (e.g., CPAs, prominent economists)
5. Reward Power -- power to provide positive reinforcement (e.g., boss gives raises)
6. Coercive Power -- short-term power (e.g., intimidating sales people)

All bases of power are relevant to marketing.

2. Why is referent power an especially potent force for marketing appeals? What are factors that help to predict whether reference groups will or will not be a powerful influence on a person's purchase decisions?

Referent power is a potent force in marketing strategies because consumers voluntarily change behaviors to please or to identify with people they admire. The success of the referent power, therefore, will depend on whether a person admires the qualities of a person or a group.

3. Evaluate the strategic soundness of the concept of affinity marketing. For what type of linkages is this strategy most likely to be a success?

Have the students refer to the Marketing Opportunity example in the text. Affinity marketing is a strategy that allows consumers to underscore their identification with some organization by attaching the group's identification to aspects of their personal lives. It is a recent and widespread application of reference group influence.

For affinity marketing to be successful the consumer must have a strong identification with a group such as a college, zoo, church, neighborhood, place of employment, or pro sports team.

4. Discuss some factors that determine the amount of conformity likely to be observed among consumers.

Conformity refers to a change in beliefs or actions as a reaction to real or imagined group pressure. Factors that determine the amount of conformity among consumers are:

a. cultural pressures: teenagers tend "to follow the crowd"
b. fear of deviance: group applies penalties to "rule violators"
c. commitment: the more dedication, the more stronger the followers
d. group unanimity, size, and expertise: "law of large numbers"
e. sex differences: those who possess feminine personality traits conform more

[Students should be encouraged to give examples of these factors in their own conformity, or lack of conformity to norms]

5. Under what conditions are we more likely to engage in social comparison with dissimilar others versus similar others? How might this dimension be used in the design of marketing appeals?

In social comparison we look at the behavior of others and use it as a yardstick about reality: what is the right music, art, or clothes to be in the "in" group. What should I avoid so I won't be an outcast. We also like to choose the comparison groups whom we want to be compared with--"level the playing field," "birds of a feather".

However, we are likely to engage in social comparison with dissimilar others when we are reasonably certain of our own views. Encourage students to find examples of social comparison in a wide variety of promotional messages, particularly in advertising.

6. Discuss some reasons for the effectiveness of home-shopping parties as a selling tool. What factors might reduce the power of this strategy?

Student should incorporate information in the chapter Marketing Opportunity example about Tupperware and UndercoverWare. Home-shopping parties capitalize on group pressure to boost sales, and are effect as a selling tool because of (1) informational social influence, (2) normative social influence, and (3) deindividuation. Students should delineate these influences.

In contrast, factors that might reduce the power of this strategy include (1) anti-conformity, (2) independence, (3) the need for freedoms and (4) the need for uniqueness.

7. Discuss some factors that influence whether or not membership groups will have a significant influence on a person's behavior.

Students should recognize that a number of factors influence whether or not membership groups will have a significant influence on a person's behavior. These include whether the group is primary or secondary, positive or negative, as well as the general strength of the groups influence. The instructor should encourage students to categorize different membership groups in their own lives and assess their relative influence.

8. Why is word-of-mouth communication often more persuasive than advertising?

Word-of-mouth communication is more persuasive than advertising because information obtained from those we know or talk with tends to be more reliable and trustworthy. Unlike advertising, word-of-mouth communication often is backed up by social pressure to conform to this information/recommendation.

9. Is there such a thing as a generalized opinion leader? What is likely to determine if an opinion leader will be influential with regard to a specific product category?

There is no such thing as a generalized opinion leader but a market maven comes about as close as you can get. Very few people are capable of being expert in a number of fields and, therefore, the same individual rarely will be sought out for information for all types of purchases. Opinion leaders are viewed as valuable information sources because they:

a. are technically competent (expertise)
b. have prescreened, evaluated and synthesized, unbiased product information
c. are socially active and have a nice social position
d. are similar to the consumer in values and beliefs
e. are often among the first to buy new products
f. like to take risk

10. The adoption of a certain brand of shoe or apparel by athletes can be a powerful influence on students and other fans. Should high school and college coaches be paid to determine what brand of athletic equipment their players will wear?

Student opinion will vary. You might want to raise the issue of consumer needs versus wants, the role of advertising in determining needs and wants, and the general ethics of marketing products to children and youth.

11. The power of unspoken social norms often becomes obvious only when these norms are violated. To witness this result first hand, try one of the following: stand facing the back wall in an elevator; serve dessert before the main course; offer to pay cash for dinner at a friend's home; wear pajamas to class; or tell someone not to have a nice day.

Students can be creative here. Encourage them to conduct these investigations and use a debriefing session in class to discuss some of their finding, reactions and attitudes. (See Field Project #4.)

12 . Identify a set of avoidance groups for your peers. Can you identify any consumption decisions that are made with these groups in mind?

Students will think of many diverse examples. Two potential avoidance groups may be a local gang and students who fail this course. If you are against gangs, you will try to avoid using any products that are associated with gangs; if you don't want to fail this course, you will avoid many of the behaviors that are associated with failing students. (Possible Field Project)

13. Identify fashion opinion leaders on your campus. Do they fit the profile discussed in the chapter?

The class might agree to focus on a particular group of fashion opinion leaders. After deciding on the group, they could go through the opinion leader profile found in the text under Opinion Leaders Versus Other Consumer Types on page 360 and determine whether or not the group members actually are fashion experts. (Possible Field Project)

14. Conduct a sociometric analysis within your dormitory or neighborhood. For a product category such as music or cars, ask each individual to identify other individuals with whom they share information. Systematically trace all of these avenues of communication, and identify opinion leaders by locating individuals who are repeatedly named as providing helpful information.

Students should include a discussion of sociometry in their responses and recognize that sociometric methods allow researchers to systematically point out the interactions that take place among group members. Conducting a study of this type should highlight for students how difficult and expensive such activities can be. (Possible Field Project)

15. The chapter discusses a situation where professional actors are paid to order a certain drink in a bar to stimulate word of mouth. Some marketing executives defend this practice. As one commented, "Twenty years ago, the way you expanded sales at a bar was to give the bartender a hundred bucks. This is moving the power from behind the bar to in front of the bar." On the other hand, some critics of the strategy view this as unethical behavior. One commented, "People have the right to know when they're being advertised to." What do you think?

Student opinions will vary. Students will be able to compare the "push and pull" strategies in marketing. Sometimes when you pay someone to push your product it is called "Payola," and at other times it is call "slotting allowances." How different are they? Are either one of them ethical (unethical)? How do you determine what is ethical or unethical? You might have students role play this making sure both sides are represented. (Possible In Class Activity)

16. Innovators are a small minority of consumers, yet marketers are very interested in identifying and reaching them. Why? How might you go about locating innovators?

As stated in the text, even though innovators represent only 2.5 percent of the population, marketers are always interested in identifying them. They are extremely influential in their risk-taking role as the first consumers to try new products. They also act as a link to the more general population of potential consumers. In their attempts to identify innovators, marketers might use self-designation, reputational, and objective techniques.

17. Provide an example of a discontinuous innovation currently vying for adoption. What are the factors working for and against its eventual success in the marketplace?

Students should be challenged to identify discontinuous innovations currently vying for adoption. They are likely to consider alternative fuels, electric cars, and communications technology, among a number of other "true" innovations. In their responses, students should recognize that the biggest factor working against the adoption of discontinuous innovations is the fact that they create major changes in the way we live.

ENDNOTES

[1] H.A. Cross, C.G. Halcomb, and W. Matter, "Imprinting or Exposure Learning in Rats Given Early Auditory Stimulation," *Psychonomic Science* 10 (1967): 223 34; R.B. Zajonc, H.M. Markus, and W. Wilson, "Exposure Effects and Associative Learning," *Journal of Experimental Social Psychology* 10 (1974): 248-63

[2] Terry L. Childers and Akshay R. Rao, "The Influence of Familial and Peer-based Reference Groups on Consumer Decisions," *Journal of Consumer Research* 19 (September 1992): 198-221.

[3] Tamar Lewin, "Sex in America: Faithfulness in Marriage is Overwhelming," *The New York Times* (October 7, 1994): A1 (2).

[4] Harold Garfinkel, *Studies in Ethnomethodology* (Englewood Cliffs, N.J.: Prentice-Hall, 1967).

[5] Randall L. Rose, William O. Bearden, and Jesse E. Teel, "An Attributional Analysis of Resistance to Group Pressure Regarding Illicit Drug and Alcohol Consumption," *Journal of Consumer Research* 19 (June 1992): 1-13

[6] Michael Lynn, George M. Zinkhan, and Judy Harris, "Consumer Tipping: A Cross-Country Study," *Journal of Consumer Research* 20 (December 1993): 478-488.

[7] W. Thomas Anderson, Jr., and Linda L. Golden, "Bank Promotion Strategy," *Journal of Advertising Research* 24 (April/May 1984): 53-65.

[8] Barnaby Feder, "Those With Things to Sell Love Word-of-Mouth Ads," *New York Times* (June 23, 1992): D18.

[9] Barbara Kantrowitz and Jennifer Tanaka, "Beware of Im-Posters," *Newsweek* 1994.

[10] B.S. Greenberg, "Diffusion of News of the Kennedy Assassination," *Public Opinion Quarterly* 28 (1964): 225-32.

[11] Marcus Mabry, "Do Boycotts Work?" *Newsweek* (July 6, 1992)3: 56.

[12] G. Appa Rao and Everett Rogers, "Caste and Formal Education in Interpersonal Diffusion of an Innovation in Two Indian Villages," *Indian Journal of Extension Education* 16 (1980): 1 9.

[13] Eben Shapiro, "Getting a Running Shoe in the Door," *New York Times* (August 13, 1992)2: D1.

[14] Rebecca Piirto, "The Influentials," *American Demographics* (October 1992)6: 30.

[15] Jack Robbins, "How Schering Won Pharmacist Loyalty," *Medical Marketing & Media* (March 1994): 58 (3).

[16] Hirokazu Takada and Dipak Jain, "Cross-National Analysis of Diffusion of Consumer Durable Goods in Pacific Rim Countries," *Journal of Marketing,* 55 (April 1991): 48-54.

Instructor's Notes:

CHAPTER 11

Organizational and Household Decision Making

SUMMARY BULLETS

- Many purchasing decision are made by more than one person. Collective decision making occurs whenever two or more people are involved in evaluating, selecting, or using a product or service.

- Organizational buyers are people who make purchase decisions on behalf of a company or other group. Although they are influenced by many of the same factors that affect how they make decisions in their personal lives, organizational buying decisions tend to be more rationally based. They are also likely to involve more financial risk, and as they become more complex, it is probable that a greater number of people will be involved in making them.

- The amount of cognitive effort that goes into organizational decisions is influenced by internal factors, such as individuals' psychological characteristics and by external factors, such as the company's willingness to tolerate risk. One of the most important determinants is the type of purchase being considered: The extent of problem-solving required depends on whether the product or service to be procured is simply to be reordered (a straight rebuy), ordered with minor modifications (modified rebuy), or if it has never been purchased before or is complex and risky (new task).

- In organizations and in families, several different roles must be played during the decision making process. These roles include the gatekeeper, who determines the flow of information within the group, influencers, buyers, and users.

- Demographics are statistics that measure a population's characteristics. Some of the most important of these relate to family structure, e.g., the birth rate, the marriage rate, and divorce rate.

- A household is an occupied housing unit. The number and type of U.S. households is changing in many ways, including increasing movement by consumers to southern and western states, delays in getting married and having children, and in the composition of family households, which increasingly are headed by single parents. New perspectives on the family life cycle, which focuses on how people's needs change as they move through different stages in their lives, are forcing marketers to more seriously consider such consumer segments as homosexuals, divorcees, and childless couples when they develop targeting strategies.

♦ Families must be understood in terms of their decision-making dynamics. Spouses in particular have different priorities and exert varying amounts of influence in terms of effort and power. Children are also increasingly influential during a widening range of purchase decisions.

♦ Children undergo a process of socialization, whereby they learn how to be consumers. Some of this knowledge is instilled by parents and friends, but a lot of it comes from exposure to mass media and advertising. Since children are in some cases so easily persuaded, the ethical aspects of marketing to them are hotly debated among consumers, academics, and marketing practitioners.

LECTURE/DISCUSSION IDEAS

I. **Organizational Decision Making**

(Use Color Transparency 30 Here)
- organizational buyers: people who purchases goods and services for organizations (manufacturers, retailers, government)
- business-to-business marketers: those who sell to organizations
- buyer's perception is affected by: expectations, organization climate, "organizational memory"

A. **Organizational Decision Making Versus Consumer Decision Making**
- purchase decision frequently involve may people
- products often bought according to precise specifications
- impulse buying is rare
- decisions are high-risk
- dollar volume of purchases is often substantial
- more emphasis on personal selling than other types of promotion
- guided by long-term relationships

Discussion Topic: How are decisions made by organizations and decisions made by individuals the same? How are they different?

B. **The Organizational Buyer Behavior Process** -- internal and external stimuli

1. **Type of Purchase** -- complex decision usually made by a group

Discussion Topic: If you were in charge of your university, who are the people you would want involved in making a decision about a purchase of a new mainframe computer?

Real World Application
☯ For an interesting discussion of the decision processes underlying the establishment of corporate art collections, see reference.[1]

---

a. **The Buyclass Framework** -- buying considerations
  - level of information that must be gathered
  - the seriousness of all possible alternatives
  - the buyers' familiarity with the purchase

b. **Straight Rebuy** -- automatic decision regarding inventory

c. **Modified Rebuy** -- repurchase with minor modifications

d. **New Task** -- extensive problems solving (team often makes this decision)

Discussion Topic: Give examples of products that would be classified as "straight rebuys", "modified rebuys," and "new task" products for a business organization.

2. **Decision Roles** -- players in the decision process are:

(Use TM 11-1 Here)

  - initiator: the person with the idea or need
  - gatekeeper: person who controls the flow of information to the group
  - influencer: person who tries to sway the outcome of the decision
  - buyer: the one who makes the decision
  - user: the person who winds up using the product

C. **Trends in Organizational Buying Behavior** -- relationship marketing

  - building strong lasting bonds with suppliers
  - consolidating inventory
  - emphasis on the user, not the buyer
  - shift from technology to marketing orientation

Discussion Topic: What is your understanding of relationship marketing and how do you think it is practiced by businesses?

II.   **The Family** -- out of fashion in 1960 and 1970's, but today 90% say it is most important

---

Real World Application
- Trying to position a trip to the ball park as a family activity, the Oakland A's ball club opened Foster Farms Family Place in the stadium. The facility allows parents to give their kids a break during a game . It features easels for painting, Legos, and a special menu including peanut butter and jelly sandwiches and milk. Parents can watch the game on monitors during these time-outs.[2]

A. Defining the Modern Family

(Use TM 11-2 Here)

- extended family: three generations living together
- nuclear family: mom, dad and kids

Discussion Topic: How do you define a family?

1. **Just What is a Household?** -- at least two people who are related by blood or marriage

2. **Growth and Distribution of Family Households** -- cities, suburbs, exurbs, edge cities, south and west

3. **Age of the Family** -- since 1980:
   - under-25, married couples declined buy one-third
   - age 65+ increased 15%
   - ages 35-44 increased 40%
   - average marrying age is 24 for women and 26 for men

4. **Family Size**
   - average American household is 2.6 people
   - families with 3 or more kids at home is 20%

5. **Sex of the Family Head**
   - about 80% of family households headed by a man and 20% headed by a woman
   - about 39% of adult population is unmarried

6. **Who's Living at Home?** -- "the sandwich generation" cares for parents and kids

Discussion Topic: Do you think the concept of "the sandwich generation" existed before now? When? Explain.

   a. **Boomerang Kids** -- children returning home after college, divorce, job loss

Discussion Topic: Is the phenomenon of "boomerang kids" new? What brought kids back to the nest in previous years?

Real World Application
☯ While economic conditions clearly contribute to the increase in boomerang kids, it appears that many return home because they have been spoiled by their parents' affluence and are unwilling to accept a lower standard of living if they live on their own. Males from households with annual incomes greater than $50,000 are the most likely to remain at home. As one father complained, "You think you've done your bit and put them through college, and here they come."[5]

---

7. **Alternate Family Structures**

   a. **Household** -- whomever is occupying a housing unit
      - stepfamilies
      - singles same sex roommates
      - POSSLQ--Persons of Opposite Sex Sharing Living Quarters)

   b. **Changes in Family Classifications** --
      - worldwide: smaller and less traditional
      - U.S. Census included three new categories of family members in 1990 survey:
         1) natural-born or adopted child,
         2) foster child, and
         3) unmarried partners

B. **Effects of Family Structure on Consumption** -- higher expenses if the family has kids and the mother works

Discussion Topic: What additional expenses are incurred by a family if the mother works outside the home?   (You might ask teams of students to prepare a list. If you have time, they might put a dollar amount on the budget items.)

1. **The Family Life Cycle** -- combines trends in income, family composition and time
   - Young Married
   - Full Nest I: young married with young kids
   - Full Nest II: married with yound adults at home
   - Divorced
   - Single Parent
   - Empty Nest: kid have moved away from home
   - Solitary Survivor: one spouse is deceased

   a. **Updating the Life Cycle Approach** -- must include: age, marital status, the presence or absence of children at home, and their ages (Delayed Full Nest: middle-aged parents with youngest child under six.)

Discussion Topic: Are there any other categories that you think might be added to the Family Life Cycle that aren't yet included?

Real World Application
- The J. Walter Thompson advertising agency developed an alternative typology, called Lifestages, to better describe the growing numbers of single consumers who do not fit into traditional FLC categories. The five stages include such classifications as At-Home Singles (average age 22) and Mature singles (divorced or separated, average age 45).[6]

III.   **The Intimate Corporation: Family Decision Making** -- family similar to business

---

- Children's input tends to be greatest in the early stages of the decision-making process where they play an important role in problem recognition and information search.[7]

- Prompted by research showing that children exert a major influence on family vacation decision, travel-and-leisure firms are getting into the act. Hyatt Hotels recently initiated a Camp Hyatt Kids Council to evaluate its Camp Hyatt program, Delta Air Lines formed a Fantastic Flier Club (complete with a mascot: Dusty the Delta Air Lion), and Embassy Suites has licensed Garfield the cartoon cat as its spokescharacter.[8]

A. **Household Decisions**

(Use Color Transparency 31 Here)
- consensual purchase decision: group agrees on the desired purchase
- accommodative purchase decisions: bargaining, coercion, compromise takes place

1. **Sources of Conflict**

(Use TM 11-3 Here)

- money--the most common source of conflict
- interpersonal needs
- product involvement and utility
- responsibility
- power

B. **Sex Roles and Decision-Making Responsibilities**
   - autocratic decision: made by one or the other spouse
   - syncratic decision: made jointly

Discussion Topic: In your family are there certain categories of products that tend to be purchased by mom? dad? mom and dad? the kids?

1. **Identifying the Decision-Maker** --nature of product is determining factor

   a. **The Family Financial Officer** -- newlyweds (joint); eventually (either)

Real World Application

☯ The "sex-role revolution" is more apparent than real. Women still spend two-to-three-times as much time on housework and child-rearing activities as their husbands, and perform more than three-fourths of the work that needs to be done. Men on average have fifteen hours more leisure time per week than their wives. On the other hand, more than a third of primary grocery shoppers are men.[9]

---

   b. **Who Decides?**

(Use Color Transparency 32 Here)
(Use TM 11-4 Here)

- sex-role stereotypes: men buy masculine product; women buy feminine products
- spousal resources: the spouse who contributes the most has greater influence
- experience: time constraints and expertise establishes one decision maker
- socio-economic status: middle class families make more joint decisions

Discussion Topic: For those who are not yet married: When you get married, how will you determine who will make various family purchase decisions?

☯ For a study that looked at marital decision making issues in Saudi Arabia, see reference.[10]

---

2. **Heuristics in Joint Decision Making**

(Use Color Transparency 33 Here)

- husband and wife take common view and act as joint decision makers
- a couple "reaches" rather than makes a decision
- a couple agrees on a system of task specialization
- concessions based on intensity of each spouse's preferences

---

Real World Application

☙ Spouses are generally unable to accurately identify how much influence they and their partners have in the decision-making process, much less predict their partners' preferences. Indeed, because spouses tend to be fairly similar, research suggests that they are better off relying upon their own preferences rather than inferring their mates' when predicting what their spouses will like.[11]

☙ One recent study on the adoption of product innovations found that a wife tends to exert more control over the new product adoption decisions of her husband rather than vice-versa. [12]

IV. **Children as Decision Makers: Consumers-in-Training**

(Use TM 11-5 Here)

- parent yielding: parental decision maker is influenced by child's request
- Born to Shop: children rank shopping as one of their top seven interests

---

☙ In one study of Singaporean families, almost half of the families surveyed felt that their children had significantly influenced major purchase decisions, including the family's dwelling.[13]

☙ Shopping goods (e.g., clothing) tend to be purchased jointly by parent and child, but specialty goods such as record and movie tickets are likely to be purchased by the child alone.[14]

A. **Consumer Socialization** -- acquiring skills, knowledge, and attitude toward shopping

1. **Influence of Parents**
   - direct: instill in children the value of a dollar
   - indirect: children watch and imitate parents

   a. **Parental Style** --
      - authoritarian parents: restrictive with negative view about ads
      - neglecting parents: detached from kids and exercise little control
      - indulgent parents: less restrictive and want children to learn about buying

Discussion Topic: How do you plan to teach your children how to become well informed buyers?

2. **Influence of Television** -- teaches children about culture's values and myths

B. **Sex-Role Socialization** -- learn gender identity at an early age

---

Real World Application

ॐ The candy industry thrives on products that stress mild rebellion. Big sellers include Slime Slurps, Big Thumbs, Gummy Worms, and Sneaky Snacks. The later are candies that come in a box disguised as a notebook, accompanied by messages like "Just say no to lunch." As a candy executives explained, "Kids are always looking to do things that their parents mildly disapprove of. The child gets to distance himself from the parents and become somewhat more independent, and what's nice about candy is that it allows you to do without any of the real anxiety associated with true separation."[15]

ॐ While kids aged 5 to 14 make up about 14 percent of the European population, a problem in reaching them is that only 15 percent have their own television, as compared to 40 percent of kids in the United States.[16]

---

1. **Child's Play: Sex-Role Rehearsal** -- about age five, girls choose domestic toys and boys choose action toys

Discussion Topic: Do you think that toys reflect or teach children what society expects from males and females?

ॐ Expectations regarding sex-typed toys also are reinforced at the time of purchase. Sales people in toy stores have been found to recommend stereotypical choices when asked for advice by shoppers.[17]

C. **Cognitive Development** -- children learn consumption related information well

1. **Piagetian Stages of Development** -- e.g. pour water from one glass to another
    - at five years, the shape of the glass determined amount of content
    - at six, the child was unsure
    - at seven, the child knew the amount had not changed

2. **An Alternative to Piaget** -- no longer believe the fixed stages
    - limited: below six, children do not employ storage and retrieval strategies
    - cued: between 6 and 12, children employ these strategies--when prompted
    - strategic: 12 and older, people spontaneously employ these strategies

D. **Marketing Research and Children** -- hard to research because they can't remember and do not understand abstract questions

Discussion Topic: Should business be allowed to conduct market research with children under six?   between six and twelve?   between twelve and sixteen? Why?

1. **Product Testing** -- kids can predict what toys other kids will like (Playlab)

2. **Message Comprehension** -- kids think what they see on TV is real

   a. **Is It a Program or a Commercial?** -- at times, it is hard to tell

E. **Advertising to Children: An Ethical Minefield** -- Children's Advertising Review Unit (CARU) of the Council of Better Business Bureaus, Inc.

Discussion Topic: Should companies be able to advertise to young children? Should there be any restrictions? Who should determine this?

1. **Are Promotions Targeted to Children Unfair?** --Consumer Union/ads at school

   a. **The Response** -- schools and parents like the contributions to the school

2. **Is Children's Television Advertising Unfair?** --FTC/brand loyalty of 8 years olds

   a. **The Response** -- kids over 7 have right to tasteful advertising information

3. **Does Advertising Encourage Poor Product Choices?** -- FTC/poor nutrition

   a. **The Response** -- parents decide which products are inappropriate

4. **Does Advertising Create Parent-Child Conflict?** -- critics/kids nag parents

   a. **The Response** -- products are a natural part of parent/child relationship

5. **Does Advertising Contribute to Undesirable Socialization?** -- teaches materialism, impulsive choice, an immediate gratification

   a. **The Response** -- actually helps child prepare for the real world

FIELD PROJECT IDEAS

Individual Assignments

1. Have a student bring in ads for two different product categories in which the family is targeted. Find another set of ads for two different brands of the same items in which the family is not targeted. Evaluate the ads as to their effectiveness. Why do you prefer one ad over another?

2. Ask a student to go to a toy store or a toy department and watch several interactions between a parent and child. Have the student make an oral report on how the children "made their wishes known" and how parents reacted to their children's "needs and wants."

3. Have a student make a list of ten product/service categories (i.e. window treatments, china, appliances, lawn mower, children's toys, cookware, automobiles, dental care, groceries, vacations, insurance, bedroom furniture, garden supplies) Now ask the student to interview two married couples (one in their 20's and one in their 50's or more). Without conferring with each other, have them indicate whether decisions to purchase products in each category are likely to be made by primarily by the wife, by the husband, or a jointly.

4. Ask a student to select a few people in a defined age category (middle school students, high school students, or retired seniors--not college students) to compile a list of purchases that they typically make in a week. Find out about how much they usually spend. Can you see any patterns developing?

5. Encourage one of your students to visit three local restaurants that seem to target clientele in three different family life cycle stages--e.g., young singles; young married without children, married with young children; married with youngest child over six; empty nesters with the breadwinner still in the work force; empty nesters out of the work force; sole survivors. How does each establishment attract its target market? Sometimes it is fun to run about a 2 minute video of the clientele entering and leaving each different type of restaurant.

6. Ask a student to visit a clothing store, shoe store, furniture store, appliance store, restaurant, **or** whatever, and interview the store manager regarding how the family life cycle concept is employed in their inventory selection, pricing, and/or advertising and sales promotion.

7. Have someone go in search of 'mall rats'. Interview four or five consumers in their early teens. Find out what types of purchases, typical and special, they usually make. See if they will tell you about how much they spend each week. How do they get their spending money each week--job, allowance, save lunch money, etc.? About how much do they have to spend in an average week?

8. Have a student bring to class three advertisements which show the changing roles of men and women. Also bring in three ads that show the traditional roles of men and women. Which ads do the class like best? Which do they find more credible? Try to analyze their responses.

9. Ask a student to do some observational research on children playing. How are the children using their toys (balls, dolls, dress up, cars, guns, stuffed animals, etc.) to rehearse future social interactions. Have the student comment on how fantasy in play helps kids to "grow up".

Group Assignments

10. Distribute a list of 10 products/services, and then have the class indicate on the sheet whether the decision to purchase each product is probably made by the husband alone, the wife alone, either husband or wife alone, or jointly made by both parties. Does there seem to be a trend developing? If so, what evidence does the class have that they are probably correct?

11. Have a group bring to class four or five ads in which teenage girls are targeted. A magazine that appeals to this group can be found in a book store. How are these appeals similar and/or different from appeals to women in their twenties? You might bring in a magazine that appeals to them? Does the class think the teenage ads were designed for older children or young adults? Have them speculate.

Individual or Group Assignments

12. Ask a student or a group of students to describe different purchase situations in which they (or another family member) plays the role of (1) initiator, (2) influencer, (3) information gatherer, (4) decision maker, (5) purchaser, or (6) user.

13. Have students bring to class some woman's magazine such as *Good Housekeeping, Ladies' Home Journal, Family Circle, Woman's Day*, etc. Discuss how advertisements aimed at women have changed over the past 20 years. (Perhaps you could photocopy older ads from magazines in the library; therefore it might be a good idea to choose black and while ads.) Show how advertisers have adapted their copy and art work to account for the changing roles of women.

14. You or one or more of your students should select a product category such as a car, tie, jewelry, restaurant, shoes, apartment. Using the life-cycle stages given in the chapter, ask the class to explain the variables that will affect a purchase decision by consumers in each stage of the cycle.

15. Hop aboard the Information Superhighway! In segmenting the market for customer telecommunication services (e.g. CompuServ, Modems, Faxes, caller ID, call return, call blocker, three-way calling, speed calling, call forwarding, and call waiting) what stage of the family life cycle, sex, age, education, or some other factor would be more important? What marketing and promotional strategies would you devise to reach the segment(s) you selected? Why?

CONSUMER BEHAVIOR CHALLENGE

1. Do you think market research should be performed on children? Give the reasons for your answer.

Discussion of this issue will most likely revolve around the student's opinion and experiences with children as consumers. As the chapter made clear, children are a large part of the economy both as consumers, and as influences on consumption. Therefore, a firm would be careless not to gather and use information on the tastes and habits of children. However, many students may object to this line of reasoning by stating that children are a particularly susceptible group and so marketing efforts aimed at them should not exist, or should be controlled. An important distinction that needs to be made in this matter is the difference between marketing research and marketing communication; while the former is done to assist the latter, the two concepts are separate. Discussion could best be focused on the suitability of market research using children and then proceed to the propriety of marketing to children as a market.

2. What do you think of the practice of companies and survey firms collecting public data from marriage licenses, birth records, or even death announcements to compile targeted mailing lists? State your opinion from both a consumer's and marketer's perspective.

Ethics questions, such as this and others in this section, are best presented and framed as an opportunity for students to analyze both sides of the issue. Many students will use their own ethical framework, and also their own experiences, to answer these types of questions. There should not be any attempt to state "the" correct answer, but listing and discussing the advantages and disadvantages of the practice is the goal. This also can be done by considering the different perspectives of consumers and marketers. Students likely will view such practices as reasonable from the marketer's perspective, but as potential violations of privacy from the individual consumer's perspective.

3. Marketers have been criticized for donating products and services to educational institutions in exchange for free promotion. Is this a fair exchange, in your opinion, or should corporations be prohibited from attempting to influence youngsters in school?

Here again, discussion of this question will reflect the student's attitude towards marketing towards younger consumers, but with a twist: donating products to schools has obvious positive consequences for those students. Some students will view this as a positive exchange, as the school and the students receive educational materials they otherwise might not. On the other hand, some will see this as a cynical attempt to ensnare a captive audience. There would appear to be some truth in both positions, as the donation of products can contribute to a child's education and it also can promote current and future purchases of those goods.

For example, Apple Computer Corporation made special efforts to provide computer equipment to schools, and they developed special promotions to sell equipment to teachers and school-age children. It would be hard to deny that such efforts contributed to Apple's success, but the benefits to both parties also are obvious. Discussion of this topic should be aimed at setting some guidelines that both groups could benefit from, while safeguarding the practice from exploiting children's less-developed discriminatory abilities.

4. For each of the following five product categories--groceries, automobiles, vacations, furniture, and appliances--describe the way in which you believe a married couple's choices would be affected if they had children.

The question provides an excellent opportunity to exhibit the direct and indirect influence that children have on purchases. If possible, students who have children should be encouraged to contribute to the discussion by relating their experiences. Students who do not have children should be encouraged to relate their own attempts to influence their parents, purchase decisions in these and other areas. In addition, discussing the types of product categories that children are more likely to influence would be interesting. Of the product categories listed, the presence of children in the household will produce the need for more of each product--more room in the car, more groceries to consume, more variety of foods, more capacity in the appliances. etc.

However, what also will be influenced is the type of product bought under each category, and this aspect should form the basis for discussion.
- **groceries**--baby food, snack foods, health foods
- **automobiles**--two-door, four-door van or station wagon
- **vacation**--if the destination has recreation facilities (pool, tennis courts, etc.) or is appropriate for children of different ages
- **furniture**--baby furniture, special beds for younger children (e.g., bunk beds, canopy beds), new furniture for older children
- **appliances**--microwave ovens and other convenience appliances for busy children and families

5. In identifying and targeting newly divorced couples, do you think marketers are exploiting these couples' situations? Are there instances where you think marketers may actually be helpful to them? Support your answer with examples.

This question is much like questions 1-3 in that it asks the student to consider a specific target market and whether marketing to it is appropriate. In addition to examining each of these groups separately, a more general question may be: What are the limits, or the parameter, of appropriate targeting? At a broader level, the whole notion of target marketing may be reexamined as to whether it is appropriate to attempt to persuade a group to purchase a product. A discussion of this scope could quickly get so broad and unfocused that students become confused, so care must be taken to keep the discussion centered on one topic at a time. Those students who accept target marketing should be asked to describe situations where target marketing should be curbed and why. Those students who feel that target marketing is wrong should be encouraged to consider that it is a necessary tool for firms to market their products. They should be encouraged to describe their set of guidelines for properly using target marketing. The situation described here, that of divorced couple, could be used to exemplify the use and abuse of target marketing. Students should also be able to describe the advantages and disadvantages of target marketing to this particular group and how other sensitive situations should be handled by marketers.

6. Arrange to interview two married couples, one younger and one older. Prepare a response form listing five product categories—groceries, furniture, appliances, vacations, and automobiles—and ask each spouse to indicate, without consulting the other, whether purchases in each category are made by joint or unilateral decisions and to indicate whether the unilateral decisions are made by the husband or the wife. Compare each couples' responses for agreement between husbands and wives relative to who makes the decisions and compare both couples' overall responses for differences relative to the number of joint versus unilateral decisions. Report your findings and conclusions.

Students' discussion of this question should consider the text material on spousal influence. Married students should be encouraged to provide their insight into these issues.

7. Collect ads for three different product categories in which the family is targeted. Find another set of ads for different brands of the same items in which the family is not featured. Prepare a report on the effectiveness of the approaches.

You might encourage students to look at magazines that target different social groups to see if there is a difference. (Possible Field Project)

8. Observe the interactions between parents and children in the cereal section of a local grocery store. Prepare a report on the number of children who expressed preferences, how they expressed their preferences, and how parents responded, including the number who purchased the child's choice.

If a student stands near a family in the cereal aisle, he/she could note who actually picks up the cereal and puts it in the basket or otherwise chooses the brand. You might also ask that student who made the cereal choices when he/she was young. (Possible Field Project)

9. Watch three hours of children's programming on commercial television stations and evaluate the marketing techniques used in the commercials in terms of the ethical issues raised in the final section of this chapter. Report your findings and conclusions.

This is a project for a true couch potato. Make sure the student has a pad of paper and makes good notes from the beginning. Find out how the student reach his conclusions concerning the ethical issues. (Possible Field Project)

10. Select a product category, and using the life-cycle stages given in the chapter, list the variables that will affect a purchase decision for the product by consumers in each stage of the cycle.

You might encourage students to develop their own list of categories in the family life cycle, define them, and then determine the types of product people in each of those categories would probably need. (Possible Field Project)

11. Consider three important changes in modern family structure. For each, find an example of a marketer who has attempted to be conscious of this change as reflected in product communications, retailing innovations, or other aspects of the marketing mix. If possible, also try to find examples of marketers who have failed to keep up with these developments.

If students have trouble getting information for this project, you might ask them to contact various retailers (department stores, specialty stores, discount houses, etc.) and ask the manager if he/she is aware of any product modification, promotions, or displays that have been made. (Possible Field Project)

12. Industrial purchase decisions are totally rational. Aesthetic or subjective factors don't -- and shouldn't -- play a role in this process. Do you agree?

The buyer's perception in organizational marketing is affected by expectations, organization climate, and "organizational memory". In most cases: 1) purchase decision frequently involve may people, 2) products are often bought according to precise specifications, 3) impulse buying is rare, 4) decisions are high-risk, 5) dollar volume of purchases is often substantial, 6) there is more emphasis on personal selling than other types of promotion, and 7) transactions are guided by long-term relationships.

However, aesthetic or subjective factors do enter the picture because the people who make purchase decisions are human and consequently make decisions based both on thinking (cognitive) and feeling (affect). Business knows that pleasant surroundings do affect the amount and quality of work. Many times an organizational buyer is buying more than a product or service, he/she is really buying the salesperson and the company--relationship marketing.

ENDNOTES

[1] Annamma Joy, "The Modern Medicis: Corporations as Consumers of Art," *Research in Consumer Behavior.* 6 (1993): 29-54.

[2] Bradley Johnson, "A's Take Swing at Family Marketing." *Advertising Age* (June 4, 1990): 16.

[3] Lori Kesler, House of the 90's Opens Up," *Advertising Age* (March 12, 1990); Susan Krafft, "The Heart of the Home," *American Demographics* (June 1992) 5:46.

[4] Glenn Collins, "One Magazine for American Parents is Making Marketers Think Twice," *The New York Times* (July 26, 1994): D18.

[5] Alison Leigh Cowan, "Parenthood II" The Nest Won't Stay Empty," *New York Times,* (March 12, 1989): 1.

[6] Gary Levin, "JWT Researchers Stages, Not Ages," *Advertising Age* (June 26, 1989): 30.

[7] George Belch, Michael A. Belch, and Gayle Ceresino, "Parental and Teenage Child Influences in Family Decision Making," *Journal of Business Research* 13 (April 1985); 163-76; D. R. Howard and R. Madrigal, "Who Makes the Decision: The Parent or the Child? The Perceived Influence of Parents and Children on the Purchase of Recreation Service," *Journal of Leisure Research* 22 (1990) 3: 244-58.

[8] Claudia H. Deutsch, "Younger Set Leads the Way on the Road," *New York Times* (December 1, 1991); F10; Betsy Spethmann, "Young Travelers Exposed to Hyatt Touch," *Advertising Age* (February 10, 1992) S-6: 294.

[9] "What Are All Those Men Doing in Grocery Stores? *Adweek* (July 13, 1992): 10; D.H. Berardo, C. L. Shehan, and G. R. Leslie, "A Residue of Tradition: Jobs Careers, and Spouses Time in Housework," *Journal of Marriage and the Family* 49 (May 1987) 10: 381; John Skow, "The Myth of Male Housework: For Women, Toil Looms from Sun to Sun," *Time* (August 7, 1989) 62; Evan Thomas, The Reluctant Father: Dad Didn't Ask for His New Role: It Just Kinds of Fell into His Lap," *Newsweek* (December 19, 1988) 3: 64.

[10] Ugur Yavas, Emin Babakus, and Nejdet Delener, "Family Purchasing Roles in Saudi Arabia: Perspectives from Saudi Wives," *Journal of Business Research* 31 (1994): 75-86.

[11] Harry L. Davis, Stephen J. Hock, and E. K. Easton Ragsdale, "An Anchoring and Adjustment Model of Spousal Prediction," *Journal of Consumer Research* 13 (June 1986): 25-37; Rosann L. Spiro, "Persuasion in Family Decision-Making," *Journal of Consumer Research* 9 (March 1983); 39-402; J.S. Hopper, C. Burns, and N.L. Sherrell, "An Assessment of the Reliability and Validity of Husband and Wife Self Report Purchase Decision Making Measures," *Journal of the Academy of Marketing Science* 17 (Summer 1989): 227-34.

[12] David J. Burns, "Husband-Wife Innovative Decision Making: Exploring the Effect of Family Power," *Psychology & Marketing* 9 (May-June 1992): 175-89.

[13] William R. Swinyard and Cheng Peng Sim, "Perceptions of Children's Influence on Family Decision Processes," *Journal of Consumer Marketing* 4 (Winter 1987): 25-38.

[14] George P. Moschis, "The Role of Family Communication in Consumer Socialization of Children and Adolescents," *Journal of Consumer Research* 11 (March 1985): 898-913.

[15] Dena Kleiman, "Candy to Frighten Your Parents With," *New York Times* (August 23, 1989): C1.

[16] Patricia Sellers, "The ABC's of Marketing to Kids," *Fortune* (May 8, 1989): 4.

[17] Glen Collins, "New Studies on 'Girl Toys' and 'Boy Toys'," *New York Times* (February 13, 1984): D1.

Instructor's Notes:

CHAPTER 12

Income and Social Class

SUMMARY BULLETS

◆ The field of behavioral economics considers how consumers decide what to do with their money. In particular, discretionary expenditures are made only when people are able and willing to spend money on items above and beyond their basic needs. Consumer confidence—the state of mind consumers have about their own personal situation, as well as their feelings about their overall economic prospects—helps to determine whether they will purchase goods and services, take on debt, or save their money.

◆ In this decade, consumers overall have been relatively pessimistic about their future prospects. A lower level of resources has caused a shift toward an emphasis on quality products that are reasonably priced. Consumers are less tolerant of exaggerated or vague product claims, and they are more skeptical about marketing activities. Consumers in their twenties are particularly skeptical about the economy and marketing targeted to their age group.

◆ A consumer's social class refers to his or her standing in society. It is determined by a number of factors, including education, occupation, and income.

◆ Virtually all groups make distinctions among members in terms of relative superiority, power, and access to valued resources. This social stratification creates a status hierarchy, where some goods are preferred over others and are used to categorize their owners' social class.

◆ While income is an important indicator of social class, the relationship is far from perfect since social class is also determined by such factors as place of residence, cultural interests, and worldview.

◆ Purchase decisions are sometimes influenced by the desire to "buy up" to a higher social class or to engage in the process of conspicuous consumption, where one's status is flaunted by the deliberate and nonconstructive use of valuable resources. This spending pattern is a characteristic of the nouveau riches, whose relatively recent acquisition of income, rather than ancestry or breeding, is responsible for their increased social mobility.

◆ Products often are used as status symbols to communicate real or desired social class. Parody display occurs when consumers seek status by deliberately avoiding fashionable products.

LECTURE/DISCUSSION IDEAS

I. **Consumer Spending and Economic Behavior** -- George Katona studied the "human side" of economic decisions (self-fulfilling prophesy applied to economics)

   A. **Income Patterns** -- real *per capita* income almost doubled between 1960 and 1990

      1. **Woman's Work** -- getting more high paying jobs

      2. **Yes, It Pays to Go to School!** -- college grads earn 50% more than high school grads

   B. **To Spend or Not to Spend, That is the Question** -- consumer demand depends on both ability and willingness to buy

Discussion Topic: Can you think of some item that you have the ability to buy but you don't intend to buy the object? Why won't you buy it?

Discussion Topic: Can you think of some item you would be willing to buy but you just don't have the means to buy it? What do you think the final outcome will be?

      1. **Discretionary Spending** -- money spent for non-necessary items

         a. **The Household Budget** -- *more* money is now being spent on shelter, transportation, entertainment, and education and *less* on food and clothes

      2. **Individual Attitudes Toward Money** -- money is equated with security and comfort

Discussion Topic: How do you "feel" about money? What does it represent to you? Would you classify yourself as a saver or a spender? Do you think other people would agree with this?

   C. **Consumer Confidence** -- reflects optimism and pessimism about the future

      1. **Forecasting Consumer Confidence** -- questions used by the Survey Research Center at the University of Michigan

- Would you say that you and your family are better or worse off financially than a year ago?
- Will you be better off or worse off a year from now?
- Is not a good time or a bad time for people to buy major household items, such as furniture or a refrigerator?
- Do you plan to buy a car in the next year?

Discussion Topic: Do you think these four questions are good ones? Do you think people would truthfully answer all these questions? Would you?

2. **The Savings Rate** -- affected by consumer's optimism and pessimism about the economy.

3. **Consumers Adapt to Changing Times** -- in a recession, both discounted goods and luxury items tend to sell well

   a. **Value Versus Quality: A Shift in Priorities** -- the 1990s seem to reflect a "back to basics" orientation
      Grey Advertising Poll:
      - majority believe that they have no control over economic or political events.
      - three out of four wonder if dreams will come true
      - majority are resigned to the fact that they cannot afford the lifestyle they want
      - only 52% are optimistic about future
      - they are cautious about spending

Real World Application

☯ Generation X captures the occupational frustrations of young people who invented jargon like a McJob, which is defined as a low-pay, low-prestige, low-benefit, no-future job in the service sector, frequently considered a satisfying career choice by people who have never held a job. This book provides a good mechanism to tap into the economic concerns of college students, and the raising of these issues in class is sure to inspire a heated discussion about students' prospects in a consumption society. Further discussion of college students as consumers can be found in Chapter 15.[1]

---

4. **Marketers Adapt to Changing Times**--Sharper Image is a yuppie toy store and more

II.   **Social Class** -- variables includes: family income, background, and occupation
                                                            (Use TM 12-1 Here)

☯ Choose your parents wisely. Although people do improve their standing through their own effort, one's background exerts a strong influence on later outcomes. A survey of American CEOs, for example, showed that two-thirds came from upper-middle-class or upper-class backgrounds.[2]

A. **A Universal Pecking Order** -- in most animal species the most assertive or aggressive animals exert control over the others

1. **Social Class Affects Access to Resources**
   - Karl Marx: the "haves" control the resources and the "havenots" provide labor
   - Max Weber: multidimensional people are ranked by social status, power, wealth, and property

Discussion Topic: Do you believe that all men are created equal? If so, why are we studying this chapter?

2. **Social Class Affects Taste and Lifestyles** -- people in each group tend to socialize with each other, share many ideas and values, and have similar education

B. **Social Stratification** -- refers to the artificial divisions in society (e.g. "those who have, gets!")

Real World Application

☙ Reflecting the British redistribution of wealth away from the aristocracy and toward self-made business-people, the richest man in the United Kingdom is now Paul Raymond, who deposed the Duke of Westminster for the title. Raymond's business ventures include ownership of several nightclubs, and he publishes the sex magazines Men Only, Club International, and Mayfair. The London Times noted that there is more money these days in pornography than inherited property.[3]

☙ The popular British television series, *Upstairs, Downstairs,* is an example of the explicit portrayal of class differences. An impenetrable gulf separates the upstairs characters from those who reside downstairs.[4]

---

1. **Achieved Versus Ascribed Status** -- status is either earned or inherited
   - status hierarchy: some are better off than others (more authority and power, more respect or simply better liked)

Discussion Topic: Do you think that those who achieve should have authority, power, money, and respect?

Discussion Topic: Can you think of an achiever that you admire? Who? Can you think of an achiever that you don't admire? Who? Who should decide which achievers are rewarded and which are not?

2. **Class Structure in the United States** -- proposed by Lloyd Warner (1941)
   (Use Color Transparency 34 Here)
   (Use TM 12-2 Here)

   - Upper Upper (old rich)
   - Lower Upper (new rich)
   - Upper Middle (professional and owners)
   - Lower Middle (lower paid white collar and high paid blue collar)
   - Upper Lower (blue collar workers)
   - Lower Lower (underemployed and unemployed)

3. **Class Structure Around the World** -- markers of success
   - Chinese: hiring a bodyguard to protect oneself and one's possessions
   - Japanese: wearing designer labels, owning a rock garden, belonging to a golf club
   - England: birth, education, speech patterns, polo, House of Lords
   - India: birth

C. **Social Mobility** -- passage of individuals from one class to another

Discussion Topic: Do you think that you are in a different socio-economic class than your grandparents were at your age? What type of work did your grandfather perform? Did your grandmother work outside of the home?

1. **Direction of Movement** -- type of mobility
   - horizontal: nurse becomes an elementary school teacher
   - downward: farmers and displaced workers end up on welfare or homeless

---

Real World Application
❧ A recent ethnographic study gives a poignant account of how homeless women adapt to life in a shelter.[5]

   - upward: child of a blue collar worker becomes physician or college professor

---

❧ Kuwait is a highly materialistic country, and car ownership is a major form of status. The social lives of many young Kuwaitis revolves around cars. Kuwaitis are the largest per capita importers of luxury American sedans outside of North America. The average household owns 3.7 vehicles. Most cars are sold with a powerful V-8 engine, and without catalytic converters.[6]

D. **Components of Social Class** -- (occupation, income and education)

1. **Occupational Prestige**
   - high prestige: CEO, physician, college professor
   - low prestige: shoe shiner, ditch digger, garbage collector
   - indicators: leisure time use, allocation of family resources, political orientation

Discussion Topic: Do you think of Republicans as being rich or poor? Democrats? Can you think of examples that refute your beliefs?

2. **Income** -- those in the top 20% control 75% of all assets

3. **The Relationship Between Income and Social Class**
   - more income doesn't necessarily result in increased status or changed consumption patterns
   - income predicts purchase of expensive products without status (e.g. major appliance)
   - social class can predict the purchase of low to moderate priced symbolic products (e.g. liquor, cosmetics)
   - both social class and income are needed to predict purchase of expensive symbolic products (e.g. cars, homes)

Discussion Topic: What are some products (brands) that typical college students buy which tend to indicate their social class?

E. **Measurement of Social Class** -- difficult to do

(Use TM 12-3 Here)

1. **Problems With Measures of Social Class** -- outdated measures

   a. **Changes in Family Structure** -- two-income families, singles, single parents

   b. **Anonymity** -- people won't share pertinent information

   c. **Status Inconsistency**

      - person from a low status ethnic background has a high-status job
      - person who did not finish high school lives in a fancy part of town
      - overprivileged consumer (lottery winners)
      - underprivileged consumers (sacrifice in order to look proper--beautiful home but no furniture)

Discussion Topic: Can you think of someone who "suffers" from status inconsistency?
(Hint: Sports and entertainment figures.)

   d. **Women and Social Class**
      - traditionally, women borrowed their social status from their husband
      - today, more women are marrying without regard to social position of man
      - realistically, social class differences still present dilemmas to couples

Discussion Topic: Do you think a male taxi driver and a female physician would have a happy marriage? Do you think a male physician and a female bus driver would have a happy marriage? What problems would their relationship face?

2. **Problems with Social Class Segmentation: A Summary** -- marketers have failed to use social class information effectively because they ignored:

- status inconsistencies
- intergenerational mobility
- subjective social class (the class a consumer identifies with rather than the one he or she objectively belongs to)
- consumers' aspirations to change their class standing
- social status of working wives

III.   **How Social Class Affects Purchase Decisions** -- products and stores are perceived to belong to certain social classes

(Use TM 12-4 Here)

A. **Class Difference in Worldview**
- working classes concerned with immediate needs are more dependent on relatives for emotional support, are family-oriented, and the appearance of home is a priority
- higher classes tend to focus on more long-term goals, quest for riches often results in depression and deviant behavior

---

Real World Application
- Because the higher classes have broader social networks and control of informational resources, it has been proposed that consumers from these strata will more readily adopt technological innovations that permit information flow and communication. For a discussion, see reference.[7]

---

1. **Taste Cultures** -- subtle distinctions in consumption choices
- lower-status home: religious objects, artificial flowers, still-life portraits
- higher-status home: abstract paintings, sculptures, and modern furniture

2. **Codes and Social Class** -- how meanings are expressed and interpreted
- restricted codes: focus on content of objects not on relationship among objects
- elaborated codes: focus on more complex issues and has a worldview.

Discussion Topic: What are some physical cues that you can observe to determine whether a person is in the upper, middle, or lower socio-economic class? Do you think you can easily be misled?

- Social class codes are often used to classify women by their appearance. A lower social class code may contain such elements as flashy dress, deep décolletage, long nails, and so on. The French sociologist Pierre Bourdieu has correlated many attributes with social class (e.g., he claims that waist measurements go up as one goes down the class ladder). The working-class girl was epitomized by Melanie Griffith in the film *Working Girl*: high heels, short skirt, gum-chewing, big hair . . . . Students will enjoy discussing the accuracy and fairness of such characterizations.[8]

B. **Segmenting by Social Class: Targeting the Rich** -- social class is more than money
- few rich people equate wealth with success
- success is related to high self-esteem (being a good parent, happy marriage, solid ethics)
- achievement such as being in charge of a cultural or educational institution
- luxury products are important
- enjoy socializing, particularly at country clubs
- buy products that are high in value and durable

Real World Application
- One way to determine where money is concentrated is to rank markets in terms of Effective Buying Income (EBI), a measure that adjust income levels for local tax rates. The five metro markets with the largest number of affluent households are New York, Los Angeles-Long Beach, Chicago, Washington, and Philadelphia.[9]

---

1. **Old Money** -- inherited money
- not how much money, but *where* did it come from and *how* is it spent
- people who earned their money are not usually included in this group
- history of public service and philanthropy

- The emphasis on lineage and ancestry is trickling down. The majority of college-educated consumers in America report that they have furnished at least part of their homes in antiques, and almost half prefer objects that evoke an early-American feeling.[10]

---

2. **The Nouveau Riches** -- "rags to riches"; not accepted by old rich

- **Status Anxiety** -- wearing the "right" clothes; seen in the "right" places; using the "right" caterer

Discussion Topic: How do spending patterns differ between the "old rich" and the "new rich"?

3. **The "Get Set"** -- sacrifice in some areas so they can have the best in others

IV. **Status Symbols** -- equate themselves with others i.e., "keeping up with the Joneses" or "he who dies with the most toys, wins."

(Use Color Transparency 35 Here)
(Use TM 12-5 Here)

- The Japanese status craze is largely driven by the spending power of single women in their twenties. A typical clerical job pays about 170,000 yen per month (about $20,000 per year with bonus), but these consumers have a large amount of disposable income. They often live at home for free, and commuting costs are typically paid by their companies. As a result, they may be left with about 135,000 yen per year to spend on consumer goods.[11]

A. **Conspicuous Consumption** -- Thorstein Veblen: visible evidence of wealth (e.g. banquets for pet dogs, hundred-dollar bills folded into guests' dinner napkins, etc.)
(Use Color Transparency 36 Here)

Discussion Topic: What are some current examples of conspicuous consumption among your friends? . . . for your parents?

Real World Application
☙   Parallels to the parties thrown by the robber barons can be found in modern-day birthday bashes for the rich and famous: Publisher Malcolm Forbes flew over 600 guests to Tangiers for a weekend of lavish feasts and entertainment, while a party for financier Saul Steinberg included nude actresses posing in re-creations of Flemish paintings.   See ABC video for this chapter.
---

1. **The Trophy Wife** -- high-heeled shoes, long finger nails, elaborate hairstyles, etc.

2. **The Modern Potlatch** -- a feast where the host gives elaborate gifts to guests and guests are expected to reciprocate, forcing poor guests into bankruptcy. (Today's elaborate wedding ceremony and reception parallels this practice!)

Discussion Topic: What are some obvious expenses that could be eliminated from the average wedding? Why won't people eliminate these?

3. **The Leisure Class** -- people for whom productive work is taboo and engage in conspicuous waste i.e., use up as many resources as possible in non-constructive pursuits

---
☙   Another contemporary example of conspicuous waste is the well-chronicled abuses of Imelda Marcos, the wife of the former Philippine ruler. Mrs. Marcos kept no less than 2700 pairs of shoes in her closets in Lalacanang Palace.[12]

B. **Is Status Symbolism Dead?** -- reputation alone is not sufficient to indicate status

1. **Fraudulent Symbolism** -- symbol has become so widely used that value is depleted (e.g. designer jeans)

Discussion Topic: What are some examples of fraudulent symbols today?

☙   There has been a change in values regarding materialism from the 1980s to the 1990s. The construct of materialism as a social value will be further discussed in Chapter 16. While many marketers are moving toward simplicity, advertising for the upscale Charivari clothing stores bemoans this new trend and says: "Ripped jeans. Pocket Tees. Back to basics. Wake us up when it's over." Students can discuss whether "it" really is over: Is there still a market for status symbols? Is the yuppie (or some new incarnation) really dead?
---

2. **Parody Display** -- avoid status symbols (e.g. pipes and support beams were deliberately exposed in home construction; ripped blue jeans; Jeeps owned by the rich)

Discussion Topic: What are some of the new status symbols that are being created by mocking traditional status symbols?

FIELD PROJECT IDEAS

Individual Assignments

1. Have a student compile a list of ten colleges and universities (or academic majors) and ask a few individuals to rank each according to its prestige. Have them comment on the results. Are there any marketing implications to the results?

2. Ask a student to bring in an ad in which the brand being marketed was formerly a status symbol (e.g. Cadillac, Parker Pen, etc.). Have the student discuss whether the ad still attempts to create that perception. What new product, if any, has replaced the featured product as a status symbol?

3. Have a student interview small business owners, large business owners, or a couple of both for their opinions of the state of the economy. How they think an increase in Social Security Taxes (American Disabilities Act, Flat Tax Proposal, NAFTA, or some currently proposed federal regulation or mandate) would affect them? Have the student find out what major signals the owners study and watch before making their business forecasts.

4. Encourage one of your students to read the book (or reviews of the book) *Generation X* and tell the class about their reactions to it. Does the student think that Coupland accurately represents the feelings of the people fitting into this category?

5. Have a student visit with a representative of a local consumer protection agency (e.g. Better Business Bureau, an investigative reporter from the newspaper or television station, etc.) and ask their opinion on how lower-class and middle-class consumers differ in terms of the type of the consumer protection that they need.

6. Have a student interview one or more salesperson(s) from one of the following product categories--new or used cars, stereo equipment, clothing, insurance, or real estate. Ask the student to determine the social classes or status of their customers. Does the student recommend that the sales approach will vary depending on the customer's social class?

7. Have a student visit two sections of a community--one where residents are professionals and business people and one where residents are mostly working class. Ask them to note of how the homes vary in terms of color, architecture, and the general appearance of the lawn and landscape. Have them check the paper or call a realtor to find the general value of homes in the area. What types of stores are in the neighborhood and how are they promoted?

8. Ask a student to bring in a collection of magazines aimed at different social classes. Have the student comment on the products advertised, the physical appearance and layout, and the editorial content of the magazines.

Group Assignments

9. Bring to class copies of the types of magazines described in the chapter that appeal to various social classes. Pass the magazines around and have students look through them. Ask the class to discuss the differences and similarities that they noted.

10. Prepare a list of 15 occupations and distribute copies to the class. Ask each student to rank the occupations according to prestige. Give the list to some students and ask them to calculate averages for each occupation. Discuss the results with the class.

Individual or Group Assignments

11. Ask a student (or a group) to find at least two manufacturer's ads for the same generic product (such as clothing, food product, personal care product, etc.) that they think are aimed at different social classes. Have them explain how they differ.

12. Have some students (or just one) make a list of fraudulent symbols and then construct a profile of individuals who are still using or wearing these symbols. Have them also make a list of some of the new "status symbols" that have become proper.

13. Ask a group of students (or an individual) to compile a collection of ads that depict consumers of different social classes. Have them generalize about the reality of the stories told in these ads. Do the ads appear to be in the right media?

14. Students usually enjoy this project. Ask a group to classify the major retail stores (department and specialty stores) in your community according to their estimation of the social class of their target market. Have them explain how the marketing strategy is different for each of the stores profiled.

CONSUMER BEHAVIOR CHALLENGE

1. Sears, J.C. Penney, and, to a lesser degree, K-Mart, have made concerted efforts in recent years to upgrade their images and appeal to higher-class consumers. How successful have these efforts been? Do you believe this strategy is wise?

According to the text, J.C. Penney has not been very successful in changing its image. Because consumers have always thought of stores like J.C. Penney, Sears, and K-Mart as discount or low-price stores, it is likely that these stores will have difficulty changing their images among the general public. Attempting to change a store's image when consumers have a strong perception of the store's image, and one that is largely inconsistent with the proposed image, can be a very risky strategy. As in the case of J.C. Penney, retailers run the risk of alienating a significant group of loyal consumers with these attempts.

2. What are some of the obstacles to measuring social class in today's society? Discuss some ways to get around these obstacles.

Some of the obstacles in measuring social class in today's society are changes in family structure, anonymity, and status inconsistency. Students should refer to the text discussion for suggestions on how to get around some of these obstacles.

3. What consumption differences might you expect to observe between a family characterized as underprivileged versus one whose income is average for its social class?

An example of the consumption differences one might expect to observe between a family characterized as underprivileged versus one whose income is average for its social class include the brands of clothing worn, the types of cars driven, types of vacations (flying versus driving, hotels versus camping), and vacation destinations (local state park versus Hawaii). Students likely will identify a number of factors in their own lives that distinguish them a members of the "middle" class.

4. When is social class likely to be a better predictor of consumer behavior than mere knowledge of a person's income?

Students should recognize that social class is likely to be a better predictor of consumer behavior than mere knowledge of a person's income when level of income masks real differences in behaviors due to educational achievement, occupational prestige, and other factors incorporated into an overall measure of social class.

5. How do you assign people to social classes, or do you at all? What consumption cues do you use (e.g., clothing, speech, cars, etc.) to determine social standing?

As discussed in the text, people are assigned to social classes by virtue of their social standing in the community. People are grouped according to their occupation, lifestyle, ideas and values, and income. Consumption cues that may be used to determine people's social standing include their cars, homes, clothing, speech, and types of people with whom they socialize.

6. Thorstein Veblen argued that women were often used as a vehicle to display their husbands' wealth. Is this argument still valid today?

The instructor should expect students to differ in their level of agreement with Thorstein Veblen's notion that women often are used as a vehicle to display their husbands' wealth. They should be encouraged to defend and support their views with examples from today's society.

7. Given present environmental conditions and dwindling resources, what is the future of "conspicuous waste?" Can the desire to impress others with affluence ever be eliminated? If not, can it take on a less dangerous form?

The goal of this question is to make the student think about current environmental conditions, depleting resources, and how "conspicuous waste" plays a major role in this decay process. The view of conspicuous waste from both consumer and marketer perspectives should be included.

8. Some people argue that status symbols are dead. Do you agree?

To begin the exercise, the instructor might ask students to list items that they perceive to be status symbols. Each item could then be analyzed to determine its history and evolution as a status symbol, and its position today.

9. Using the Status Index presented in Figure 12–4, compute a social class score for people you know, including their parents if possible. Ask several friends (preferably from different places) to compile similar information for people they know. How closely do your answers compare? If you find differences, how can you explain them?

Students should enjoy using this exercise to analyze their parents' social class standing, as well as that of their peers' parents. They might be encouraged to compute a hypothetical score for themselves, based on expectations for the future. (Possible Field Project)

10. Compile a list of occupations, and ask a sample of students in a variety of majors (both business and nonbusiness) to rank the prestige of these jobs. Can you detect any differences in these rankings as a function of students' majors?

The student should be encouraged to try this exercise with a variety of individuals, not just students in different majors. It would be interesting to see differences in perceptions of prestige due to gender, age, current occupation, level of education, etc. (Possible Field Project)

11. Compile a collection of ads that depict consumers of different social classes. What generalizations can you make about the reality of these ads and about the media in which they appear?

The instructor might review this exercise after students have completed it and attempt to identify the aspects of the advertisements that students used to classify consumers a members of different social classes. A discussion of how our attitudes and perceptions are influenced by stereotypical beliefs could then be used with the students' own examples as evidence of stereotypical beliefs and their potentially negative consequences. (Possible Field Project)

12. Identify a current set of fraudulent status symbols, and construct profiles of consumers who are wearing or using these products. Are these profiles consistent with the images portrayed in each product's promotional messages?

Students should draw from the text discussion of fraudulent symbolism at the end of the chapter. They are likely to identify a wide variety of fraudulent symbols, related to a wide variety of product categories. (Possible Field Project)

13. The chapter observes that some marketers are finding "greener pastures" by targeting low-income people. How ethical is it to single out consumers who cannot afford to waste their precious resources on discretionary items? Under what circumstances should this segmentation strategy be encouraged or discouraged?

Student opinions will vary. Possible ethical issues include: Do people with low incomes need special protection? Does low income equate with low intelligence? Do you take away freedom of choice from people with low incomes? Who should decide how people use their money? Will society have to provide essential items if those with low incomes spend their money on discretionary items? The argument of what discretionary items should not be promoted to low-income people seems to be centering around "sin products" (tobacco, alcohol, etc.). When a special cigarette, a special wine, and a special ale were targeted toward people who live in the inner-city, many groups spoke out saying that it was immoral to use billboards in these neighborhoods to encourage sales. The companies involved have either dropped the product or changed their promotional strategies, but these same products with different brand names are still appearing on billboards in the inner-city. Some argue that since low-income people have the right to use tobacco products and alcoholic beverages, manufacturers should have the right to communicate about their products to every potential consumer.

ENDNOTES

1 Douglas Coupland, *Generation X: Tales for an Accelerated Culture* (New York: St. Martin's Press, 1991): 5.

2 Louis E. Boone, David L. Kurtz, and C. Patrick Fleenor, "The Road to the Top," *American Demographics* (March 1988): 34.

3 "Duke is No Longer Britain's Richest Man," *New York Times* (December 1, 1992): D5.

4 Arthur A. Berger, *Signs in Contemporary Culture: An Introduction to Semiotics* (New York: Longman, 1984).

5 Ronald Paul Hill, "Homeless Women, Special Possession and the Meaning of 'Home,' An Ethnographic Case Study," *Journal of Consumer Research* 18 (December 1991): 298

6 Chris Hedges, "A V-8 for Victory: It's Kuwait's Way of Celebrating," *The New York Times* (February 9, 1993): A4.

7 James E. Fisher and Paul D. Boughton (1991), "Information, Technology and Social Class," in Marketing: Toward the Twenty-First Century, ed. Robert L. King, (Richmond, Va.: Southern Marketing Association, 1991), 11.

8 Joan Kron, "Secret Beauty Codes," *Allure* (August 1992)3: 54.

9 *Sales & Marketing Management 1994 Survey of Buying Power* (August 30, 1994).

10 Jeremy Schlossberg, "Sitting Pretty," *American Demographics* (May 1988): 24-29.

11 "Japan's Consumer Boom: the Pricey Society," *The Economist* (September 9, 1989): 21.

12 Lance Morrow, "The Shoes of Imelda Marcos," *Time* (March 31, 1986): 80.

Instructor's Notes:

CHAPTER 13

Ethnic, Racial and Religious Subculture

SUMMARY BULLETS

♦ Consumers identify with many groups that share common characteristics and identities. These large groups that exist within a society are subcultures, and membership in them often gives marketers a clue about individuals' consumption decisions. A large component of a person's identity is often determined by his or her ethnic origins, racial identity, and religious background. The three largest ethnic/racial subcultures are African-Americans, Hispanic-Americans, and Asian-Americans, but consumers with many diverse backgrounds are beginning to be considered by marketers as well.

♦ Recently, several minority groups have caught the attention of marketers as their economic power has grown. Segmenting consumers by their ethnicity can be effective, but care must be taken not to rely on inaccurate (and sometimes offensive) ethnic stereotypes.

♦ African-Americans are a very important market segment. While in some respects the market expenditures of these consumers do not differ that much from whites, blacks are above average consumers in such categories as personal-care products. In the past, blacks were either ignored or portrayed negatively in mainstream advertising, but such depictions are changing as more blacks actually work on the development of campaigns and as specialized black media increase in importance.

♦ Hispanic-Americans and Asian-Americans are other ethnic subcultures that are beginning to be actively courted by marketers. The size of both groups is increasing rapidly and in the coming years will dominate some major markets. Asian-Americans on the whole are extremely well educated, and the socioeconomic status of Hispanics is increasing as well.

♦ Key issues for reaching the Hispanic market are consumers' degree of acculturation into mainstream American society and the recognition of important cultural differences among Hispanic subgroups (e.g., Puerto Ricans, Cubans, Mexicans).

♦ Both Asian-Americans and Hispanic-Americans tend to be extremely family-oriented and are receptive to advertising that understands their heritage and reinforces traditional family values.

♦ While the impact of religious identification on consumer behavior is not clear, some differences among religious subcultures do emerge. In particular, cultural characteristics of Protestants, Catholics, and Jews result in varied preferences for leisure activities and orientations toward consumption. Some of these factors are closely related to social class. White Anglo-Saxon Protestants (WASPs) in particular have played a dominant role in the formation of American cultural values largely due to their cultural emphasis on achievement and early domination of the American power structure.

♦ The market power of the growing numbers of born-again Christians is uncertain at this point, but opportunities exist to cater to the unique needs of this segment.

LECTURE/DISCUSSION IDEAS

I.   **Subcultures and Consumer Identity** -- subcultural identifications affect consumer behavior and types of products and services purchased

(Use Color Transparency 37 Here)

Real World Application
☯ One study has compared the validity of ethnicity scales.[1]

II.   **Ethnic and Racial Subculture** -- self-perpetuating groups held together by cultural and/or genetic ties

(Use TM 13-1 Here)

Discussion Topic: What are some of the ways that members of ethnic and racial minorities identify with and support each other? What implications does this have for marketers?

A. **Why Ethnic Groups Should be Segmented** -- spend over $600 billion a year

1. **Ethnicity and Marketing Strategies** -- membership shapes needs and wants
    • high-context cultures: (most minorities) tightly-knit, symbols and gestures carry much weight, sensitive to nuances in ads
    • low-context cultures: (Anglos) the above is less important

2. **The "Big Three" American Subculture** -- projections for 2013
    • Hispanic-Americans--42.1 million
    • African-Americans--42 million
    • Asian-Americans-- smaller in absolute number, but the fastest growing

B. **Ethnic and Racial Stereotypes: The Dark Side of Multicultural Marketing** --
    same trait can be viewed two ways (e.g. is a Scottish person "thrifty" or "stingy.")

Discussion Topic: Identify a specific ethnic or racial minority and make a list of some of the negative stereotype descriptions that are associated with the group. In a column next to the negative word, write a positive word that describes the same behavior or characteristic. How might this analysis be useful to marketers?

1. **Do Advertisers Perpetuate Ethnic and Racial Stereotypes?** -- blacks were subservient (e.g., Aunt Jemima); Mexicans were bandits (e.g., Frito Bandito)

Real World Application
- Recently, Colt 45 Malt Liquor modified its ad campaign that depicted the black actor Billy Dee Williams in glamorous scenes surrounded by status symbols and sophisticated women. As one industry consultant put it, "Blacks resent 'malt-liquor macho.' They don't want to see black women portrayed as sex symbols or homebound frumps, or black men as footloose, irresponsible studs."[2]

---

2. **De-Ethnicitization** -- product is detached from its roots (e.g. jalapeno bagels) Ethnic restaurants: Chinese, Mexican, Italian (70% of all ethnic restaurants)

Discussion Topic: What are some ethnic products (food, clothes, accessories, etc.) that have become a part of the mainstream culture?

- Sales at sit-down ethnic restaurants totaled $8 billion in 1991. Mass market companies like General Mills are aggressively entering the ethnic restaurant market in a big way. After scoring a hit with its Olive Garden chain, the company is testing the marketing for mass-produced Chinese food at its China Coast units in Florida and Indianapolis.[3]

C. **New Ethnic Groups** -- most now are Asian and Hispanic

- Long-distance telephone carriers are cashing in on immigrant groups, who tend to call home frequently. Revenue from overseas calling is expected to reach $8.6 billion by 1996. In 1991, international telephone traffic accounted for 20 percent of the calls placed in the United States.[4]

---

1. **Classifying Ethnic and Racial Membership** -- federal agencies use these races: 1. American Indian or Alaskan native 2. Asian or Pacific Islander 3. Black 4. White. Problem: How do you classify multiracial, Arabs, and Hispanics?

III. **African-Americans** -- 12% of U.S. population

(Use Color Transparency 38 Here)
(Use TM 13-2 Here)

- Memphis is the American city with the highest percentage of black population (41.4%). It is followed by New Orleans (35.8%) and New York (29.9%).[5]

Real World Application
❧ Several major mass-market retailers, including K-Mart, Toys 'R' Us, and J.C. Penney, are making a concerted effort to woo minority shoppers. J.C. Penney, for example opened "Authentic African" boutiques in 120 of its stores in 1991, and the company has plans to expand this operation to 350 of its outlets.[6]

A. Black/White Consumption Differences
- blacks buy only 2% of trucks and vans
- blacks account for a quarter of all spending on mass transit
- blacks buy 17% of all encyclopedias and references books sold
- blacks buy one half of all cognac sold in U.S.
- blacks comprise 34% of the market for hair-care products

❧ Glory Foods, Inc., announced plans to offer the first national line of packaged soul food (e.g., okra, collard greens).[7]

1. **The BUPPIE** --exhibit attitudes of white middle-class but hold on to black heritage

Discussion Topic: What are some of the attitudes and characteristics that middle-class blacks have adopted that mirror attitudes and characteristics of middle-class whites? What are some of the aspects of their black heritage that they seem to retain? How might a marketer make use of this information?

❧ Coca-Cola found that black consumers had trouble relating to its Max Headroom campaign for Sprite so it developed a separate campaign for this market. In two years, Sprite became the number one lemon-line drink among blacks. Occasionally specialized advertising actually turns out to be so universal it is adapted for the general market. The Kentucky Fried Chicken theme of "We Do Chicken Right," for example, was originally developed by a black agency exclusively for black consumers in the New York area.[8]

B. Blacks and the Media -- average 10 hours of TV a day, read local morning newspaper, read classified ads and circulars

1. **Black Representation in Mainstream Media** -- now account for one fourth of all people in ads and portrayed in network shows as middle-to-upper class

❧ Ethnic segmentation of the cigarette market is hardly a new phenomenon. A content analysis of cigarette ads appearing in *Life* and *Ebony* between 1950-1965 showed that the *Ebony* ads almost exclusively featured black models (primarily athletes), while none of these endorsements appears in *Life*. This advertising also was on average two to three years tardy in offering filtered cigarettes to black consumers.[9]

2. **Black-Oriented Media** -- Jet (90% black males), Ebony, Essence, and Black Enterprise. Multicultural romance novels. (e.g. test marketing of Uptown menthol cigarette to black community was controversial)

a. **Family Emphasis** -- ads promote positive images of black males as fathers

b. **Black Celebrities** -- Black version of "Bart Simpson" is popular

Discussion Topic: Who are some of the most popular black celebrities appearing as spokespersons in ads for various products? Why do you think these particular persons were chosen? Evaluate the choices. Do black youths identify with Bill Cosby?

◐ As part of its Neighborhood KFC program, Kentucky Fried Chicken outfitted employees in new uniforms inspired by African designs and piped in R&B music to KFC stores in urban areas. The program boosted sales an average of 5%-10%.[11]

◐ The Olmec Company makes a Sun Man collection of black action figures and recently introduced a line called the Bronze Bombers, inspired by all-black units in World War I and II.[12]

IV. **Hispanic-Americans** -- increasing affluence of this group is being noticed by corporations
(Use TM 13-3 Here)

◐ Reflecting the prevalence of Hispanics in major league baseball, the Florida Marlins are making a concerted effort to woo Hispanic fans to the stadium. The team is also aggressively marketing the club in Latin American countries. According to the Marlins' Vice-President of sales and marketing, "We strive to be the team of the Americas...."[13]

◐ Comic pages are to be integrated. DC Comics, Inc., is planning to produce a line of comic books that will feature members of diverse ethnic and racial groups. The company is contracting with Asian and Hispanic writers to produce books tailored to their culture.[14]

A. **The Allure of the Hispanic Market**
- young market (median age is 23.6)
- larger families (3.5 people)
- brand loyalty (45% buy their usual brand)
- they are highly concentrated geographically by national origin
- education levels are increasing dramatically

Discussion Topic: Why do you think that marketers have recently become more interested in the Hispanic market? What makes this market so attractive?

1. **Appealing to Hispanic Subcultures** -- need for status, strong sense of pride, self-expression, and familial devotion. Assertive role models are effective.

Discussion Topic: What should marketers emphasize when trying to appeal to the Hispanic market? What should they avoid?

☯ For a discussion of techniques for conducting market research on Hispanics see reference.[17]

☯ The boom in the Hispanic population, coupled with non-Hispanic consumers' passion for Hispanic foods, has ignited the tortilla industry. Sales of tortillas quintupled between 1980-1990. Tortillas sales have surpassed those of pita bread, English muffins, and bagels. One survey of non-Hispanics showed that 25 percent of respondents consider Mexican to be their favorite ethnic food, and 41% had eaten Mexican food in the last month.[18]

a. **Subsegmenting Hispanic Consumers**
   - Mexican-American--fastest growing
   - Cuban-Americans--wealthiest

☯ For data on particular cities where different Hispanic groups are concentrated, see reference.[19]

b. **Marketing Blunders** -- translation errors
   - Chevy Nova: "no va" means "won't go"
   - Budweiser was promoted as the "queen of beers"
   - Braniff: "Sentado en cuero" was interpreted "sit naked"
   - Coors: "get loose with Coors" translated to "get the runs with Coors."

B. **Understanding Hispanic Identity** -- native language and culture are important

1. **The Role of the Church** -- predominantly Catholic, now one in five have joined an evangelical Protestant sect because U.S. Catholicism is not emotional enough

2. **The Role of the Family** -- strong preference to spend time with family.

Real World Application

☙ After discovering that Hispanics tend to eat at home more than Anglos, Campbell's Soup developed a line of more than fifty food products under the Casera name, targeted to consumers of Caribbean origin.[20]

☙ Toyota created an ad campaign specifically for Hispanics that emphasized more traditional family roles. Its commercial for the Toyota Camry showed a pregnant woman being taken to the hospital in the car and even included the woman's mother-in-law in the scene. The tagline: "When it comes to family, Toyota quality . . .."[21]

---

3. **Level of Acculturation** -- process of adapting to one' adopted country's cultural environment (38% of Hispanics live in *barrios*.)

a. **Differences in Cultural Integration**
- highly educated Cubans who fled from Castro
- poorly educated illegal aliens

Discussion Topic: How are the various Hispanic groups different from each other? What can marketers do to avoid embarrassing and costly cultural blunders in their promotions?

b. **Progressive Learning** -- people learn a new culture over a period of time
Traditionally, Hispanics
- have negative attitudes toward business in general
- make high use of Spanish language media
- are brand loyal and store loyal (prefer prestige labels)
- buy brands specifically advertised to Hispanics

☙ Recent evidence indicates that most minorities and a substantial portion of Anglo consumers believe Hispanics are underrepresented in the media. However, despite indications that Hispanic characters tend to be portrayed in a negative light, most consumers do not perceive that they are portrayed unfairly.[22]

---

4. **Atravesando Fronteras: Crossing to a New Life** -- i.e. "border crossings"
- entering a strange culture leaving family members behind; must keep in touch
- immigrants happy about job and educational opportunities
- they miss their family, friends, holidays and food
- ads done exclusively in Spanish create negative feelings

☙ The insulation of some Hispanics creates obstacles for conventional marketing research, due to such factors as low incidence of telephone ownership and the tendency to have unlisted numbers when a phone is available. The phone is primarily used to call only family and friends, and these consumers see no reason to publicize their number. A personal interview technique, using bilingual Hispanics as interviewers, is much more effective.[23]

---

5. **Adjustment Process**
- acculturation agents: people and institutions that teach the new culture
- culture or immigration: learn about public schools and English-language media
- movement: physically uprooting themselves from one location to another
- translation: master a set of rules for operating in the new environment
- assimilation: adopt products that are identified with mainstream culture
- maintenance: practices associated with culture of origin (food, newspapers, etc.)
- segregation: live and shop in places physically separated from Anglos

V. **Asian-Americans**

(Use TM 13-4 Here)

- still relatively small, but the fastest-growing minority group in U.S.
- average household income is $2,000 greater than whites, $7,000 to $9,000 more than blacks & Hispanics
- college graduation rate is twice that of whites and quadruple that of blacks and Hispanics

☯ For demographic data on Asian-Americans, see reference.[24]

A. **Segmenting Asian-Americans** -- 20 different ethnic groups (Chinese--largest Filipino--2nd; and Japanese--3rd)
- diverse languages and dialects
- birth rate increase almost four times the rate of other groups
- save more of their wages and borrow less
- status conscious and buy premium brands
- buy technically oriented products

Discussion Topic: How are the various Asian groups different from each other? What can marketers do to avoid embarrassing and costly cultural blunders in their promotions?

1. **Marketing Blunders**
- "Coke Ads Life" translated to "Coke brings your ancestors back from the dead"
- KFC: people in Korea and Japan don't lick fingers when food is good

B. **Reaching the Asian-American Consumer**
- English is used in broadcast ads; Asian languages work best in print ads
- Filipinos predominantly speak English among themselves
- most frequently spoken languages: Mandarin Chinese, Korean, Japanese and Vietnamese

Discussion Topic: What should marketers emphasize when trying to appeal to the Asian market? What should they avoid?

1. **One Success Story**
   - Asians are leery of buying insurance--associated with old age and death.
   - Met Life stressed the role of insurance in protecting children--22% increase in premiums

Discussion Topic: How is the Asian subculture different from the African-American or Hispanic subcultures? What are the marketing implications? (e.g., who takes lead role in buying a car?)

VI.   **Religious Subcultures** -- religion impacts consumer behavior (e.g. religious articles)
                                        (Use Color Transparency 39 Here)
                                        (Use TM 13-5 Here)

A. **The Impact of Religion on Consumption** -- religion influences attitudes toward sexuality, birthrates, household formation, income, and politics

   - more than 90% of Americans say they believe in God
   - 40% say they attend weekly church services
   - Roman Catholics dominate New England
   - Baptists--the South
   - Lutherans--the Midwest
   - Nonbelievers--Pacific Northwest and Southwest

Discussion Topic: What impact does religion have on family purchase decisions?

Real World Application
- It is not that unusual for marketers to appropriate religious symbolism to imbue their products with a "sacred" quality. Most recently, The Russian Orthodox Church decided to cooperate with a California businessman to bottle water from the Saint Springs in Russia. The bottle even includes the Russian Archbishop's signature to convey an air of authenticity.[25]

B. **The Catholic Subculture** --
   - approximately one quarter of Americans are Catholics
   - Catholics have more children than Protestants and Jews
   - lower socioeconomic status
   - emphasis on collective rather than individual initiative
   - committed Catholics are usually more conservative, while others are liberal

Discussion Topic: Can you think of some products that appeal primarily to Catholics? How should these be marketed?

C. **The Protestant Subculture**
- approximately 10% identify themselves as Protestants
- dogma stresses the faith of the individual
- some sects emphasize industriousness and hard work
- low fertility rate facilitates the upward mobility of children
- historically part of the power elite
- over represented in science, education, government, and military
- this group is not monolithic

Discussion Topic: Can you think of products that would appeal more to Protestants than to any other religious subculture? e.g. Mormons, Baptists, Lutherans, Pentecostals

D. **The Jewish Subculture**
- 2% of the American population identify themselves as Jews
- incorporates both cultural and religious dimensions
- emphasis on education
- American Jews have relatively high socioeconomic status
- family size is relatively low (except Orthodox)
- high product innovation tendencies, need for achievement, somewhat emotional, and exercise individualism
- kosher foods because of dietary requirements

Real World Application
- One study has examined the effect of including a kosher claim in a breakfast cereal ad on consumer information processing.[26]

- When Coors displayed the small U in a circle to indicate that the beer had obtained rabbinical certification and compiled with kosher dietary laws, sales increased by 15 percent in New York and a whopping 38 percent in Philadelphia.[27]

Discussion Topic: What products appeal more to the Jews than to members of other religious subcultures?

E. **The Moslems Subculture**
- 3-4 million Moslems in America
- Arab is an ethnic identity while Moslem is a religious affiliation
- they tend to be conservative and value close-knit family structure
- individual's "bad acts" can be a reflection on the family

F. **The Born-Again Subculture**
- one third of American adults say they are born-again
- primarily women, older adults, and Southerners
- numbers decrease as education level and income increases
- has led to *demarketing* of certain products and services (sin products)

Discussion Topic: How do the values and attitudes of a born-again Christian affect consumer behavior and consumption?

1. **Consumption Characteristics of the Born-Again Segment**
   - endorse traditional sex-role orientations
   - below average consumers of credit
   - place low emphasis on national brands
   - prefer gospel and contemporary Christian music

Real World Application
- ☯ An ad by a German clothing manufacturer aroused a great deal of controversy. The ad parodies the Last Supper by showing a female Jesus sitting at a table surrounded by 12 women disciples, each of whom is wearing only a pair of jeans. The ad ran once in German *Elle*, and German's Office for Unfair Competition took legal action to stop it from running again.[28]

---

2. **Christian Media**
   - 12% of all U.S. radio stations have a religious format
   - 200 local television station regularly feature religious programming
   - television preachers have an estimated audience of 15 million people
   - subscribe to religious magazines and home-oriented magazines
   - 37 million people spend $1.4 billion annually in Christian bookstores

Discussion Topic: What are some of the cultural icons of religious, ethnic and racial subcultures?

FIELD PROJECT IDEAS

Individual Assignments

1. Ask a student to interview a member of a subculture other than his or her own (e.g. Hispanic, Asian, Black, White, Catholic, Mormon, Jewish, etc.) to discover what types of products or services are purchased because of membership in this particular group. What are some marketing implications?

2. Have a student interview a member of an ethnic or religious subculture (e.g. Black, Hispanic, Asian, Lutheran, Jewish, Baptist, etc.) to see if the person can identify additional subcultures within the subculture! What are the subtle differences and are any of these significant to marketers?

3. Ask a student to assume that he or she is the product manager in charge of developing a promotional strategy for Jiffy peanut butter, Surf detergent, Hallmark greeting cards, or some other product of their choice. Have the student use the knowledge gained while reading this chapter to design an effective campaign for an ethnic or religious subculture.

4. Have a student visit two local supermarkets to find out if either has segmented their market on the basis of the subculture or ethnic background of their customers. How many subcultures are recognized by each supermarket?

5. Have a student visit a toy store to observe the various types of toys that are for sale to ethnic subcultures. Have them give a report on the range of toys available and specify the intended racial or ethnic markets.

6. Ask a student to visit with an Account Executive from an advertising agency and ask this person about marketing to ethnic subcultures, particularly the black and Hispanic markets.

Group Assignments

7. Bring to class (or ask your students to do so) some magazines that are primarily targeted toward either black audiences or white audiences. Ask the students to look through the black-oriented magazines and select three advertisements that are similar, except for the models, to those appearing in the predominantly white-oriented media. Are there any other differences between the ads, such as language, models, social situation, etc.? Explain.

8. Bring to class (or have your students do so) several ethnic publications and discuss the differences in articles, advertisements, and layout from general audience media.

9. So that students can better understand the power of ethnic stereotypes, have them conduct a poll. For a set of ethnic groups (e.g. white, black, Hispanic, Asian), have students ask people to anonymously provide attributes (including personality traits and product purchases) most likely to characterize each group. Was much agreement obtained? Now have them compare the ;information they received for each ethnic group with actual members of that group. Any differences?

Individual or Group Assignments

10. Have the class prepare a list of holidays that are oriented toward a particular subculture (e.g., Cinco de Mayo, Martin Luther King's Birthday, Passover, Easter, St. Patrick's Day, etc.). Now have them ask a few people if they celebrate or commemorate these holidays. What are the marketing implications? (Make sure that some of the people interviewed belong to the subcultures chosen.)

11. Ask each member of the class to identify one of the ethnic or religious groups that they belong to and have them design a list of products or services that are purchased or used because of their membership.

12. Have the students bring to class print ads aimed at a particular subculture and show how the ads attempt to address the group. Do the students think they are effective?

CONSUMER BEHAVIOR CHALLENGE

1. R.J. Reynolds' controversial plan to test-market a cigarette to black consumers raises numerous ethical issues about segmenting subcultures. As one observer noted, "The irony is that if R.J. Reynolds made shoes or shirts and specifically marketed to blacks, they would probably be regarded as progressive and socially positive." Does a company have the right to exploit a subculture's special characteristics, especially to increase sales of a harmful product like cigarettes? What about the argument that virtually every business that follows the marketing concept designs a product to meet the needs and tastes of a preselected segment? For example, the chapter also notes that Maybelline developed a makeup line specifically for black women, yet this did not seem to bother anyone. What do you think?

The instructor should anticipate a high level of interest and involvement with the issues represented in the R.J.R. case. As in the case of targeting gays and the handicapped, there is likely to be a difference of opinion. It would be particularly interesting to hear the perspectives of both white and black students on this specific case. Generally, students should be able to think about and critically examine the issues regarding segmentation (on any basis) in order to meet the unique needs and wants of consumers and to increase overall sales of the product.

2. The chapter notes that products can function as socialization agents for ethnic groups, citing the example of the air freshener product category. What other examples can you find that serve this important function? What special problems do these create for marketers?

Students should review the text discussion on products as socialization agents. They likely will generate a long list of products that function this way. Students will be more challenged to think in terms of the problems that marketers face in the development and advertising of these products.

3. Describe the progressive learning model and discuss why this phenomenon is important when marketing to subcultures.

The progressive learning model states that people gradually learn a new culture as they increasingly come in contact with it. As stated in the text, this model leads us to expect the consumer behavior of Hispanic-Americans, for example, to be a mixture of practices taken from their original culture (Spanish, Mexican, etc.) and those of the new host culture (U.S.). Students should focus their discussions on the implications of this model for marketing strategy.

4. Born-again Christian groups have been instrumental in organizing boycotts of products advertised on shows they find objectionable, especially those that, they feel, undermine family values. Do consumer groups have a right or a responsibility to dictate the advertising a network should carry?

As with many of the previous exercises, the answer to this question is a matter of individual opinion. As always, the instructor should encourage students to consider both sides of the argument, and develop examples or cases to defend both positions, regardless of their personal opinions.

5. In a related issue, an official with a Christian organization defended the Christian Members Buying Plan described in the chapter, arguing that "We are sick and tired of Christians and Christian values being expunged from every area of public life. This isn't separation of church and state; this is a private merchant." Do you agree?

Students will either feel that this practice is fair or that it discriminates against non-Christians. Answers will likely be drawn from the student's personal beliefs about whether different groups of individuals should be targeted by a variety of marketing practices, whether the segmentation basis is religious beliefs or anything else.

6. Can you locate any current examples of marketing stimuli that depend upon an ethnic stereotype to communicate a message? How effective are these appeals?

Students are likely to identify beer companies for their practice of ethnic segmentation in advertising. In order to target Hispanic- or African-Americans, for example, advertisers are employing well known Hispanic- and African-American personalities (movie stars, professional athletes, etc.) to promote their products. It is likely that these appeals are effective when the consumer feels a sense of identity or affinity with the spokesperson. (Possible Field Project Idea)

7. To understand the power of ethnic stereotypes, conduct your own poll. For a set of ethnic groups, ask people to anonymously provide attributes (including personality traits and products) most likely to characterize each group using the technique of free association. How much agreement do you obtain across people? Compare the associations for an ethnic group between actual members of that group and nonmembers.

Students should be encouraged to conduct their own research for this exercise and many others. This may be a good time for the instructor to emphasize the importance and value of market and consumer research efforts. (Possible Field Project Idea)

8. African-American singer Gladys Knight recently took a lot of heat for agreeing to serve as a spokesperson for the Aunt Jemima brand. One commentator said, "You have a famous black singer perpetuating the stereotypes that go along with the trademark...." On the other hand, the singer stated, "...What matters to me is what's inside the box. I'm simply saying, 'This is a good product.'" Which side do you take, and why?

Students opinions will vary. Some students will discuss social responsibility and ethical situations while other students will stress individual rights. This might be a good time to talk about how the Aunt Jemima icon has changed to look less like a slave and more like a grandmother (you might also note that she has lost some weight--using more lite syrup).

9. Locate one or more consumers (perhaps family members) who have immigrated from their country of origin. Interview them about how they adapted to their host culture. In particular, what changes did they make in their consumption practices over time?

Note: You might want to ask the class if anyone personally knows someone who has immigrated to the U.S. or if they personally know a foreign student at your university before making this assignment. The class will be able to discuss this question in more depth if someone who personally knows an immigrant conducts this interview. (Possible Field Project Idea)

ENDNOTES

[1] Michel Laroche, Annamma Joy, Michael Hui, and Chankon Kim, "An Examination of Ethnicity Measures: Convergent Validity and Cross-Cultural Equivalence," *Advances in Consumer Research* 18, eds. Rebecca H. Holman and Michael R. Solomon (Provo, Utah: Association for Consumer Research, 1991): 150-57.

[2] Mary Westerman, "Death of the Frito Bandito," *American Demographics* (March, 1989): 28.

[3] Annetta Miller and Saren Springen, "Egg Rolls for Peoria," *Newsweek* (October 12, 1992): 59.

[4] Jonathan Burton, "The Millions of New Immigrants Yearning to Call Home," *New York Times* (September 6, 1992): F4.

5 "1994 Survey of Buying Power," *Sales & Marketing Management* (1994): A-8.

6 Carrie Goeme, "Retailers Boost Efforts to Target African-American Consumers," *Marketing News* (June 22, 1992): 2.

7 "Packaged Soul," *Newsweek* (September 14, 1992): 6.

8 Trudy Gallant-Stokes, "Black Marketing Marksmanship," *Marketing Insights* (Spring 1990): 101-4; Jeffrey L. Kovach, "Minority Sell: Ads Target Blacks, Hispanics, but . . .," *Industry Week* (November 11, 1985): 29.

9 Richard W. Pollay, Jung S. Lee, and David Carter-Whitney, "Separate, But Not Equal: Racial Segmentation in Cigarette Advertising," *Journal of Advertising* 21 (March 1992).

10 Jeffery L. Kovach, "Minority Sell: Ads Target Blacks, Hispanics, but . . . ," *Industry Week* (November 11, 1985) 29.

11 John P. Cortez, "KFC Stores Boast Flavor of Neighborhood," *Advertising Age* (May 31, 1993): 3.

12 Allyson Reid-Dove "Toy Makers Make Do with Mixed Blessings," *Black Enterprise* (December 24, 1988).

13 Jeffrey D. Zbar, "Reeling in Fans: From Players to Stadium Food, Florida Marlins Target Hispanics," *Advertising Age* (August 9, 1993): 12.

14 Veronica Byrd, "The Men Behind the Superheroes," *NewYork Times* (September 13, 1992): F8.

15 Kate Fitzgerald, "Hair-Care Eyes Ethnic Babies," *Advertising Age* (February 11, 1991): 8.

16 "Bilingual Mice To Hollywood," *American Demographics* (July 1987): 25.

17 Gonzalo R. Soruco and Timothy P. Meyer, "The Mobile Hispanic Market: New Challenges in the '90s," *Marketing Research: A Magazine of Management & Applications* 5 (Winter 1993)1: 6-11.

18 Calvin Sims, "Tortillas Gain Aficionados in U.S.," *The New York Times* (September 23, 1992): D1.

19 Morton Winsberg, "Specific Hispanics," *American Demographics* (February 1994): 44 (8).

20 Howard LaFranchi, "Media and Marketers Discover Hispanic Boom," *Christian Science Monitor* (April 20, 1988): 1.

21 Ruth Stroud, "Toyota Shifts Gears After First Effort Doesn't Translate," *Advertising Age* (February 13, 1989): S-9.

22 Ronald J. Faber, Thomas C. O'Guinn and Timothy P. Meyer, "Televised Portrayals of Hispanics: A Comparison of Ethnic Perceptions," *International Journal of Intercultural Relations* 11 (1987): 155-69.

23 Sigredo A. Hernandez and Carol J. Kaufman, "Marketing Research in Hispanic Barrios: A Guide to Survey Research," *Marketing Research* (March 1990): 11-27.

24 William P. O'Hare, William H. Frey, and Dan Fost," Asians in the Suburbs," *American Demographics* (May 1994): 32-38.

25 Alessandra Stanley, "A Russian Bottled Water with a Saintly Twist," *The New York Times* (August 23, 1994): D1 (2).

[26] Michael A. Kamins and Lawrence J. Marks, "The Perception of Kosher as a Third Party Certification Claims in Advertising for Familiar and Unfamiliar Brands," *Journal of the Academy of Marketing Science* 19 (1991): 177-185.

[27] Andrew Murr, "Move Over, Matzos," *Newsweek* (July 1, 1991): 45.

[28] "New Last Supper Guests," *Advertising Age* (December 20, 1993).

Instructor's Notes:

212

6. Is it practical to assume that people age 55 and older constitute one large consumer market? What are some approaches to further segmenting this age subculture?

Marketers have become convinced that the over 55 age segment is diverse, with a minimum of four sub-segments represented by the 55-64, 65-74, 75-84, and 85 and older categories. Clearly, with people living longer lives, there is going to be considerable differences in the health and general welfare of these individuals. Many will have more income relative to expenditures than any other time in their lives, affording opportunities for full and rich lifestyles. Ultimately, the most influential characteristic of elderly consumers is their perceived age, or how old they feel.

7. Find good and bad examples of advertising targeted to elderly consumers. To what degree does advertising stereotype the elderly? What elements of ads or other promotions appear to determine their effectiveness in reaching and persuading this group?

This will be an interesting exercise for students and is likely to draw their attention to issues they have not carefully considered to date. Encourage them to find examples of what they view as both positive and negative treatment of the elderly in the media. (Possible Field Project Idea)

ENDNOTES

[1] Neil Howe and William Strauss, "The New Generation Gap," *The Atlantic Monthly* (December 1992)16: 67.

[2] Stuart Elliott, "Mass-Marketing to a Nation That Thinks Middle-Aged," *New York Times* (June 11, 1992): D20; Jim Kirk, Bud Tries to Bridge Generational Gap, Adweek (September 14, 1992): 4.

[3] William Dunn, "Sinatra Has the Last Dance," *American Demographics* (July 1994): 39.

[4] Yankelovich Clancy Shulman, "Getting Hip to Free-Spending Teens," *Adweek* (June 15, 1992): 70.

[5] Kate Fitzgerald, "Marketers Drawn to Comics," Advertising Age (September 14, 1992): 12; Laurie McLaughlin, "Tweens Blossom as Consumer Group," *Advertising Age* (October 14, 1991): 33.

[6] Carol Terrizzi, "At the Movies," *American Demographics* (November 1987): 58-60.

[7] Michael B. Mazis, Debra Jones Ringold, Elgin S. Perry, and Daniel W. Denman, "Perceived Age and Attractiveness of Models in Cigarette Advertisements," *Journal of Marketing* 56 (January 1992): 22-37.

[8] Peter Flax and James Chung, "Marketing 101: Introduction to the Student Consumer," *Marketing Communications* (March 1989): 32-35.

[9] Suzanne Alexander, "You Can Call This Study Cheesy, But It Gives a Slice of Campus Life," *Wall Street Journal* (September 14, 1992): B1.

[10] Susan Krafft, "Who Slams the Door on Research?" *American Demographics* (September 1991): 14.

[11] Alan J. Greco, "The Elderly as Communicators: Perceptions of Advertising Practitioners," *Journal of Advertising Research* 28 (June July 1988): 39.

[12] "Study Finds Lively 'Geromarket'," *Advertising Age* (May 18, 1987): 89.

Instructor's Notes:

1. **Interdependence Among Product Meanings**
   - costumes worn by political figures affect the apparel and accessory industries industry (the movie, *Urban Cowboy* and cowboy boots)
   - Russians launch Sputnik and U.S. companies introduce futuristic designs in cars and clothes to convince ourselves that we are equal to the Russians

Discussion Topic: What are some fashions (fads) that have been started by popular movies?

☯ People's postures seem to be affected by dominant clothing fashions, a phenomenon sometimes remarked upon by photographers and historians. Even when posing nude, models in the late-Victorian era tended to protrude the rear portion of their anatomies to resemble bustles, while nudes in the 1920s tended to slouch like the debutantes of the time, and their counterparts in the 1940s stuck out their chests while tucking in their stomachs, producing the period's popular hourglass figure.[18]

B. **Collective Selection** -- process by which certain symbolic alternatives are chosen over others. Competing products adhere to a dominant theme or *motif.*

C. **Behavioral Science Perspectives on Fashion** -- fashion products are aesthetic objects and rooted in art and history

1. **Psychological Models of Fashion** -- people conform to the basic outline of fashion but add their personal touch to be unique

Discussion Topic: How did you decorate your room? What are some of the items you have on display? What is in your room that almost everyone your age has in their rooms? How is yours different? Does your room reflect your personality?

a. **Fashion and Sexuality** -- shifting erogenous zones account for fashion changes
   - Victorian era emphasized shoulders
   - early 20th century emphasized ankle
   - 1930s emphasized the back
   - 1960s emphasized legs
   - 1970s emphasized the breasts
   - today we seem to emphasize the midriff

2. **Economic Models of Fashion** -- rare objects command respect and prestige

a. **Conspicuous Consumption** -- the wealthy consume to display their property

Discussion Topics: Can you think of items people buy that seem to display their wealth? How do you know that these people have these items?

3. **Sociological Models of Fashion** -- relationship between product adoption and class structure.

   a. **The Trickle-Down Theory**
- dominant styles originate with upper class and trickle-down
- subordinate groups try to adopt upper-class symbols
- subordinate groups look below them and change fashion when they are copied

Discussion Topic: Can you think of a product that went "out of fashion" because too many people in subordinate groups started buying the product?

   b. **Modifications to the Trickle-Down Theory** --
- because of technology, modern consumers have more choices
- mass fashion has replaced elite fashion
- trickle-across effect: consumers copy leaders similar to them
- trickle-up: some fashions originate with lower classes (urban youth)

D. **Cycles of Fashion Adoption** --range from a month to a century (e.g. Power Rangers)

1. **Up the Charts with a Bullet: Stages of Acceptance** -- diffusion of innovations
- introduction stage: song listened to by a small number
- acceptance stage: song increases social visibility and accepted by many (Top 40)
- regression stage: song reaches social saturation (overused) and drops off charts
a. **Classics** -- a fashion with an extremely long acceptance cycle (e.g., Keds)

Real World Application
- Some fads can have dangerous consequences before they decline. In the mid-1980s, there was a brief craze in some urban areas for Cazals, eyeglass frames imported from West Germany which retailed for $85 to $200. At least four slayings were linked to youths desperate to obtain the frames.[19]

---

   b. **Fads** -- a very short-lived fashion (e.g. hula hoops, "pet rocks", streaking)
- non-utilitarian--does not perform any meaningful function
- adopted on impulse
- diffuses rapidly, gains quick acceptance, and dies

Discussion Topic: What are some of the latest fads? Who is someone who was responsible starting a fad? How did this happen?

FIELD PROJECT IDEAS

Individual Assignments

1. Ask a student to give a report on some fad that the student is familiar with (pet rocks, coon skin caps, hula hoops, streaking, leisure suits, hair styles, clothing, food, etc.) Have the student try to find some documentation of the rise and fall of this fad.

2. Have a student interview three friends about a new product they recently purchased for the first time. Find out how they first heard about. See if they know why they bought it? Did personal influence play a role?

3. Ask a student to compare and contrast two products--one an American product and one a foreign product. Does the student think that the marketing concept is present or absent in the design or promotion of each product design?

4. Ask a student to interview a person from a different culture or foreign culture. During the interview have the student observe any nonverbal communication that is taking place, ask then what similarities and differences he or she has noticed between the nonverbal language of his culture and the American culture. Have the student report on these similarities and differences.

5. Have a student interview two people from two different foreign cultures. Have the student ask what major differences they see between the cultural values in their country and those in the American culture. Ask the student to explain these to the class.

6. Ask a student to identify an American custom, more, and convention and then determine several products that are needed because of these crescive norms.

Group Assignments

7. Bring to class (or have the group do so) a least three magazine advertisements that incorporate one or more the American Core Values (Table 15-1) as a basis for their appeal. Have students explain the nature of the appeal in each ad.

8. Ask the class to prepare a list of products that people tend to buy more for what the products mean than for what the products do. Are there other products that could satisfy the same need and even perhaps sell for less? What makes these products have lesser status?

9. Ask the class to compare a list of rituals that will probably be performed (or that were performed) at their wedding ceremony and reception. What are the marketing implications of these rituals? (It is interesting to point out the different rituals based on a religious, ethnic or racial subcultures and rituals that seem to be solely American.) An added question might be: How are wedding plans affected when people from different subcultures get married?

10. Invite a person from a foreign culture to come to your class to discuss products commonly used in the guest's country that are seldom used in this country. In preparation, have the students develop a list of products commonly used in the U.S. Ask the guest how available these products are in the guest's country, where they can be purchased, and the frequency of use.

Individual or Group Assignments

11. Since many fads seem to originate on the West Coast, ask students who have friends or relatives who live there to query them about the latest products, services, and fashions. Do the students think that these fads will become popular across the country?

12. [In Class Activity] Have a student briefly summarize an episode of a weekly television series which he or she watched recently. Have the class describe how the program transmitted cultural beliefs, values and customs.

13. Ask a student or the entire class to survey their friends to determine what activities and products are used to demonstrate masculinity and femininity in our culture. How do others tend to react when they see a person ignoring these norms? What are the marketing implications?

14. Have an individual or class members interview a ball player, an actress or actor, a student preparing for exams, a trial lawyer, or others you might choose, to see if they have a certain ritual or superstition that they tend to follow in preparing for and performing their activity. Do they remember when they first started performing this ritual?

15. Have a student or the class interview a middle school, junior high or high school student (and, if possible, that person's closest friend). Find out what new words their group is using this year. What do they mean? What new products are they using to prove that they are "in"? How can they spot persons that obviously do not belong to their groups? What words or products are now "out"?

CONSUMER BEHAVIOR CHALLENGE

1. Culture can be thought of as a society's personality. If your culture were a person, could you describe its personality traits?

Students likely will describe the U.S. culture as young, aggressive, independent, healthy, and fit.

Some of the following American core values will probably be discussed:
freedom; youthfulness; achievement; materialism; activity; conformity; individuality; mastery over the environment; efficiency; equality; humanitarianism; religious orientation, etc.

In contrast, other cultures may be described in ways that are equally as distinctive and reflective of their unique (or stereotypical) characteristics. Instructors may be alerted to students' tendencies to describe the U.S. culture as positive and other cultures are negative, in which case a discussion of ethnocentrism may be beneficial.

2. What is the difference between an enacted norm and a crescive norm? Identify the set of crescive norms operating when a man and woman in your culture go out for dinner on a first date. What products and services are affected by these norms?

Students should draw on the definitions and discussion provided in the text. Norms, by definition, are rules dictating what is right or wrong, acceptable or unacceptable.

Enacted norms are explicitly decided upon, such as the rule that a green traffic light means "go" and a red one means "stop." Crescive norms, however, are more subtle. They are embedded in a culture and are only discovered through interaction with other members of that culture. The crescive norms include customs, mores, and conventions.

In the situation of a man and a woman going out for dinner on a first date, the set of crescive norms operating might include the man driving the woman in his car, opening the car door for her, selecting a nice restaurant (rather than fast food or using a coupon) or a casual rather than romantic spot (because it is a first date), and paying for the meal. More and more, these conventions are being called into question due to both the women's and the men's movements of recent years.

241

3. How do the consumer decisions involved in gift giving differ from other purchase decisions?

In responding to this question, students should consider the general discussion of gift giving in the text as well as the specific outline of the gift-giving process:

- gift-giving rituals involve obtaining the "perfect gift" and removing the price tag to make it unique
- the giver transfers a gift to a receiver who in turn is obligated to reciprocate (*exchange gifts*)
- the gift-giving process
  - gestation: the giver is motivated by an event to buy a gift
    - structural: prescribed by culture (e.g. Christmas present)
    - emergent: decision is more personal (e.g. husband brings home flowers)
  - presentation: recipient responds to gift and donor evaluates the response
  - reformulation: bonds between parties are adjusted (looser or tighter)

(Students should recognize the "ritualistic" aspects of gift-giving, and symbolism inherent in the gift exchange.)

4. The chapter argues that not all gift giving is positive. In what ways can this ritual be unpleasant or negative?

The text clearly states that negativity can arise if the recipient feels the fit is inappropriate or of inferior quality. The giver/donor may feel the response to the gift was inadequate, insincere, or a violation of the reciprocity norm, which obliges people to return the gesture of a gift with one of equal value. Both participants may feel resentful for being forced to participate in the gift-giving ritual.

5. Construct a ritual script for a wedding in your culture. How many artifacts can you list that are contained in this script?

Student will probably be able to generate a fairly complete ritual script for a wedding quite readily. A large number of ritual artifacts might be included ranging from those attached to the engagement (pre-wedding ritual), the rehearsal dinner, the wedding ceremony, the reception, and the honeymoon. Examples include wedding rings, gowns, tuxedoes, flowers, photographs, music, unity candles, wedding cakes, etc.

6. What are some of the major motivations for the purchase of self-gifts? Discuss some marketing implications of these.

As stated in the text, people commonly find reasons to give themselves gifts. Many people are motivated to purchase self-gifts as personal rewards, a way of consoling themselves over disappointments, or as an incentive to accomplish some goal. The instructor might ask students to find examples of advertisements that reflect various motivations for self-gifts, in addition to considering the more general marketing implications.

7. Describe the three stages of the rite of passage associated with graduating from college.

Rites of passage include three phases:
- separation: detached from original group (e.g. college freshman leaves home)
- liminality: person is literally in-between statuses (e.g. freshman during orientation)
- aggregation: person reenters society after rite-of-passage (e.g. goes home for Christmas as a "college veteran")

For the college graduation example:
- students should recognize the college graduate's separation involves detachment from his or her college friends, roommates, fraternity brothers/sorority sisters, professors, etc.
- during the liminality phase, the college graduate is in between stages--college and career-- and experiences a period of adjustment to the new environment
- aggregation occurs when the graduate comes part of the professional society, identifying with his or her career, rather than college

8. Identify the ritualized aspects of football that are employed in advertising.

Students should be able to generate a long list of ritualized behaviors associated with high school, college, and professional football. These include wearing school/team colors, pre-game tailgating activities, singing school/team songs, cheers, the "wave," half-time entertainment (including performance by the marching band), etc. Any and all of the rituals can be employed in advertising.

9. Some people have raised objections to the commercial exploitation of cultural figures. For example, many consumers deplore the profits that filmmakers and business people have made off of films like Malcolm X (e.g., by selling a "Malcolm X" air freshener). Others argue that this commercialization merely helps to educate consumers about what such people stood for, and is inevitable in our society. What do you think?

The instructor could encourage students to consider both positions on this issue and, perhaps, ask groups to defend each, irrespective of their personal positions.

10. Construct a "biography" of a product, tracing its progress from the time it was introduced. How long did it take to diffuse to the mass market? Do the same consumers use the product now as did those who first adopted it? What are its future prospects—is it destined for obsolescence? Would you characterize the product as either a classic or a fad?

Students' responses to this exercise should vary considerably. They are likely to reflect individuals areas of particular interest and experience, or merely reflect products that are highly visible due to marketing/advertising efforts. The instructor might assign students to consider examples of either fad or classic products so that these differences can be highlighted. (Possible Field Project)

11. Some consumers complain that they are "at the mercy" of designers: They are forced to buy whatever styles are in fashion, because nothing else is available. Do you agree that there is such a thing as a "designer conspiracy?"

Students will have different views on this issue. It might be interesting for the instructor to discuss the issue in class by soliciting opinions from a diverse set of students--different ethnic backgrounds, social status, gender, religion, age, size, etc.

12. What is the basic difference between a fad, a fashion, and a classic? Provide examples of each.

Definitions:
- fashion (or style): a particular combination of attributes
- classic: a fashion with an extremely long acceptance cycle
- fad: a very short-lived fashion.

(While the text includes good examples of each of these types of products, students should be encouraged to think of additional examples.)

13. What is the difference between an art and a craft? Where would you characterize advertising within this framework?

- art: primarily an object of aesthetic contemplation without any functional value. A piece of art is original, subtle, and valuable and is often associated with the elite of society.
- craft: is admired because it is both beautiful and functional. A craft tends to follow a formula that can permit rapid production.

After reviewing these definitions with students, select various types of advertisement (TV, billboard, magazine, point-of-purchase, etc.) and ask students to express their views of advertising within this framework.

14. The chapter mentions some instances where market research findings influenced artistic decisions, as when a movie ending was reshot to accommodate consumers' preferences. Many people would most likely oppose this use of consumer research, claiming that books, movies, records, or other artistic endeavors should not be designed to merely conform to what people want to read, see, or hear. What do you think?

The instructor should encourage students to review the relevant discussion in the text concerning aesthetic marketing research and then express their thoughts and feeling regarding the use of consumer research for these purposes. Considering this practices in light of the marketing concept should generate an interesting discussion.

ENDNOTES

1 John Maines, "The Box That's Challenging MTV," *American Demographics* (July 1992): 10.

2 John Leland, "The Big Hunk of Country," *Newsweek* (June 22, 1992): 53.

3 Abraham Rosenblatt, Jeff Greenberg, Sheldon Solomon, Tom Pyszczynski, and Deborah Lyon, "Evidence for Terror Management Theory: I. The Effects of Mortality Salience on Reactions to Those Who Violate or Uphold Cultural Values," *Journal of Personality and Social Psychology* 57 (1989)4: 681 90.

4 Doris Walsh, "Foreign Leisure," *American Demographics* (February 1987): 60.

5 Martha Ann Overland, "What Ails Europeans? Everything," *New York Times* (November 26, 1991): C3.

6 David Diamond, "Translating Taste: Tokyo Woes and Other Tales of Global Marketing," *Avenue* (March 1990): 105.

7 Laurel Anderson and Marsha Wadkins, "The New Breed in Japan: Consumer Culture," unpublished manuscript, Arizona State University, Tucson, 1990.

8 Michael Heistand, "Mom, the Flag, and Apple Pie," Adweek's *Marketing Week* (November 28, 1988): 4.

9 William Blake Tyrrell, "Star Trek as Myth and Television as Myth-maker," in the *Popular Culture Reader,* eds, Jack Nachbar, Deborah Weiser and John L. Wright (Bowling Green, Ohio: Bowling Green University Press, 1978), 79-88.

10 Sharon E. Beatty, Lynn R. Kahle, and Pamela Homer, "Personal Values and Gift-Giving Behaviors: A Study Across Cultures," *Journal of Business Research* 22 (1991): 149 57.

11 Russell W. Belk, "A Child's Christmas in America: Santa Claus as Deity, Consumption as Religion," *Journal of American Culture* 10 (Spring 1987): 87 100.

12 "A Tricky Business, But Often a Treat," *The New York Times* (October 28, 1993): D1 (2).

13 Elizabeth C. Hirschman and Michael R. Solomon, "Competition and Cooperation Among Culture Production Systems," in Marketing Theory: Philosophy of Science Perspectives, eds. Ronald F. Bush and Shelby D. Hunt (Chicago: American Marketing Association, 1982), 269 72.

14 Paul M. Hirsch, "Processing Fads and Fashions: An Organizational Set Analysis of Cultural Industry Systems," *American Journal of Sociology* 77 (1972) 4:639-59; Russell Lynes, *The Tastemakers* (New York: Harper and Brothers, (1954); Michael R. Solomon, "The Missing Link: Surrogate Consumers in the Marketing Chain," *Journal of Marketing* 50 (October 1986); 208-19.

15 Alice Kahn, "A One-time Bimbo Be-comes a Muse," *New York Times* (September 29, 1991)3: H1.

16 Caryn James, "Casting for Dollars," *New York Times* (December 6, 1992): H12.

17 Fred Davis, "Clothing, Fashion, and the Dialectic of Identity," in Communication and Social Structure, eds. David R. Maines and Carl J. Couch (Springfield, Ill.: Charles C. Thomas, 1988), 23 38.

18 Alison Lurie, *The Language of Clothes* (New York: Random House, 1981).

19 William Robbins, "Fad for Eyeglass Frames Linked to 4 Slayings," *New York Times* (April 1, 1984): L23.

Instructor's Notes:

a. **Lifestyle as a Standard of Living** -- the good life includes: two or more cars, exotic vacations, TVs, VCRs, CD players, microwaves, cellular phones, 3-4 bedroom homes, boats, credit cards, etc.

Discussion Topic: Make a list of 10 items you think you must have in order to attain the good life. Why do you suppose you selected these items?

Discussion Topic: Do you think money can buy happiness? Do you feel sorry for the people who win the lottery?

II.   **Lifestyle Marketing** -- people sort themselves into groups on the following basis:
- the things they like to do
- how they like to spend their leisure time
- how they choose to spend their disposable income

A. **Products are the Building Blocks of Lifestyles** -- products are associated with social situations. In ads people, products, and settings represent consumption style.

1. **Product Complementarity** -- symbolic meanings of certain products are related
- some products seem to go together (suit and tie)
- some do not (a can of snuff in an executive's pocket)

Discussion Topic: What are some products that seem to "go together"? What are your thoughts when these items are not together?

Discussion Topic: What are some products that you just don't expect to see together? Why?

Real World Application

☙ Students will enjoy discussing the many products and services included in the yuppie constellation as depicted on the cover of the Yuppie Handbook. Published in 1984, the Handbook was a popular satirical treatment of yuppies during the 1980s.

☙ The Sisters Rosensweig, a popular recent play by Wendy Wasserstein, relies heavily on product complementarity and brand imagery to develop three sisters who are the play's main characters. Sara is a bank president and Radcliffe graduate who reads The Financial Times and buys products of understated elegance. Pfeni is a travel writer who wears Birkenstock sandals and carries her possessions in plain shopping bags. Gorgeous is a bargain-basement shopper who wears Chanel knock-offs, carries an imitation Louis Vuitton handbag, and mispronounces the names of Italian shoe brands. Other specific products mentioned in the script that are used to define the characters range from Wedgwood, Ralph Lauren shirts, and Sacher torte to Diet Coke, Retin-A, and Fruit of the Loom. A lively discussion can be generated by asking the class to identify other movies, plays, or novels in which products play a central role in defining the characters. This issue is also considered in the discussion of the role of product placement and its influence on consumers' perceptions of reality in Chapter 17.[2]

B. **Psychographics** -- use of psychological, sociological, and anthropological factors to segment target markets

  1. **The Roots of Psychographics**
- motivational research: use in-depth interviews & projective techniques to probe.
- demographics tell us "who" buys and psychographics tell us "why" they buy

C. **Conducting a Psychographic Analysis** -- ask pertinent consumer questions

(Use TM 16-2 Here)

  1. **AIO** -- (Activities, Interests, and Opinions) demographic information based on:
- how people spend their time
- what they find interesting and important
- how they view themselves and the world around them

Discussion Topic: Why would AIOs be important to marketers? How could marketers use this information to promote their products?

    a. **The 20/80 Rule** -- 20% of customers use 80% of the products; therefore:
- identify heavy users
- identify the different reasons they have for using product or service
- subdivide the heavy users in terms of the benefits they seek

  2. **Uses of Psychographic Segmentation**
- to define the target market
- to create a new view of the market
- to position the product
- to better communicate product attributes
- to develop overall strategy
- to market social and political issues

Discussion Topic: Can you think of a company that uses psychographic segmentation to position its product in the marketplace? Do you think it is effective? Why or why not?

D. **Psychographic Segmentation Typologies** -- based on AIOs and other perceptions

  1. **VALS** -- (Values and Lifestyles)
- administered to 1600 U.S. households in 1980
- uses Maslow's Hierarchy: physiological, safety, belongingness, ego-needs, self-actualization
- combined with David Reisman's study of inner-directed people (who value personal expression and individual taste) and outer-directed people (who tend to be swayed by the behavior and reactions of others.)

a. **Throwing the Bull: VALS in Action** -- e.g. Merrill Lynch changed advertising slogan from "Bullish on America" to "A Breed Apart"

b. **VALS 2** -- divides people into eight groups that are determined by psychological characteristics, income, education, energy levels, and eagerness to buy

(Use Color Transparency 46 Here)
(Use TM 16-3 Here)

- Actualizers: successful with many resources open to change
- Fulfilled: satisfied, reflective, comfortable, practical
- Achievers: career-oriented, avoid risk, self-discovery
- Experiencers: impulsive, young, offbeat, love risk
- Believers: strong principles, favor proven brands
- Strivers: like achievers but with fewer resources, need approval
- Makers: action-oriented, self-sufficiency, do-it-yourselfers
- Strugglers: bottom-of-ladder, immediate gratification

Discussion Topic: In which of the eight VALS 2 categories do you think a researcher would place you? Where do you think your parents would be placed?

Real World Application
- ☯ VALS 2 has been used by some local broadcasters to create ads that will boost sales. The new system was used by WISH-TV in Indianapolis to develop a campaign for a sporting goods store whose sales were being threatened by a national chain. The station's consultant used results yielded by a VALS 2 analysis to recommend that the store get rid of items like stuffed moose heads and the dark-paneled walls in order to attract more women. Sales rose by 37% in six months.[3]

E. **International Lifestyle Segmentation** -- designed to better understand buyer behavior in other countries.

1. **Non-American Lifestyle Typologies** --
   - ConsumerBank: data base with 240 pieces of information on 40 million consumers
   - McCann-Erickson London segments men and women into four categories
   - Socioconsult: attempts to develop typology for England, Wales and Scotland
   - Japanese culture values conformity
   - Eastern Europe is becoming increasingly consumption-oriented
   - Australian firm identified 10 segments

III. **Geographic Influences on Lifestyles** -- unique climates, cultural influences, and resources shape consumption patterns in different regions

(Use Color Transparency 47 Here)
(Use TM 16-4 Here)

A. **Regional Consumption Differences** -- e.g., snow skis, houses built with a steep slope to the roof in heavy snow areas, flat roofs in dessert areas, dehumidifiers, humidifiers, etc.

Discussion Topic: What are some consumption differences that you will find in various regions of the country? What accounts for this?

Real World Application
☻ The results of one study indicate that the top ten states with the highest tension levels are all in the West and South. Nevada is the most stressful state, while Nebraska boasts the lowest "tension level."

---

1. **Food Preferences** -- e.g., jalapeño peppers, barbecue sauce, pretzels, pork rinds

Discussion Topic: What are some regional food preferences of which you are aware?

☻ Denny's Restaurants, a national chain based in California, adapts its menu to the different regions it serves. For example, although chili is served in many outlets, this dish takes a variety of forms: In Texas, it contains no beans and is very spicy; in Cincinnati, five-way chili is served with chili sauce, cheese, raw onions, beans, and spaghetti; and on the West Coast, the same dish is served with a side order of salsa. Similarly, a Denny's customer can only order a bagel and cream cheese if he or she is in Hawaii, southern Florida, or the region north of Virginia and east of Harrisburg, Pennsylvania. Those customers, however, can't take advantage of the catfish special, which is only available in parts of the South and Midwest.[5]

---

2. **The Arts and Entertainment**
   - country/western music is most popular everywhere, blues and soul is gaining
   - jazz and classical music is most popular in West and Midwest
   - consumers in the West attend museums and theater more than other Americans

B. **The Nine Nations of North America** -- Joel Garreau's book (1981)

Breadbasket: Midwest, middle American, conservative, hardworking; Kansas City (Capital)
Ectopia: Northwest, environmentally oriented, New Age philosophy; San Francisco (Capital)
MexAmerica: Southwest, Hispanic roots; Los Angeles (Capital)
The Island: Southern Florida and the Caribbean islands, Hispanic influence; Miami (Capital)
Dixie: the South, genteel, wave to strangers, optimistic; Atlanta (Capital)
The Foundry: Great Lakes, also "Rust Belt", losing population; Detroit (Capital)
New England: Northeast, oldest "Anglo" nation, tolerant, political, elitist; Boston (Capital)
Empty Quarter: Rockies, smallest population, government owned land, frontier; Denver (Capital)
Quebec: Quebec, "The French Quarter", French speaking, ethnic pride, Quebec City (Capital)

3. Ask a student to interview two people from two different cultures. Have the student determine the extent to which products such as toothpaste, perfume, beer, ice, personal computers, bicycles, VCRs and the like are used in those cultures. Do variations in the values or traditions of those cultures seem to have an effect on how the product is used and the frequency of use?

4. Have a student bring in three ads for the same basic type of product (e.g., pens, clothes, cars, watches, restaurants, etc.) which use "lifestyle" segmentation in their advertising to differentiate each product. How do the companies achieve differentiation? Are the products really different?

5. Ask a student to examine several foreign magazines and newspapers in the library. Have the student comment on the similarities and differences that were observed in advertising from various countries. Then have the student speculate on the reasons for differences.

6. Have a student locate an article on a marketing failure by an American company operating in a foreign market. What was the reported reason for the failure? Could an improved cultural understanding have prevented this failure? How?

7. Ask a student to do a comparative analysis of various promotions used for Disney parks in the U.S., Japan, and Europe. See if they can point out some of the similarities and differences in the way the parks position themselves.

8. Have a student interview people from other countries (fellow employees, fellow students, neighbors, etc.) about their attitudes toward the American popular culture. Do they believe their own cultures are being polluted by American culture or do they welcome the change? Find out whether American products are popular or unpopular in the native's countries.

Group Assignments

9. Bring in some magazines targeted toward specific regional or local groups (*Southern Living, Midwest Living, Progressive Farmer, Sunset, Ingrams*, etc.) and ask the students to look through the magazine and describe the types of articles and advertisements contained in each magazine. How effective are they in reaching their target market?

10. Ask your students to compile a selection of recent ads that attempt to link consumption of a product with a specific lifestyle. How is this goal usually accomplished?

11. Have your students find three advertisements in popular magazines that they believe are targeted toward a particular psychographic segment. See if they think the ads are achieving their goal. What criteria did they use in their evaluation?

Individual or Group Assignments

12. This chapter mentions that psychographic analyses can be used by politicians to market themselves. What are some of the marketing strategies and techniques use by politicians in recent elections? Did the candidates design special appeals to attract the attention of special target markets? What communication strategies were used? Have your students discuss their observations.

13. Ask your students to construct a consumption constellation for the social role of a college student (**or** a young married couple, parents, an elderly couple, a solitary survivor.) What set of products, activities, and interests tend to be directed toward the group they selected? What factors might be operating that could distort the students' concept of reality with reference to this group?

14. Have students assume that the owners of a fast-food chain have asked your class to prepare a psychographic profile of families living in the communities surrounding a new location they are considering. (Select any area that the students would mostly likely know.) Ask students to construct a 10-question psychographic inventory appropriate for segmenting families in terms of their dining-out preferences.

CONSUMER BEHAVIOR CHALLENGE

1. Compare and contrast the concepts of lifestyle and social class.

Students should recognize the similarities and differences between lifestyle and social class based on the definitions provided in the text.

- Lifestyle: the shared values or tastes exhibited by a group of consumers, including their consumption patterns.
- Social class: the classification of individuals according to their level of education, level and source of income, and occupational prestige.

2. In what situations is demographic information likely to be more useful than psychographic data, and vice-versa?

Demographic information is likely to be more useful than psychographic data when simple, objective criteria are sufficient in defining and distinguishing potential consumers. Demographic data are more clearly defined and directly measurable than psychographics and, therefore, make segmentation on these bases more straightforward. In contrast, psychographics are used to understand consumers' motivations for purchasing and using products. These data reflect people's tendencies to sort themselves into groups on the basis of the things they like to do, how they like to spend their leisure time, and how they choose to spend their money. Many of these characteristics are more complex and less overt than demographics, but often address the underlying motivations for individuals' behaviors.

3. Alcohol drinkers vary sharply in terms of the number of drinks they may consume, from those who occasionally have one at a cocktail party to regular imbibers. Explain how the 20/80 rule applies to this product category.

According to text, the 20/80 principle states that only 20 percent of a product's users account for 80 percent of the product sold. For this question, alcohol drinkers vary according to the number of drinks consumed. Consumers may be heavy, moderate, or light users. Applying the 20/80 principle, we assume that 80 percent of the alcohol is drunk by 20 percent of the drinkers (who constitute the heavy-drinker segment).

4. Describe the underlying principles used to construct the VALS system. What are some positive and negative aspects of this approach to lifestyle segmentation?

The underlying principles used to construct the VALS systems were (1) Maslow's Hierarchy of Needs and (2) Riesman's distinction between inner-directed people and outer-directed people. The instructor should have the students review these concepts in order to identify both negative and positive aspects of the VALS system. Some of the following issues might be raised:

- Negative aspects include the fact that consumers are put into only one VALS category, the system assumes that a person never changes categories, and many product decisions are not that closely related to personal values.
- Positive aspects include the fact that marketers can use this method to segment the market for their products, design specifically targeted promotional messages, and address specific consumer needs via tailored product offerings.

5. Compile a set of recent ads that attempt to link consumption of a product with a specific lifestyle. How is this goal usually accomplished?

Students should be able to find a variety of advertisements to represent the link of product consumption with specific lifestyle. Examples include luxury cars, cruises, and golf linked to an affluent lifestyle; used cars and furniture, small apartments, stereos and books linked to the 'university student' lifestyle; Miller beer linked to the young, single, sports fanatic male lifestyle. (Possible Field Project)

6. The chapter mentions that psychographic analyses can be used to market politicians. Conduct research on the marketing strategies used in a recent, major election. How were voters segmented in terms of values? Can you find evidence that communications strategies were guided by this information?

Students should recognize the power of psychographic analyses in defining target consumers and positioning political candidates for office. They should search for campaign literature that is designed for different targets and which might even contradict each other, looking for obvious and subtle differences. This type of polling data is difficult to get because it is closely guarded by the candidates and their pollsters, but often just by viewing the ads one can identify the target audience. (Possible Field Project)

7. Construct separate advertising executions for a cosmetic products targeted to the belonger, achiever, experiential, and societally conscious VALS types. How would the basic appeal differ for each group?

Students should review the information in the text before trying to design advertising campaigns for the various VALS types.

- Belongers: upper-lower to lower-middle class, want to "fit in", family-oriented, traditional, conservative, blue-collar jobs, high school graduates, optimistic.
- Achievers: affluent, well educated, hard workers, believe in the American dream, self-confident, view life as a challenge they can master, optimistic and happy
- Experientials: consider themselves liberated, willing to try new things, impulsive, fairly mature, receive pleasure from non-work related activities.
- Societally Conscious: very high educational level, mature individuals, successful professionally, influential, liberals, more interested in non-material rather than material goods.

(Possible Field Project)

8. . Using media targeted to the group, construct a consumption constellation for the social role of college students. What set of products, activities, and interests tend to appear in advertisements depicting "typical" college students? How realistic is this constellation?

Students should enjoy developing a consumption constellation for their role segment. The instructor might point out how the students serve as "experts" with respect to this segment, and how their constellation might differ from that constructed by their professors, parents, or business executives. (Possible Field Project)

9. The principle of market segmentation implies that a group of people sharing some set of characteristics will be singled out as the focus of a marketing strategy. Critics of targeted marketing argue that this is discriminatory and unfair, especially if such a strategy encourages a group of people to buy a product that may be injurious to them or that they cannot afford. On the other hand, The Association of National Advertisers argues that banning targeted marketing constitutes censorship and is a violation of the First Amendment. Is segmentation an ethical marketing practice? Give the reasons for your answer.

The question of the ethics of segmentation practices has been addressed in previous exercises. Students should be asked to recall their position with respect of this issue when segmentation involved black and Hispanic consumers and handicapped consumers.

10. Administer the Materialism Scale in Table 16–1 to a sample of business majors and another group of liberal arts majors. What predictions might you make regarding group differences on this value? For each statement, ask respondents to circle a number on a scale:

Strongly disagree 1 2 3 4 5 Strongly agree

<u>Note</u>: When scoring, be sure to remember that items marked with an asterisk are reverse scored. That is, a response of "5" should be scored as a "1," a "4" as a "2," and so on. Sum each person's score for each scale item, and calculate the average response for each sample. Do the two groups differ in terms of their mean responses?

Students are likely to hypothesize that business students will score higher on the materialism scale than nonbusiness students. The instructor should encourage a discussion of this hypothesized relationship. Why do students expect to find a difference? Why do they expect business students to be more materialistic? If the relationship is evidenced, what are the implications? (Possible Field Project)

11. If you were segmenting a consumer group in terms of their relative level of materialism, how might your advertising and promotional strategy take this difference into account? Construct two versions of an ad for a suntan lotion, one to appeal to a high materialism segment and one to appeal to a low materialism segment.

The instructor should encourage students to consider their findings from question 10 in generating their responses to this exercise. It is likely that the position they adopt on the previous question will influence their approach to this exercise. (Possible Field Project)

12. Due to increased competition and market saturation, marketers in industrialized countries increasingly are trying to develop Third World markets by encouraging people in underdeveloped countries to desire Western products. Should this practice be encouraged, even if the products being marketed may be harmful to consumers' health (e.g., cigarettes) or divert needed money away from the purchase of essentials? If you were a trade or health official in a Third World country, what guidelines, if any, might you suggest to regulate the import of luxury goods from advanced economies?

This question represents a controversial aspect of marketing activities that has received considerable attention from many and diverse parties. Students should be encouraged to review popular press commentaries and raise this question with others, both within and outside the business arena. An interesting discussion is likely to ensue.

13. Geodemographic techniques assume that people who live in the same neighborhood have other things in common as well. Why is this assumption made, and how accurate is it?

While members of the U.S. culture share a common national identity, purchase and consumption patterns of different regions have been shaped by unique climates, cultural influences, and resources. For example, a student from Minnesota going to a university in the South will quickly recognize that the regional drink is ice tea or "Coke," rather than hot chocolate or "pop." Similarly, the easterner will have a very different attitude toward space and crowding than residents of Texas or New Mexico. Just as we have come to realize that cultural differences between countries are significant, regional differences are recognized as influential. (For example, different names for the same thing: pop, soft drink, soda, soda pop, soda water, "coke", tonic.)

14. Single-source data systems give marketers access to a wide range of information about a consumer, just by knowing his or her address. Do you believe this "knowledge power" presents any ethical problems with regard to consumers' privacy? Should access to such information be regulated by the government or other bodies? Should consumers have the right to limit access to these data?

Students will differ in their responses to this question. Many may view single-source data as a threat of the Orwellian Big Brother nature. Others will view it as part of the public domain. The instructor should encourage students to examine both sides of the argument.

ENDNOTES

[1] Chester A. Swenson, "How to Sell to a Segmented Market," *Journal of Business Strategy* 9 (January February 1988): 18.

[2] Joan Kron, "All-Consuming Art," *New York Times* (December 6, 1992): 12V.

[3] Rebecca Piirto, "Pulse of the City," *American Demographics* (June 1990): 6.

[4] "States of Stress, " *American Demographics* (February 1987): 18.

[5] Brad Edmondson, "Chili Recipes," *American Demographics* (April 1987): 22.

[6] Susan Krafft, "Who Slams the Door on Research?" *American Demographics* (September 1991): 14.

[7] Tim Padgett, "The Gringos are Coming!" *Newsweek* (November 30, 1992): 55.

[8] Calvin Trillin, "Uncivil Liberties: American Fast Food Restaurants Around the World," *The Nation* (April 10, 1989): 473.

[9] William E. Schmidt, "West Sets Up Store and the Russians are Seduced," *New York Times* (September 27, 1991): A4.

[10] Andrew Pollack, "Export News: 'Twin Peaks' Mania Peaks in Japan," *New York Times* (August 2, 1992): H18.

[11] David Kilburn and Julie Skur Hill, "Western Barbie: Mattel Makes Japan Push with Revamped Doll," *Advertising Age* (October 7, 1991): 40.

[12] Nicholas D. Kristof, "The Voice of Taiwan Speaks English," *New York Times* (January 4, 1992): L4.

Instructor's Notes:

Chapter 17

Sacred and Profane Consumption: Cultural Trends and Ethical Issues in Consumer Behavior

SUMMARY BULLETS

♦ Consumer activities can be divided into sacred and profane domains. Sacred phenomena are "set apart" from everyday activities or products. People, events, or objects can become sacralized.

♦ Objectification occurs when sacred qualities are ascribed to products or items owned by sacred people. Sacralization occurs when formerly sacred objects or activities become part of everyday life, such as when "one-of-a-kind" works of art are reproduced in large quantities.

♦ While textbooks often paint a picture of the consumer as a rational, informed decision maker, in reality many consumer activities are harmful to the individual or to society. The dark side of consumer behavior includes excessive materialism, addiction, the use of people as products (consumed consumers), and theft or vandalism (anticonsumption).

♦ Much of our daily lives is affected by the actions of marketers. As the boundaries blur between commercial activities and popular culture, a wider range of mundane events are influenced by the actions of marketers. Reality engineering refers to the process where aspects of our environment are modified to reflect commercial activities (e.g., product placement, theme parks, billboards.) The cultivation hypothesis refers to the ability of the mass media to influence consumers' perceptions of reality.

♦ Some major lifestyle trends occurring in the mid-1990s include an emphasis on: environmentalism, a resurgence of importance placed on value-oriented products and services, a decreased emphasis on nutrition and exercise, a renewed interest in devoting more time to family versus careers, and more emphasis on individuality as consumer gravitate to marketers that practice mass customization (products and services are tailored to the specific needs of individual consumers.)

LECTURE/DISCUSSION IDEAS

I. **The Future of Consumer Behavior**--Disney World and Reality: complex relationships between marketing activities and consumers' everyday experiences

Discussion Topic: How have the lives of children changed since you were a kid? How did this affect marketing? What do you think this holds for the future?

II. **Sacred and Profane Consumption**

(Use Color Transparency 49 Here)

- sacred consumption--objects and events set apart from normal activities
- profane consumption--objects and events that are ordinary not special

---

Real World Application
- Money is not necessarily profane. It is invested with good powers (as when a person saves up a nest egg or makes a donation) as well as bad (as when used as a ransom or for blood money). It can be used to buy immortality (as in philanthropy, when a building is named after a donor), life (as when children are adopted or a surrogate mother is hired), or even death (contract murders or abortion).[1]

A. **Domains of Sacred Consumption**--ordinary consumption that is not "ordinary"

(Use TM 17-1 Here)

1. **Sacred Places**--"set apart" by society, e.g. Bethlehem, Ellis Island, Statue of Liberty, Disney World, Graumann's Chinese Theater, Graceland, and home.

2. **Sacred People**--people elevated to sacred status, e.g. Marilyn Monroe, Elvis, and sports heroes

---

- Many believe that The King is actually still alive. Sighting in shopping malls or fast food restaurants are frequently reported in the tabloids. As one minister put it, "This has the makings of a new religion. Elvis is the god, and Graceland is the shrine . . . And some even say he is rising again."[2]

- Marilyn Monroe has been dead for over 30 years, but consumers and marketers have kept her spirit very much alive. She has inspired numerous books (over 70 at last count, including a 1992 work written by four psychics that claims to contain an interview with her spirit), plays and television shows, and even a California wine bottle bears her likeness (the wine is called Marilyn Merlot). The Monroe estate makes over $1 million a year in licensing fees for the use of her name and likeness. At least 100 women make their living by impersonating Marilyn Monroe.[3]

Discussion Topic: Who are some of the celebrities who have become sacred? Can you think of any who have actually been created by marketing people? (Models, stars of television ad.) The creation of celebrities by marketers may generate interesting class discussion. For a fascinating treatment of the subject, see Irving J. Rein, Philip Kotler, and Martin R. Stoller. High Visibility. *New York: Dodd, Mead & Company, 1987)*

        3. **Sacred Events**--any event can be elevated to sacred status, e.g. Olympics, Super Bowl, World Series, Woodstock, and a family vacation

---

Real World Application
- Societies often devise ways to ensure that sacred things are kept separate. Legislation in Great Britain, for example was passed to prevent advertising (a profane commodity) from appearing two minutes before or after the telecast of any royal occasion (a sacred event).[4]

    B. **From Sacred to Profane and Back Again**--sacred things become profane and profane things become sacred.

(Use TM 17-2 Here)

        1. **Desacralization**--sacred item is duplicated in mass quantities or is simply demoted by society, e.g. plastic Washington Monument, burning the American flag in protest, certain religious holidays, televangelists

        2. **Sacralization**--ordinary objects, events and people become sacred to a culture, e.g., Super Bowl, "Star Trek", Barbie, baseball cards, Big Bird, and Barney

---

- The role of the souvenir as a "marker" of sacred experiences can be so compelling that it can actually supersede the experience itself. One researcher observed that 30 percent of visitors arriving on buses at a Canadian museum visited only the gift shop.[5]

Discussion Topic: Tell the class about a person who is commonly held in high esteem even though you don't have the same opinion. Why do you suppose this is so?

III. **The Dark Side of Consumer Behavior**--negative behavior due to excesses or immorality
(Use TM 17-3 Here)

- It is not uncommon for people to be addicted to more than one thing at a time. Cross-addition is found, for example, among sexaholics, who are often also addicted to drugs or alcohol. These people do not consume sex for recreation but rather to manage pain or anxiety, much as a chemical may be taken to relieve depression.[6]

    A. **Addictive Consumption**--physiological and/or psychological dependency on products, e.g. drugs, tobacco, alcohol, chocolate, shopping

1. **Gambling**--gamblers have a "high" followed by depression, e.g. lottery, slot

---

Real World Application

☯ Gamblers can be segmented by lifestyle and demographic variables. For example, slot and keno players are more likely to be Protestant who go to church regularly, while the craps table has a better chance of being patronized by non-practicing Catholics (the religious group with the highest gambling frequency). Fundamentalists and atheists are the two religious groups least likely to gamble at all. Gambling is more popular in urban areas than rural ones and more widespread in the northern United States than in the South.[7]

---

2. **Compulsive Consumption**--"born to shop", "repetitive and excessive shopping"

☯ Some evidence suggests that television addicts display symptoms similar to other forms of dependency such as alcoholism. These consumers, estimated to compose between 2 percent and 12 percent of the population, watch twice as much television as average, and experience attentional inertia--they feel powerless to turn off the television once it is on.[8].

Discussion Topic: What are some of the major compulsive behaviors in people your age? Why is it so hard for people to break these bad habits?

B. **Consumed Consumers**--people who are used (willingly or not) for commercial gain

1. **Prostitutes**--annual expenditures estimated to be $20 billion

---

☯ It is common in many societies for a "bride price" to be paid by a husband to the bride's father in exchange for receiving this "property". Historically, women who were in some way damaged (e.g., by virtue of being widowed or raped) had no choice but to become prostitutes--their bodies were the only asset they had to sell. These women are often regarded as profane commodities and less than human. They are, in fact, often described in various animal terms, such as chickens, beavers, or just meat. Not coincidentally, a group of prostitutes working for a pimp is referred to as his stable.[9]

---

2. **Organ, Blood, and Hair Donors** -- giving or selling of blood, organs or hair

3. **Babies for Sale** -- e.g. baby black market, surrogate mothers

C. **Illegal Activities**--consumer crimes against business, e.g. shoplifting, arson, fraud

1. **Shrinkage**--losses caused by shoplifting and employee theft

2. **Anticonsumption**--products and services deliberately defaced or mutilated, e.g. product tampering, graffiti, billboard destruction

3. **Culture resistance**--subculture modifies an object of value to the dominant class, e.g.--peace symbols on military uniforms, body piercing, codes of dress

Discussion Topic: How important do you think the virtue of honesty is in a democratic society? Can democracy survive if the citizens can't be trusted?

IV. **Blurred Boundaries:** Marketing and Reality--popular culture often shaped by marketers

(Use TM 17-4 Here)

- Disney named their hockey team "The Mighty Ducks" after the successful movie
- Hooters restaurant sponsors arena football team (the Miami Hooters)
- Movie "The Program"--young men laid down on busy highways

A. **Reality Engineering**--popular culture is appropriated by marketers, e.g. "Prego Science Challenge", "fake" Africa for affluent guests

1. **Marketing Goes to Hollywood: Product Placement**--real brands prominently displayed in movies, e.g. Reese's Pieces in the film *E.T.*

Discussion Topic: What movies or television shows have you seen lately that contained commercial products? What were they? What are your thoughts when the actor is drinking a generic product?.

2. **Types of Product Placement**

- On-set placement--product is incorporated into actual film
- Creative placement--real TV commercial playing in the background

---

Real World Application
- The cigarette industry is taking advantage of product placement strategies by planting plugs in new movies. The National Center on Television Violence reported that over 85 percent of movies contain smoking plugs. Philip Morris, Inc., paid $350,000 to place its Lark brand in the James Bond film, *License to Kill,* where smoking is shown in 13 different scenes.[10]

---

3. **Advertising Versus Editorial Content**--people personally relate to TV characters

- ☯ Some companies have even come under fire for designing highly visible cause-marketing campaigns. When the Quaker Oats Company announced plans to sponsor a series of public service announcements on behalf of the American Medical Association, some broadcasters refused to run the spots because the commercials featured company spokesman Wilford Brimley.[11]

- ☯ Commercial screeners are routinely used by advertisers to ensure that their messages are not inappropriately communicated. Objections are made to general themes, such as sexual content, in order to counteract possible pressure from religious or other groups.

- ☯ Pizza companies do not like to advertise in shows where blood flows, since they feel it will cause viewers to make negative associations with tomato sauce. Similarly, drug companies avoid placing ads on any program where a character commits suicide by overdosing on sleeping pills.[12]

    4. **"Blurmercials"**--Advertorials and infomercials

Discussion Topic: Who do you think watches infomercials on television? Do you think informercials are effective?

    5. **The Cultivation Effect**--ability of the media to distort consumer's perceptions of reality

V. **Lifestyle Trends:** What's in Store for Consumers and Marketers?--lifestyles are moving targets, e.g. "affinitization" exists when groups organize around special interests

    A. **Trend Forecasting:** Peering into the Crystal Ball of Consumer Behavior--
        e.g. The Needham Lifestyle Study

- Church attendance is slightly down
- A third of adults say that couples should live together before marriage
- Increasing majority of Americans favor legalized abortions
- Less people believe family income is high enough for important things
- Steep drop in people who say they are the first to try new products
- Steep drop in people who say that television is their primary form of entertainment

    B. **Major Consumer Trends**--trend forecasting is risky
(Use Color Transparency 50 Here)
(Use TM 17-5 Here)

    1. **Voluntary Simplicity and Environmentalism**--"outwardly simple inwardly rich" e.g. "the green movement"

Discussion Topic: Do you think that most Americans are really interested in the environment? What items do your friends (family) recycle? What do you recycle?

2. **A Return to Value**--shoppers are picking and choosing carefully, e.g. Everyday Low Prices, relationship marketing

3. **Decreased Materialism and Emphasis on Self-fulfillment**--disenchantment with accumulation of status goods and focus on acquisition of experiences, e.g. travel, virtual reality games

   a. **Time Poverty**--consumers want convenience products and services

   b. **Disillusionment of Working Women**--working outside of home is not "liberating", shift toward "neo-traditionalism" (committed to family)

Real World Application
☙ The convenience trend can be overdone. One company wanted to sell sheets in supermarkets, reasoning that working women would welcome this addition. They quickly found that consumers hated the idea. An important benefit of shopping for sheets is looking at a wide range of designs and colors, and fantasizing how one's bedroom would look with them. Consumers felt that a supermarket could not offer this diversity and that their mood would be too pragmatic while in the supermarket to fantasize. The idea was shelved.[13]

Discussion Topic: Do you know of a working woman who did not go back to work after she had a baby? What were her reasons?

   c. **Decreased Emphasis on Nutrition and Exercise**--"It's okay, in moderation"

   d. **"Cocooning"**--staying home as much as possible

Discussion Topic: Do you know any people who are working out of their homes? Do you predict more of this in the future? Why? What are the causes?

   e. **Individualization and Mass Customization**--database marketing allows marketers to target well-defined interests, e.g. Marriott's Honored Guest Program, create your own Hallmark Card

FIELD PROJECT IDEAS

Individual Assignments

1. Ask a student to sit down with a pad of paper and write down at least five actions that business or government (local, state, or federal) could take that would protect the rights of the rural or inner city poor. Then have them write down the problems that would be created if these actions were actually carried out.

2. Have a student survey approximately 10 people to find out what actions they have taken in the last two weeks that would have positive or negative effects on the environment (e.g., recycled something, bought something made of recycled materials, conserved various resources, or the number of trash bags they filled, approximately how many miles they drove, their habits in using electricity, water, fireplaces, etc.) Have them report to the class.

3. It takes a bold student to pull this one off. Ask the student to interview a local consumer or civil rights advocate about the recent initiatives their organization has undertaken to protect individual rights. See if the student thinks the organization has been effective. Does the student think the organization has gone too far or not far enough? Have the student share ideas with the class.

4. Ask a student to interview a couple of people who seem to go shopping frequently. Find out if they derive greater pleasure from the act of purchasing or from obtaining the actual product. What is the student's impression of the conversations with the respondents?

5. Have a student assume the role of Director of Customer Relations for a large organization (e.g., city, automobile manufacturer, public utility, university, accounting firm). See how this person would ensure that the complaints received from customers were communicated to proper officials. How would this person follow-up with the customer? What would the student do if consumer rights organizations got involved?

6. This project takes courage and time. Have a student visit a supermarket or drug store and select one aisle or product group, (e.g., cereal, cookies, cold medicine). Ask the student make a list of the number of different types of products and sizes that are available. Who are the major manufacturers of all these products? On the basis of this experience, does the student think the consumer may suffer from "information overload"? Why or why not?

7. Ask a student to bring to class a newspaper or magazine article related to consumerism. Have the student summarize the article for the class from a marketer's standpoint.

8. See if you can find a student who will talk with an executive from a local corporation about the role that company plays in the community. What does the company see as its responsibilities to customers? What does it see as its responsibilities to its employees and shareholders? Then report to the class on what was said.

272

"green movement"; and they both recycle and want to buy recycled products. But if recycled products and "green products" cost more, consumer motivation begins to wane. They indicate an interest in recycling, but they find it inconvenient to deliver their products to a recycling center-- so they don't. They vote against a city's recycling program if it is going to cost them.

4. Discuss the distinction between sacred and profane consumption. What are some marketing implications of positioning a product as either sacred or profane?

Students should review the definitions of sacred and profane objects provided in the text. A variety of ideas might be expressed with respect to marketing implications of positioning products as either sacred or profane. As examples, positioning a product or event as sacred might allow marketers to heighten consumer demand and increase the price a consumer is willing to pay (tickets to rock concerts, Disney World, the Super Bowl, Hard Rock Cafes). It also helps to sell trinkets to commemorate these events. Positioning a product as profane might increase the number of consumers who perceive themselves to have access to such items. In the Catholic Church many of the priests and nuns stopped wearing habits because they wanted to be viewed as part of the mainstream and more approachable.

5. Observe people in the process of watching television. Can you find any evidence of para-social interaction?

As stated in the text, people often engage in para-social interaction with television, where they actively relate to television characters and vicariously experience and evaluate the different lifestyles portrayed. Many adult males engage in such interaction when they become "armchair" quarterbacks during Monday Night Football. However, para-social interaction is also common behavior among children. Children learn from imitation and often act out whatever they see or hear,especially from their heroes. Students should be encouraged to consider the potentially negative consequences of such confusion between reality and advertising for children. (Possible Field Project)

6. Everyday objects like cars, televisions, and money may be said to have sacred qualities. How do these objects become sacred? Do you agree with this contention?

The discussion in the text suggests that the sacralization process occurs when everyday objects like cars, televisions, and money take on sacred meaning. These objects become sacred through the objectification process wherein profane products of various kinds can take on sacred qualities through contamination (association with sacred events of people). Cars, televisions and money can bring families together and create harmony. Students should be asked to think about this contention and develop personal arguments either for or against the idea.

7. "People can be marketed just like any other product." Do you agree?

Students should consider the discussion of sacred people provided in the text. In addition to the marketing of "sacred people", such as movie stars, athletes, and musicians, students might consider how corporate executives and politicians are marketed. The instructor should encourage students to develop their own position on the values and ethics of marketing people like any other product.

8. What do you personally feel are the three most significant social trends affecting consumer behavior in the 1990s? How might these developments affect your decisions as a marketer?

Students will likely identify a variety of trends as most significant in consumer behavior in the 1990s. Some trends are: voluntary simplicity, environmentalism, green movement, changing structure of the family, decrease in materialism and emphasis on self-fulfillment, time poverty, disillusionment of working women, decreased emphasis on nutrition and exercise, "cocooning", nonconsumption, individualization and mass customization, changing roles of men and women, and growth in the number of ethnic minorities. The instructor might ask students to develop marketing strategies, or suggest new product introductions in response to some of these trends.

9. Should any limits be placed on topics, events, or places that are accessible to marketers (e.g., the commercialization of holidays, advertising in schools, promoting art)?

Student responses will vary. Instructors may find a difference between students with different college majors, both within and outside the business program. Specific attitudes on this issue will likely reflect general attitudes toward marketing practices. This may offer a good opportunity for the instructor to present a lecture on marketing ethics.

ENDNOTES

[1] Russell W. Belk and Melanie Wallendorf, "The Sacred Meanings of Money." *Journal of Economic Psychology* 11 (1990): 35-67.

[2] Quoted in Richard Corliss, "The King is Dead Or is He? The Elvis Cult has the Makings of a New Religion," *Time* 110 (October, 1988) 91.

[3] Pat H. Broeske, "Marketing Monroe: Still Big Box Office," *New York Times* (July 26, 1992): H16.

[4] Russell W. Belk, Melanie Wallendorf, and John F. Sherry, Jr., "The Sacred and the Profane in Consumer Behavior: Theodicy on the Odyssey." *Journal of Consumer Research* 16 (June, 1989): 1-38.

[5] Robert F. Kelly. "Culture as Commodity: The Marketing of Cultural Objects and Cultural Experiences," *Advances in Consumer Research* 14, eds. Melanie Wallendorf and Paul Anderson (Provo, Utah: Association of Consumer Research, 1987), 347-351).

[6] Jean Seligmann, "Taking Life One Night at a Time; Sex Addicts Seek Help," *Newsweek* (July 20, 1987): 48.

[7] Brad Edmondson, "The Demographics of Gambling," *American Demographics* (July, 1986): 38.

[8] Daniel Goleman, "How Viewers Grow Addicted to Television." *New York Times* (October 16, 1990): CI.

[9] See Vern L. Bullough, *The Subordinate Sex* (Urbana, IL: University of Illinois Press, 1973); Elizabeth C. Hirschman, *Metaphor and Ideology in Profane Consumption: The Case of Prostitution and Pornography,* unpublished manuscript, Rutgers University, New Brunswick, NJ, 1990.

[10] George W. Brown, Subtle Cigarette Ads Abound in New Films. (September 1, 1991).

[11] Julie Liesse, "Line Between Public Service, Paid Ads Blurs," *Advertising Age* (October 8, 1990): 28.

[12] Bill Carter, "Screeners Help Advertisers Avoid Prime-Time Trouble" *New York Times* (January 29, 1990): D1.

[13] Judith Langer, "Where does the Consumer's Personal Style Fit It?" *American Demographics* (October, 1987): 48.

Instructor's Notes:

THE ABC CONNECTION

ABC Video Users' Guide

CHAPTER 1

PRIVACY: YOUR SECRETS FOR SALE

Running Time: 8:00

Video Summary: In the age of computers and wireless communications, the details of our lives have become big business. Information from all sorts of databases is available for sale by everyone from the government to extra-legal "information brokers." This segment focuses on concerns about how marketers' need for targeted information is balanced against possible violations of consumers' privacy. Several demonstrations of the ability of various brokers to infiltrate databases and collect personal data underscore the potential of businesses large and small to learn the intimate details of our lives. These concerns are also discussed in Chapter 1 in a Marketing Pitfalls box.

Discussion Questions:

1. If you wanted to learn about the consumption habits of a friend, business associate or neighbor, how would you go about doing this? What sources are (legally) available to you?

2. Currently our Social Security numbers provide a gateway to the information highway for many government and private enterprises. To what extent should the government have access to information about our private lives? Does the government have a right to sell this information to private businesses?

3. Many proponents of relationship marketing would argue that the key to meeting people's needs is to learn as much as possible about their preferences over time so that products and services can be tailored to these precise desires. They might say that any time you make a purchase it becomes a matter of public record. Do you agree?

CHAPTER 2

HIDDEN MESSAGES

Running Time: 12:45

Video Summary: Subliminal persuasion is a concern of many, even though ironically there is scant evidence that advertisers and others possess the ability to encode effective subliminal messages visually or audibly. This segment focuses on one facet of the subliminal industry where consumers <u>voluntarily</u> bring subliminal messages into their homes. Self-help tapes encoded with motivational messages to encourage weight loss, smoking cessation, sexual ability, and even restoration of long-lost hair are purchased by millions. Most of the evidence offered by manufacturers to attest to the effectiveness of these messages comes in the form of testimonials of users and former users; most scientists express strong doubts about these claims. However, it is possible that a form of the placebo effect is working here, since the people who buy the tapes are already motivated to change the behavior in question.

Discussion Questions:

1. What is the rationale behind self-help subliminals? How do they (supposedly) work if no one can hear them?

2. Has anyone ever purchased and/or used a subliminal self-help tape? What was the experience like? Were you happy with the results?

3. Despite research results to the contrary, many people claim to have been helped by these products. Is it possible for a product to show the desired effect even when there is no functional reason for it to work that way?

4. Should manufacturers have to produce scientific documentation to back up the claims made by products like these, or is it up to the buyer to determine if he or she is satisfied with the product?

CHAPTER 3

NIKE RECRUITS YOUNG ATHLETES

Running Time: 3:00

Video Summary: This brief segment profiles Nike's efforts to cultivate young athletes by sponsoring teams and distributing merchandise to up-and-coming stars. These kids in turn serve as role models and facilitate the observational learning of their peers, and they themselves learn strong connections between performance and the Nike name. Nike's sponsorship practices have drawn fire from some critics, who claim that the company's visibility among younger players comes at a big cost to the athletes. In some cases the eligibility of high school players has even been threatened because they have accepted Nike merchandise. Even a few coaches have expressed concern about the company's influence on impressionable young people.

Discussion Questions:

1. How might the product choices of an athlete in junior high or high school affect the preferences of his or her peers?

2. In an era of scarce resources, many schools are grateful to attract whatever outside help they can to improve upon the educational services they can provide to students. Critics argue that acceptance of these gifts creates a learning environment that is biased and places too much of an emphasis on commercial products; stimuli that should not be featured in a school setting. To what extent (if at all) should corporations sponsor activities, provide resources, or otherwise get involved in educational settings? What limits (if any) should be placed on these activities?

CHAPTER 4

MEN'S GROOMING PRODUCTS

Running Time: 6:50

Video Summary: The segment highlights the growing market for men's grooming products. Attitudes are changing, and men's involvement with their appearance is increasing. As a result, an increasing number of customers for facials, pedicures, and cosmetic surgery are male. Some fans of these services feel that their motivation to receive them is due to the increasingly strong linkage between appearance and success in the business world. Others argue that they simply are entitled to be pampered so long as they can afford to be.

Discussion Questions:

1. Has appearance traditionally been more of a concern for women than men? Why?

2. What associations might exist between such activities as getting a manicure and higher-order motivations like success or well-being?

3. Who is more vain about their appearance, men or women?

4. What changes in marketing strategy (if any) need to be made to market these products and services to men?

CHAPTER 5

HEALTH FOODS?   FAT CHANCE!

Running Time: 5:56

Video Summary: Meatless lunch meats, fruit-juice sweetened frozen yogurt, low-fat cookies. We've come a long way from thick steaks, premium ice cream and Twinkies.

Or have we? As consumers' attitudes about diet and nutrition are changing, many people are trying to modify their behavior to be consistent with the new emphasis on eating right. Unfortunately, as the old saying goes, "the road to hell is paved with good intentions." Despite people's best efforts to buy so-called health foods that are low in fat, cholesterol, and other nasty things (and often paying a premium for them), these choices may not be worth the sacrifice.

Discussion Questions:

1. How have changes in attitudes toward nutrition worked to the advantage of the health food industry? What has caused these changes? How has the industry encouraged this shift?

2. It takes a lot to get many people to change their nutritional habits, especially if this means doing without old favorites that happen to be high in fat, cholesterol, or sugar. Is it easier to change consumers' attitudes and then hope for a change in behavior, or vice versa? How does the consumers' level of involvement with snack foods relate to the hierarchy of effects discussed in the chapter?

3. As many people make a genuine effort to mend their evil nutritional ways, what effect might reports like this one have on their willingness to continue to modify their behaviors? From a public policy perspective, what are the pros and cons of revealing that new solutions to health problems may not be so effective after all?

CHAPTER 6

IT SLICES, IT DICES, IT'S AN INFOMERCIAL!

Running Time: 7:08

Video Summary: This segment chronicles the growing influence of infomercials, or program-length commercials. It provides some interesting historical footage of early infomercials, and shows how the industry is getting more sophisticated and winning the participation of major corporations such as Volvo. As noted in the Chapter, one reason for the success of infomercials is that they tend to adopt formats from talk shows or news programs and as a result their credibility may be enhanced.

Discussion Questions:

1. People have been selling things on TV since the medium was invented. Why are infomercials different?

2. Is a commercial more effective if it "borrows" a program format such as a news show or a talk show? Why or why not?

3. The U.S. Government is considering whether and to what extent it should regulate the contents of infomercials. For example, some critics want to require that a "warning label" indicating that the program is intended to sell a product or service be run continuously throughout the program. What is your stand on this controversy?

4. Many celebrities, from Lyle Wagonner to Cher, regularly appear on infomercials to hawk products. Is this an effective strategy for the advertiser? Do you see any negative aspects of these appearances for the celebrity?

CHAPTER 7

PUT ON A HAPPY FACE (?): COSMETIC TATTOOING

Running Time: 12:00

Video Summary: This segment reports on the new fashion of cosmetic tattooing, where permanent makeup is applied to women's faces by injecting color into the skin. The results can be satisfying, but in some cases the procedure has been shown to cause medical problems -- perhaps because the tattooists are only haphazardly trained and regulated.

Discussion Questions:

1. What do women perceive as benefits of cosmetic tattooing? Would you consider having this procedure done?

2. Do you feel that the pressure to always be "made up" in public justifies the convenience of this procedure?

3. What does this risky practice say about the importance of appearance in our society?

CHAPTER 8

ENVIRONMENTALISM AS A DECISION CUE: GREEN OR OBSCENE?

Running Time: 8:26

Video Summary: In the 1990s many consumers have begun to use a company's "environmental friendliness" as a decision-making cue. While this attribute is legitimately promoted by many marketers, in some cases this dimension has been abused by companies making fraudulent or exaggerated claims. These distortions have the potential to "poison the well" for legitimate companies engaged in green marketing.

Discussion Questions:

1. How does a company's claim to practice "green marketing" enter into the decision-making process?

2. Have you ever chosen a brand over others because it was environmentally friendly? How did this information affect your decision-making?

3. Are you willing to pay more for green products?

4. Should a product's "greenness" be promoted as a brand attribute? What is the best way to do this? What packaging and other cues should be used to have the most impact on consumers' decision-making?

5. Should the government regulate the claims made by supposedly green marketers? What is the best way to educate consumers about which products really are better for the environment?

CHAPTER 9

THE TOWN THAT LOVES GARBAGE

Running Time: 12:19

Video Summary: Product disposal is a major headache in the 1990s. This segment profiles the town of Riverview, Michigan, which has turned garbage into a cash cow.

Discussion Questions:

1. Most of us throw things away without really thinking about where this waste goes when we're done with it. How is product disposal handled where you live?

2. What steps can marketers take to encourage recycling among consumers and businesses?

3. How could the lessons learned by the citizens of Riverview be used to encourage other towns to be as enthusiastic about taking in people's garbage?

CHAPTER 10

ON THE ROAD AGAIN

Running Time: 12:50

Video Summary: As noted at the beginning of the chapter, Harley Davidson riders constitute an important reference group for many aspiring bikers. This segment profiles the company and the efforts it has made to broaden its appeal to affluent baby boomers.

Discussion Questions:

1. How has Harley Davidson changed its positioning strategy over the last decade? What effect has this change had for the company?

2. How do motorcycle riders function as a reference group?

3. To what do you owe the success of Harley's merchandising efforts? What is the appeal of the Harley image, both in the U.S. and overseas? Do you think this image is the same in other countries? How would you describe the Harley "brand personality?"

4. Given Harley's success, how can its competitors fight back to regain their share of the market? Is Harley too entrenched as part of the American biker mindset to ever be dethroned by Japanese companies?

CHAPTER 11

FROM THE MOUTHS OF BABES

Running Time: 4:16

Video Summary: This segment elaborates on the material in the chapter related to kids' influence on parental spending. It notes that kids increasingly are being given more responsibility for making family-related purchases, and that they also have more of their own money to spend.

Discussion Questions:

1. Do you feel that kids are more influential in shaping the spending decisions of their parents than in times past? Why or why not?

2. In what product categories are kids the most or least likely to exert an impact?

3. Should kids be held responsible if they make poor purchase decisions?

CHAPTER 12

IF YOU'VE GOT IT, SHOULD YOU FLAUNT IT?:
LIFESTYLES OF THE FILTHY RICH

Running Time: 8:45

Video Summary: This segment highlights the extravagant birthday party thrown by businessman Malcolm Forbes for himself, where over 600 guests and journalists were flown to Tangiers for a celebration weekend (this event is also mentioned in the chapter).

Discussion Questions:

1. Some people argue that people have a right to spend their hard-earned money any way they see fit, even irresponsibly. Do you agree?

2. The party in the video took place in the late 1980s, when everybody was very materialistic. Times have changed in the more sober 1990s, and this extravaganza could <u>never</u> happen now. Do you agree?

3. How is throwing a party a form of conspicuous consumption? What purposes does it serve for the host?

CHAPTER 13

ETHNIC COSMETICS: A RAINBOW OF POSSIBILITIES

Running Time: 4:07

Video Summary: This clip underscores the material in the chapter on how big businesses are beginning to develop specialized products for ethnic and racial subcultures. It describes efforts by cosmetics industry giants such as Revlon and Esteé Lauder to create and promote beauty products for black women.

Discussion Questions:

1. These major companies are only getting into the business to exploit minority consumers and drive smaller black-owned firms out of business. Do you agree?

2. What are some other product needs of ethnic subcultures not currently being addressed by major corporations? Can you identify any opportunities for new products targeted to these segments?

CHAPTER 14

TWENTYSOMETHING

Running Time: 20:10

Video Summary: Many marketers are scrambling to understand the elusive "twentysomething" generation. Some have found these young consumers to be quite unique, while others have discovered that in many ways they are not so different after all. This segment explores the issue by profiling the experiences of a set of twentysomething consumers from a variety of backgrounds. The clip is a bit longer than others, but its use in class is perhaps justified due to the intense interest of many class members in pursuing issues closely related to their own situations. The segment goes well beyond consumption activities, but it should be stressed that evolving attitudes toward relationships, work, etc. exert important influences on how people approach buying and using products and services.

Discussion Questions:

1. Are "Twentysomethings" really different? Why or why not?

2. What are some examples you've seen of firms trying to appeal to people in their twenties? How successful have these efforts been, in your opinion?

3. What are the attributes of marketing campaigns targeted to people of this generation that really turn you on or off? How could marketers do a better job of meeting your needs?

CHAPTER 15

THE TYRANNY OF FASHION

Running Time: 8:00

Video Summary: Nightline takes a close look at the wheeling and dealing of the fashion industry, from *haute couture* in Paris to fashion journalism to models to fashion as depicted in the movies. The segment underscores the influential role played by such tastemakers (or *cultural gatekeepers*, as discussed in the chapter) as editors of trade magazines, whose opinions help to shape what products will eventually appear in stores.

Discussion Questions:

1. Do fashion designers or consumers really have the last word in determining what we will buy?

2. Why are trade publications that most consumers never even see so important in determining what clothes appear in stores? How does the fashion selection process work?

3. Fashion is described as a form of seduction, where people are convinced to buy things they don't really want or need. Do you agree with this assessment? What role(s) does fashion play in our society?

CHAPTER 16

ROLLERBLADING: HAVE FUN AT YOUR OWN RISK

Running Time: 3:30

Video Summary: This brief segment highlights a hot lifestyle choice for many young Americans. They have fallen in love with inline skating, or rollerblading. But, as the number of participants goes up, so do injuries. Many skaters are reluctant to wear safety equipment, either because they are lazy or because they don't want to be encumbered while having fun.

Discussion Questions:

1. Why has rollerblading become such a popular activity? What kind of lifestyle statement does it make?

2. As people choose to go rollerblading during their spare time, what activities has this replaced? In the 1930s and 1940s, for example, bridge was the activity of choice for many college students. Today, bridge players are few and far between as most students have developed other interests. How are the leisure time choices of students evolving over time?

3. What do you predict will be the next "big" leisure time activity for active consumers?

CHAPTER 17

MALT LIQUOR ADVERTISING:
TARGET MARKETING OR PROMOTING ADDICTION?

Running Time: 14:00

Video Summary: This segment focuses on the marketing of malt liquor products to people in poor neighborhoods. It includes commercial footage from malt liquor ads that show how the product is positioned as a virile, powerful beer substitute that gets one drunk more efficiently. Critics such as rap star Chuck D rail against this practice, claiming that these campaigns are part of a conspiracy by white America to destroy the black community. Defenders argue that no one is forcing anyone to buy these products, and that the advertising is only targeted to people who exhibit high demand for them anyway.

Discussion Questions:

1. What is targeted marketing, and how does it work?

2. Should companies be allowed to promote products that have addictive qualities, even if the sale of these items is not illegal?

3. The marketing concept states that we must identify consumer needs and satisfy them. Why do people make such a fuss when beer companies do just that?

4. Some critics feel that while targeted marketing of injurious products is unethical, efforts to curtail these practices are actually an insult to the affected consumers -- This concern implies that these people have no control over their own decisions and will buy whatever is put in front of them. Which side do you take?

Instructor's Notes:

SIMMONS CONNECTION EXERCISES

Instructor Introduction

Several practical data-oriented exercises have been designed for selected chapters in the text. These exercises are designed to give students some hands-on experience with the sort of data that marketers use to better understand the behavior of consumers. Each exercise is keyed to examples and concepts covered in the chapter in which it appears. There is also a computer disk that contains real market data. In order to "solve" the various problems posed in these exercises, students will need to access the data contained on the disk. The exercises are "user-friendly" and will increase student involvement in the learning process. Most of the exercises relate directly to the opening vignette of the chapter in which they are assigned. Students may wish to reread the vignette before they begin working on an exercise. The only thing needed to run the exercises is a standard spreadsheet program and access to either a DOS or Macintosh computer.

The data come from a widely used syndicated data service -- The Simmons Study of Media & Markets. This is a very extensive study that includes data on over 800 product and service categories. A panel of 22,051 adult Americans provides the data that make up the Simmons database. The real value of this database is that it allows marketers to look at patterns of buying behavior as a function of a wide array of consumer characteristics, including demographics (age, education, income, race, and so on) and psychographics (attitudes, self-concept, buying style, and so on).

The Simmons Study of Media & Markets is conducted annually and the results are tabulated into 34 separate volumes that are offered as Simmons products. Additional tabulations are prepared on a custom basis for individual clients. Simmons also conducts studies of special groups, for example, CompPro is their study of computer professionals, STARS focuses on teens between twelve and nineteen years old, and KIDS focuses on those younger than twelve. Simmons has extracted portions of its 1994 database and provided summary data in the form of spreadsheets that contain the critical information needed to work on each exercise. Although Simmons provides a great deal of information at the brand level, for most of the exercises the data have been aggregated to the product category level.

In order to use the data from the Simmons disk, you will need access either to a DOS or Macintosh computer and a standard spreadsheet program such as Lotus, Excel, Quattro, or another comparable program. The files are saved on the disk in what is called a "WKS" format, which is like a generic format for spreadsheets. This means that any standard program should have no problem reading the information from the disk. Since the disk itself is already a DOS disk, DOS users can access the files with no prior translation. If you are using your own computer and the computer has a hard disk, then you should first copy all of the files from the floppy disk onto the computer's hard drive.

If you are using a Macintosh computer and you use some version of System 7, you should be able to insert the Simmons disk and get an immediate translation to Macintosh format. For users of earlier versions of the Macintosh operating system, you will need to run a utility program called "Apple File Exchange." All system 6 and up users should have received this program. If you do not have this program, you can obtain it either through your local Macintosh Users Group or directly through Apple. The following instructions apply whether you are copying the files onto another floppy (in Macintosh format) or onto a hard drive (only the destination changes). In order to translate the files, first open the Apple File Exchange icon. Then insert the Simmons disk into your floppy drive. The dialog box will show the Simmons files on the right-hand portion of the screen. Select all of the Simmons data files and click on the "Translate" button. The next dialog box will ask how you want the files translated -- just select the format that matches your spreadsheet program.

There is a total of 14 files on the disk. Some files are titled *Chap#* -- these are keyed to the chapters in which you will find the Simmons exercises. The other four files are labeled *Self*, *Style*, *Media1*, and *Media2*. These are general Reference Files that may come in handy for several of the exercises. The following is an example of what you will find in the spreadsheets.

MAGAZINES	CELL	BASE = ALL ADULTS TOTAL	ALL ADULTS EDUCATION GRADUATED HIGH SCHOOL	ALL ADULTS EDUCATION GRADUATED COLLEGE	ALL ADULTS POLITICS VERY CONSERVATIVE	ALL ADULTS POLITICS SOMEWHAT CONSERVATIVE	ALL ADULTS POLITICS MIDDLE OF THE ROAD	ALL ADULTS POLITICS SOMEWHAT LIBERAL	ALL ADULTS POLITICS VERY LIBERAL
	Row								
TOTAL	(000)	187747	73139	37353	19774	42039	57742	28958	10161
TOTAL	Resps	22051	8179	5832	2293	5140	6298	3610	1156
TOTAL	Index	100	100	100	100	100	100	100	100
ARCHITECTURAL DIGEST	(000)	2939	591	1414	329	537	763	580	317
ARCHITECTURAL DIGEST	Resps	883	151	488	92	182	217	188	66
ARCHITECTURAL DIGEST	Index	100	52	242	106	82	84	128	199
HUNTING	(000)	3410	1642	292	332	724	1271	471	190
HUNTING	Resps	636	323	83	66	145	222	93	23
HUNTING	Index	100	124	43	92	95	121	90	103
MADEMOISELLE	(000)	4237	1775	854	299	767	1553	748	188
MADEMOISELLE	Resps	1027	392	253	69	193	316	220	52
MADEMOISELLE	Index	100	108	101	67	81	119	114	82
MONEY	(000)	7219	1879	3307	933	1926	1801	1197	382
MONEY	Resps	1963	430	1015	208	521	486	351	105
MONEY	Index	100	67	230	123	119	81	107	98
MOTOR TREND	(000)	3858	1740	540	267	687	1362	515	282
MOTOR TREND	Resps	942	405	198	70	193	275	156	51
MOTOR TREND	Index	100	116	70	66	80	115	87	135
NATIONAL ENQUIRER	(000)	16953	7895	1149	1754	3142	6125	2334	1109
NATIONAL ENQUIRER	Resps	3392	1579	312	333	671	1114	509	225
NATIONAL ENQUIRER	Index	100	120	34	98	83	117	89	121
NEWSWEEK	(000)	19310	5475	7612	1910	4420	5642	3601	1206
NEWSWEEK	Resps	4718	1223	2179	485	1197	1195	886	264
NEWSWEEK	Index	100	73	198	94	102	95	121	115
NEW YORKER	(000)	2880	495	1638	358	579	689	687	197
NEW YORKER	Resps	1064	152	702	104	255	242	229	77
NEW YORKER	Index	100	44	286	118	90	78	155	127

Each file contains a cross-tabulation of data -- columns by rows. For example, consider the sample table shown above for three magazines broken down by the gender of the reader.

For each cell in the spreadsheet (a cell is defined as a row and column intersection) there are three pieces of information. The first number is identified by a row label of (000). This number is a projection based on the raw count for each cell and the total U.S. population. This lets marketers immediately project the Simmons sample values onto the total U.S population and thereby estimate total potential market size. In the example above, if the Simmons panel were projected onto all U.S. consumers there would be 2,939,000 readers of Architectural Digest, 3,410,000 readers of Hunting, and 4,237,000 readers of Mademoiselle magazines.

The population projections are not a simple matter of multipling the raw cell count by a constant. Instead, each respondent is assigned a weight that reflects their "representativeness" in the U.S. population as a whole (this relates to the probability of their selection in the first place). This weighting is a complex and proprietary procedure designed to provide the best possible population estimates. It is important to remember that because individual cases receive unique weights, two cells with the same raw count may have different population projection figure.

The second number listed is the actual number of respondents (out of a total of 22,051) that fit the characteristics defined by the column and row labels. In the sample above, the intersection of Architectural Digest and TOTAL shows a value of 883. This means that of the entire sample, 883 people reported that they are readers of Architectural Digest.

The last number -- the Index -- is extremely valuable for marketers because it tells them whether a particular consumer group is more or less likely than all members of a particular "universe" of consumers to consume a particular product (or product category). For example, if we are interested in magazine preferences we would consider all adult magazine readers as our universe. Each Simmons file identifies the universe of consumers that form the basis for these index values. The top-left most cell containing numerical information identifies the population base used in computing the index values in that spreadsheet (or portion of a spreadsheet when multiple bases are used).

For any breakdown defined by row labels -- say education of reader -- a value of 100 would mean that a particular group of consumers was no more or less likely to be a reader of, for example, Architectural Digest than the total universe (all adults). If you look at the intersection of Graduated College and Architectural Digest, you will see an index value of 242. This means that college graduates are 142% more likely (242 - 100) to be readers of Architectural Digest than all adult readers of the magazine. Similarly, high-school graduates are 48% less likely to be readers of Architectural Digest than all adult readers of the magazine.

The index values are always computed using the projected population values according to the following formula: The percentage value of each cell against the category listed in the column is computed. Then, the percentage value for the row total against the population base is computed. The index is arrived at by divifing the cell percentage by the row-total percentage and multipling the result by 100. For example, 3.8% of college graduates read Architectural Digest ((1414/37353) X 100 = 3.786). Readers of Architectural Digest represent 1.6% of the total population ((2939/187747) X 100 = 1.565). Dividing these values yields the cell index of 242 ((3.786/1.565) X 100 = 241.9).

Because the index values are a direct comparison of a market segment's behavior with a relevant universe of consumers, they provide extremely useful information for marketers. The index values are a particularly useful tool in defining market segments whose tastes, preferences, and past consumption behavior are particularly well-suited for a particular product or product category.

Since the data are in the form of a spreadsheet, students can be encouraged to manipulate the data themselves. For example, arriving at some of the solutions is greatly facilitated by computing percentages, while others become clear when averages are computed. Similarly, some exercises can be expanded, for example, by having students estimate market share by computing percentages for various product/segment breakdowns. Most files contain more data than needed to answer the specific questions asked in the exercises. This allows instructors to tailor the exercises to their own student needs.

The data disk also contains four Reference Files. Two of these datafiles contain media information: *Media1* provides information about magazine readership in terms of total audience for a large number of magazines. The datafile titled *Media2* provides information about radio-listening habits in terms of weekday 24-hour audience levels. Both files cross-tabulate the media information with a variety of demographic characteristics of the audiences.

The other two Reference Files contain psychographic characteristics cross-tabulated with the same demographic battery as used in the Media files. The datafile titled *Style* contains the Simmons Buying Style Inventory and the datafile titled *Self* contains the Simmons Self-Concept Inventory. For both measures, Simmons uses a five category response scale for each item in the inventory (Agree A Lot, Agree A Little, Not Sure, Disagree A Little, Disagree A Lot). The datafiles contain two categories of response - Agree (agree a lot OR agree a little) and Disagree (disagree a lot OR disagree a little). The Not Sure category of response has been omitted. The same form is used in each datafile that lists all or part of these inventories.

The solutions for the exercises appear on the following pages of this Instructor's Manual. For some exercises, especially those appearing early in the text, the solutions are relatively clear-cut. However, as the exercises become more complex, there will be more than one single correct answer. For the more complicated exercises, the solutions provided should be treated as suggested, but not as exhaustive, solutions. In all cases, instructors have been provided with enough detail in the solutions to evaluate performance and to provide guidelines for students.

CHAPTER 1: MAGAZINE READERS

Although the data file contains information about household income and marital status, it is really age of the reader that discriminates among the various magazines listed in the exercise. This is a good exercise for introducing students to the use of the Simmons index values. Since the emphasis of the exercise is on men's vs. women's magazines, the data tables are provided in two sections: each section uses a different population base (so the "male" section uses only males as the base, and likewise for the "female" section). The following table of index values is taken from the data file for Chapter 1.

Women's Magazines

Age	Better Homes & Gardens	Elle	Glamour	Harper's Bazaar	Mademoiselle	Self	Seventeen
18-22	55	398	277	126	366	158	443
(%female)	(83%)	(98%)	(96%)	(70%)	(99%)	(90%)	(98%)
25-34	94	134	151	124	131	123	102
35-44	116	67	88	113	91	88	45

Since the index values are computed on separate population bases, index values should be compared within gender group. For example, the index value of 398 for 18-22 year-old readers of Elle means 18-22 year-old women are 298% more likely to be readers of Elle, than all adult readers of Elle. (8.84% of 18-22 year-old women read Elle, and 2.22% of all adult women read Elle: (8.84/2.22)*100 = 398). 18-22 year-old women are a heavy readership group for Elle, Glamour, Mademoiselle, and Seventeen. Readership figures by age of reader show that readership for these magazines drops off with increasing age. This illustrates the distinctive appeal that they have for particular age groups. In contrast, the readership by age pattern is stable for Harper's Bazaar, while the popularity of Better Homes and Gardens grows for older reader groups.

Men's Magazines

Age	Car & Driver	Gentleman's Quarterly	Motor Trend	Penthouse	Playboy	Road & Track	Sports Illustrated
18-22	257	225	264	182	162	289	169
(%male)	(99%)	(62%)	(94%)	(93%)	(93%)	(96%)	(85%)
25-34	114	156	100	146	148	120	120
35-44	110	93	85	87	100	103	69

The percentage values are computed against the total readership among 18-22 year-olds for each magazine. All values are computed using population projections.

The second part of this exercise can be used to sensitize students to the limitations of using single demographic characteristics. Clearly, magazines such as Bride & Your New Home are very popular in the 18-22 year-old group because many people not in college are marrying at this age. So, age alone would not be very helpful in understanding the difference between a reader of Seventeen and the reader of Bride & Your New Home.

This exercise can be expanded by having students refer to the MEDIA1 datafile, which contains additional demographic information as well as additional magazines. The MEDIA1 datafile contains three population base tables -- ALL ADULTS, MALES ONLY, and FEMALES ONLY.

CHAPTER 2: PERSONAL FRAGRANCES

For this datafile, consumer characteristics are in the rows and product/brand selections are in the columns. In response to the first question concerning the most likely demographic characteristics that would describe Gary, the Simmons Index values are appropriate. These values indicate the likelihood that a consumer of a particular brand falls into a particular demographic category. Thus, of all Drakkar Noir users, 18-24 year-old men are 378% more likely to use the product than all adult men. Gary is also likely to be a single (index = 394), college graduate (index = 221). The same conclusions can be reached through computation of the appropriate percentage values.

The second part of the exercise asks students to use Gary's profile to "pick" a likely scent for Janeen. In this case, the demographic characteristics are fixed and so the question is a bit different than for the first part. The appropriate base for the percentage computations is the total number of 18-24 year-old women in the population 11,903,000. Thus, the three most popular perfumes for women in this age group are Eternity (7%), Obsession (9%), and Poison (5%).

The last question asks students to relate choice of fragrance to the personal views of consumers. Although this is relevant to the vignette at the beginning of the chapter, some instructors may feel that it is too far beyond the scope of the present chapter, and may, therefore, choose to omit this portion.

Again, using Gary as the "benchmark," the following profile would result (as hinted in the exercise, the following take only those personal views endorsed by more than 25% of Drakkar Noir users):

Personal View	Drakkar Noir	Eternity	Obsession	Poison
I am a workaholic	36%	31%	32%	27%
I keep up with new developments in technology.	57%	37%	46%	49%
I like to keep up with the latest fashions.	45%	57%	59%	54%

CHAPTER 3: MUSICAL NOSTALGIA

Students should generate some subset of the information contained in the following table. Classic rock and golden oldies formats typically cover music from the late fifties through the sixties (and sometimes beyond). Similarly album-oriented rock stations often give heavy play to music from the sixties on. There is some evidence of a "nostalgia" effect for golden oldies, less so for classic rock and album-oriented rock formats.

The values in the table also illustrate the growing importance of other formats with increasing age of the listener: all-news, news/talk all increase in appeal with age. In contrast, the contemporary hit format shows a sharp decrease in appeal with age as does album-oriented rock.

Radio Format		18-24	25-34	35-44	45-54
Album-oriented rock	Males	313	217	140	44
	Females	159	133	61	25
Classic rock	Males	218	240	137	68
	Females	138	115	110	32
Contemporary hit rock	Males	210	129	83	60
	Females	307	158	104	56
Country	Males	100	105	109	132
	Females	138	107	92	115
Golden Oldies	Males	70	80	191	148
	Females	62	89	170	105
All News	Males	45	66	100	146
	Females	86	70	77	128
News/Talk	Males	46	83	113	169
	Females	10	40	73	113

Considering the importance that popular music has for many college students, an interesting discussion can be generated by asking students whether or not they think that their own interests in music will wane as they grow older and why.

CHAPTER 6: ATTITUDES AND BEHAVIOR

● Although this exercise is assigned for Chapter 6, it draws upon material that students have studied in Chapter 5 as well. The emphasis of the questions is on attitude-behavior consistency. The Simmons datafile contains items from the Buying Style inventory - these tap attitudes that should be very relevant to their shopping behavior. Two questions in particular relate to the environment: The first is labeled ECOLOGIST - consumers either agree or disagree with the statement "All products that pollute the environment should be banned." Of all adult consumers, 47% agree with this statement. The second item is labeled ENVIRONMENTALIST - the statement associated with this item is "I buy paper products (napkins, towels, toilet paper, etc.) that are recycled." 50% of all adult consumers agree with this statement.

Several environmentally sensitive products are listed in the datafile, e.g., disposable cups, plates, diapers, razors, insecticides, insect repellents, and so on. The index values for all of these are quite close to 100. Thus, roughly one-half of all users of these products endorse the ECOLOGIST and ENVIRONMENTALIST attitude statements.

Other items in the Buying Style inventory can be used to stimulate discussion concerning when measures of consumer attitudes should/should not predict behavior.

● The exercise can be expanded further by having students use the Simmons datafile entitled STYLE to generate a demographic profile of consumers who endorse a pro-environment attitude position.

CHAPTER 7: SELF-CONCEPT AND BUYING STYLE

Instructors can easily expand this exercise to include analyses of the demographic characteristics associated with different self-concept profiles (and/or buying styles) by having students use the STYLE and SELF datafiles. These files cross-tabulate the Self-Concept and Buying Style inventories with a variety of demographic characteristics.

The exercise asks students to identify the self-concept dimensions that differentiate six different buying style groups. Instructors will find it helpful to insert additional rows in their own spreadsheets that calculate percentages for each Self-Concept item. The most appropriate way to do this (given the questions) is to use each cell's population projection and then use the total population projection for that row as the base. For example, 45,561 (000) adults identify themselves as AD BELIEVERS. Of these, 38,771 (000), or 85% agree that they are also affectionate, passionate, loving. Formulas can easily be copied across rows. Then, at the base of each section of the table (agree vs. disagree) two additional rows can be inserted to identify minima and maxima for each Self-Concept item. The results quickly identify the Self-Concept items that differentiate most among buying styles.

One possible solution (using a minimum of a 10% difference) is the following:

Egocentrism (egocentric, vain, self-centered, narcissistic) most separates CONFORMISTS (31%) from ECONOMY MINDED buyers (19%).

Tenseness (tense, nervous, high-strung, excitable) most separates EXPERIMENTERS (48%) from CAUTIOUS buyers (38%).

Not-tense (not tense, nervous, high-strung, excitable) also separates EXPERIMENTERS (33%) from PLANNERS (46%).

IMPULSIVES are not separated from any other group by 10 percentage points or more.

CHAPTER 10: HOGS AND RUBS

Students may use several approaches to answering the questions in this exercise. For the most part, the Simmons Index values can provide direct answers to the questions. The Index values in this file represent the likelihood that purchasers of a particular category of motorcycle fall into one or another of the demographic categories in the rows. However, the questions can also be answered with percentages computed within each column -- for example, percentages could be used to look at the distribution of Harley Davidson owners across the five social class categories.

Several rather sharp social class differences exist for ownership within this product category, among brands of motorcycles owned, and for size of motorcycle. Members of the upper (ISP I) and lower (ISP V)classes are less likely than others to own any motorcycles. Forty-four percent of all motorcycle owners are members of the upper lower class (ISP IV). For the other three social classes, upper middle (ISP II) and upper lower (ISP IV) classes are more likely to own larger motorcycles (1000 cc+), while members of the lower middle class (ISP III) are more likely to own mid-range motorcycles (650-999 cc). Similarly, there are some social class differences in brand preference as well (brand selections are based on index values greater than 110): upper middle class owners (ISP II) prefer Honda and Kawasaki, lower middle class owners (ISP III) prefer Honda, Suzuki, and Yamaha, and upper lower class owners (ISP IV) prefer BMW, Harley-Davidson, Kawasaki, and Suzuki.

There are also some interesting breakdowns by occupation. Five occupational categories are heavy consumers of motorcycles: Three of these are white collar categories - Technicians & Related Support Occupations (134), Manager/Administrators (144), and Proprietors (149). Two of the relevant occupation categories are skilled blue collar occupations - Crafts/Precision Production (141) and Operators/Fabricators (137). The last category is an unskilled blue collar occupation - Farm Labor (161).

Approximately 16% of all Harley-Davidson owners fall into these two skilled blue collar occupations and another 14% fall into the three white collar categories. This suggests that there are potentially two distinct sub-cultures of Harley-Davidson owners. Less than 1% of Harley-Davidson owners are unskilled farm laborers.

Finally, owners of motorcycles with engines of 1000 cc or more in displacement are more likely to fall into the two skilled blue collar categories than for either white collar or unskilled farm labor categories (index = 0 for this group).

CHAPTER 12: SOCIAL CLASS VERSUS INCOME

This exercise asks students to identify consumption patterns that are more or less sensitive to income as compared to social class differences. A simple way to find such patterns is to add several rows to your spreadsheet. One approach is to calculate the difference between the appropriate index values. For example, cell formulas could compute the index differences between ISP Class I and Class V, and other formulas could calculate the difference between high (say $150,000 - $249,999)and low ($10,000 - $19,999) income groups. Similarly, these computed values can be averaged within product category to further simplify the spreadsheet: This makes sense for all categories except sports and usage of alcoholic beverages. The solution provided below uses this approach. (Other approaches, such as average first differences between categories would also be informative).

Using differences in index values, purchases in the following categories are more sensitive to social class differences than to income differences (values are top to bottom category differences as specified above):

Product Category	ISP Difference	Income Difference
Cross-country skiing	142	83
Riding a stationary bicycle	120	77
Financial services	85	34
Women's fragrances	-56	19
Tobacco Products	-59	-4

For the following, income differences are more important than social class differences.

Product Category	ISP Difference	Income Difference
Purchase wine/liquor by the case	49	136
Downhill skiing	105	182
Tennis	134	211
Stationary rowing	27	54
Using a stair machine	84	140

Income and social class are equally important for all other categories (note that among men's fragrances, Gray Flannel is a notable exception).

Instructors can expand this by using the last portion of the datafile, which presents social class and income cross-tabulated with political outlook.

CHAPTER 13: ETHNIC AND RELIGIOUS SUBCULTURES

Students can use the Simmons index values to respond to the questions posed in the exercise. The hint provided should direct students toward looking at both categories of Spanish language usage - exclusive use of Spanish versus a mix of Spanish and English spoken in the home. This distinction can be used to generate a discussion of the concept of acculturation.

Students are also asked to compare Hispanic consumers with Asian-Americans. Instructors can expand this part of the exercise to include the other racial and language categories contained in the datafile. In addition, other product categories are provided that can be assigned and then used in class discussion. For example, there has been much controversy over the marketing of cigarettes in the Hispanic and African-American communities. Data are provided concerning usage of tobacco products.

The following table of index values provides a solution to the questions posed in the exercise:

	Only Spanish spoken	Spanish & English	Asian-Americans
Locale-Urban	208	164	154
Politics- Very Conservative	102	81	92
Very Liberal	323	129	104
Soap Operas- Another World	36	124	5
Days of Other Lives	154	106	11
Prime Time- BH-90210	61	167	171
In Living Colour	134	564	91
Home Improv.	441	86	81
Melrose Place	130	285	52
Murphy Brown	141	77	243

This datafile also contains a panel that cross-tabulated these consumption, media, and demographic variables against religion. Instructors can pose numerous additional questions that relate to religious affiliation.

CHAPTER 15: MUSICAL TASTE AND RETAIL STORE USAGE

The Simmons datafile for this chapter contains information about retail store usage and it cross-tabulates this with consumers' radio format preferences.

Students are encouraged to apply a criterion value of 150 in selecting retail stores for each musical preference group.   This indicates that shoppers in those stores selected are more than 50% more likely to listen to the radio format category that students are asked to describe. The following patterns are found in the datafile for each musical preference group:

Shopping at Bloomingdale's, Dayton's, and Marshall Fields goes along with a taste for classical music.

Shopping at Ann Taylor, Banana Republic, Benetton, Bloomingdale's, Dayton's, Dillard's, Lord & Taylor, Macy's, I. Magnin, Marshall Field's, Nordstrom's and Saks Fifth Avenue goes along with easy listening music. (Considering the number of different stores shopped at by this group, they may be the heaviest shopping group.)

Shopping at Service Merchandise, Woolworths, and Montgomery Ward's goes along with listening to ethnic radio.

Jazz relates to shopping at Bloomingdale's and Dayton's.

Contemporary Hit/Rock listeners are likely shoppers at Banana Republic and The Gap.

Rhythm & Blues relates to shopping at Banana Republic, Benetton, Dayton's, Marshall Fields, and Montgomery Wards.

This exercise can be expanded by having students examine the demographics associated with each radio format and relate this to store usage. The applied ramifications for retail store advertising can also be discussed.

CHAPTER 17: CONSUMERS ON THE ROAD -- TRAVEL PATTERNS OF AMERICAN CONSUMERS

The first part of the exercise asks students to examine theme parks and cruise-ship vacations. The sharpest distinction here is that families with one to three children are most likely to travel to theme parks, while cruises tend to appeal more to those with no children. Both destinations are more popular among college educated consumers, than other educational groups. The differences in these two forms of vacation are sharpest for ISP Class I (in favor of cruise-ship vacations) and are nearly equivalent among middle-class consumers (ISP Class III).

There are also much sharper differences among the social classes for foreign as compared to domestic travel destinations.

As family size increases, consumers are less likely to combine business and pleasure trips to foreign as well as domestic destinations. Similarly, they are less likely to travel for vacations to foreign destinations as family size increases, but travel to domestic destinations stays relatively stable as family size increases.

More highly educated consumers are more likely to travel for all categories of business, as are consumers of higher social class status.

Table of Contents
Transparency Masters
created and designed by
Lewis Hershey
for
Consumer Behavior, 3rd Edition
by
Michael R. Solomon

Defining Consumer Behavior

Definition

Consumer behavior is the process involved when individuals or groups select, use, or dispose of products, services, or experiences to satisfy needs and desires.

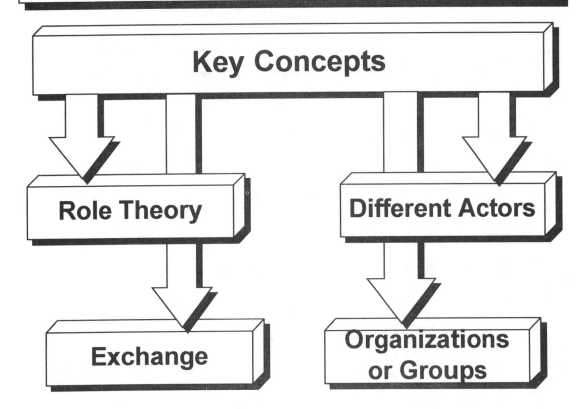

Key Concepts

Role Theory

Different Actors

Exchange

Organizations or Groups

Target Marketing

Steps in Targeted Marketing Strategy

1. Define the Market

2. Analyze Potential Customers

3. Identify Bases for Segmentation

4. Develop Segment Profiles

5. Analyze Competitor's Positions

6. Evaluate Market Segments

7. Select Market Segments

8. Finalize the Marketing Mix

Market Segmentation

Criteria For Identifying Market Segments

☞ **Are consumers within the segment similar in terms of product needs?**

☞ **Can important differences among segments be identified?**

☞ **Is the segment large enough to be profitable?**

☞ **Can the segment be reached by an appropriate marketing mix?**

☞ **Will the segment respond as desired?**

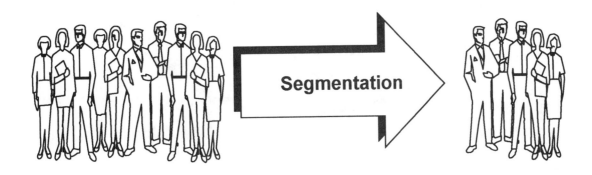

Segmentation

Marketing Impact on Consumers

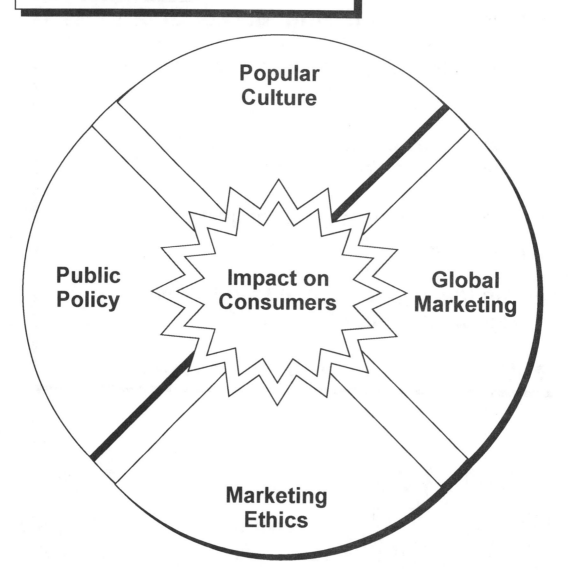

Interdisciplinary Influences

Individual Focus

Experimental Psychology
Clinical Psychology
Developmental Psychology
Human Ecology
Microeconomics
Social Psychology
Sociology
Macroeconomics
Semiotics/Literary Criticism
Demography
History
Cultural Anthropology

Social Focus

Perspectives on Consumer Research

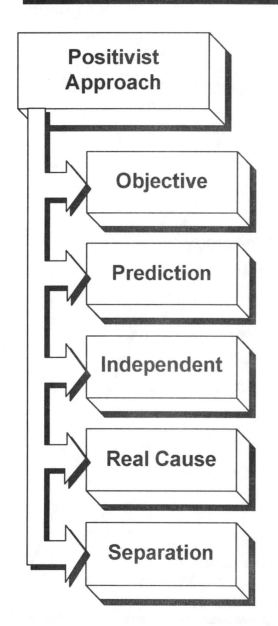

Positivist Approach

- Objective
- Prediction
- Independent
- Real Cause
- Separation

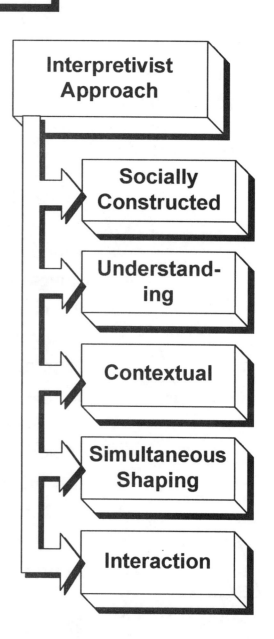

Interpretivist Approach

- Socially Constructed
- Understanding
- Contextual
- Simultaneous Shaping
- Interaction

Exploratory Research

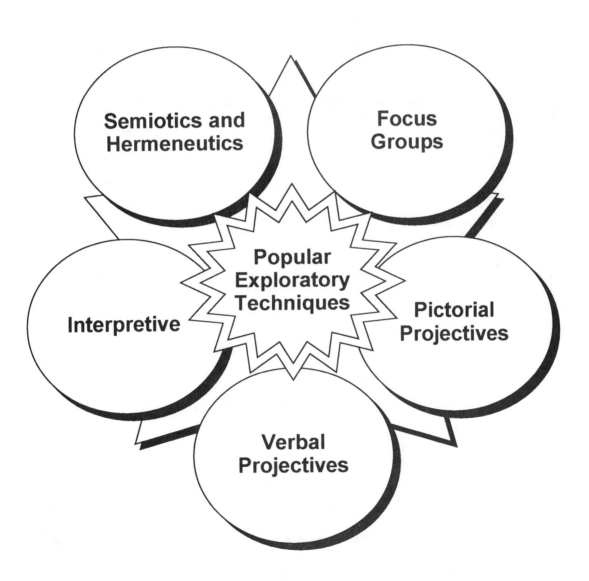

Popular Exploratory Techniques

- Semiotics and Hermeneutics
- Focus Groups
- Interpretive
- Pictorial Projectives
- Verbal Projectives

Problem-Solving Research

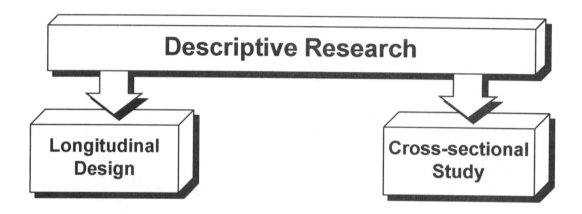

Descriptive Research

- Longitudinal Design
- Cross-sectional Study

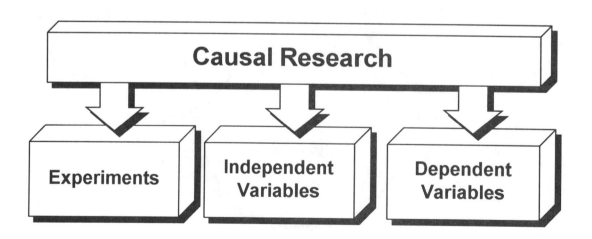

Causal Research

- Experiments
- Independent Variables
- Dependent Variables

Types of Data

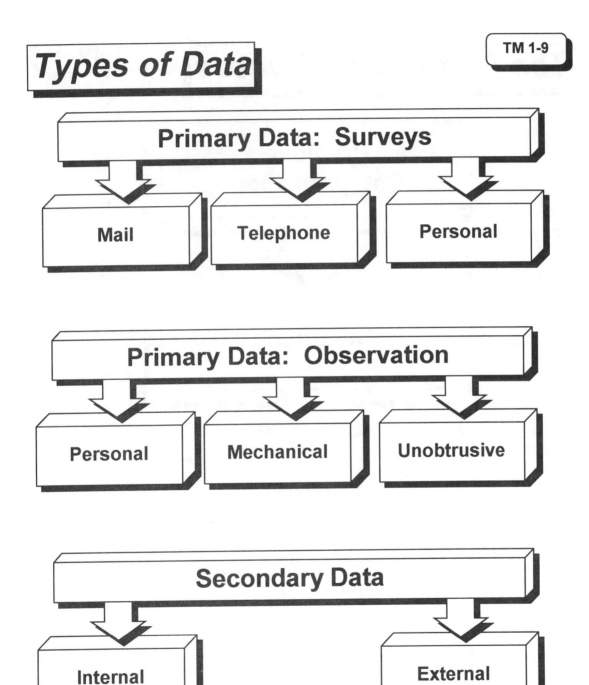

Primary Data: Surveys

- Mail
- Telephone
- Personal

Primary Data: Observation

- Personal
- Mechanical
- Unobtrusive

Secondary Data

- Internal
- External

The Perceptual Process

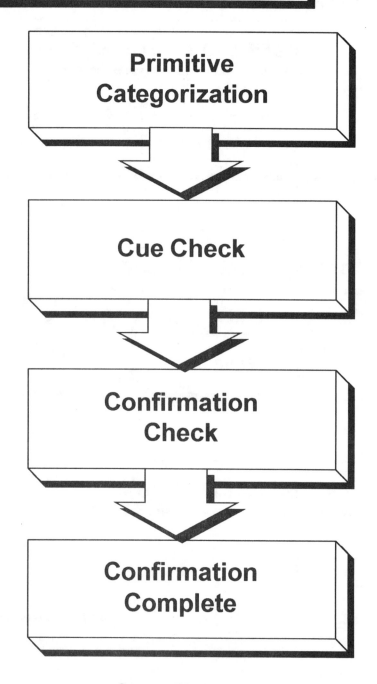

Primitive Categorization

Cue Check

Confirmation Check

Confirmation Complete

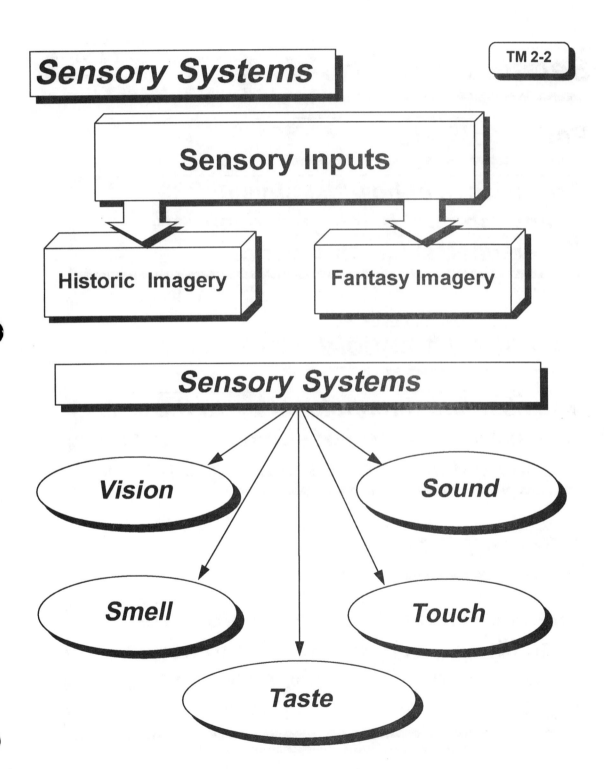

TM 2-2

Sensory Systems

Sensory Inputs

Historic Imagery

Fantasy Imagery

Sensory Systems

Vision

Sound

Smell

Touch

Taste

Sensory Thresholds

Psychophysics

The science of how the physical environment is integrated into our personal, subjective world.

Absolute Threshold

The absolute threshold refers to the minimum amount of stimulation that can be detected on a sensory channel.

Differential Threshold

The differential threshold refers to the ability of a sensory system to detect changes or differences between two stimuli.

Subliminal Persuasion

Subliminal Perception

Subliminal Perception Occurs When The Stimulus Is Below The Level Of The Consumer's Awareness.

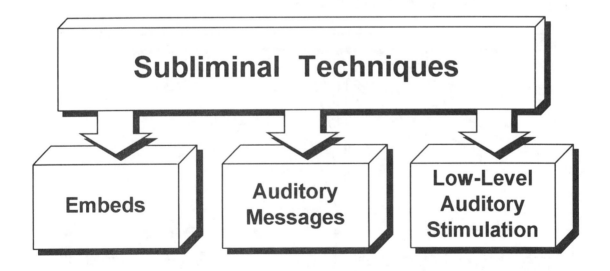

Subliminal Techniques

| Embeds | Auditory Messages | Low-Level Auditory Stimulation |

Evaluating Subliminal Techniques

Threshold Differences

Distance and Position Control

Subliminal Marketing ??

Viewing Attention Control

Generalized Effect

Exposure and Adaptation

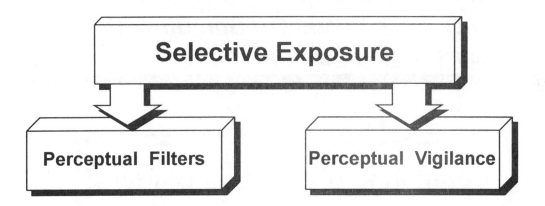

Selective Exposure

Perceptual Filters

Perceptual Vigilance

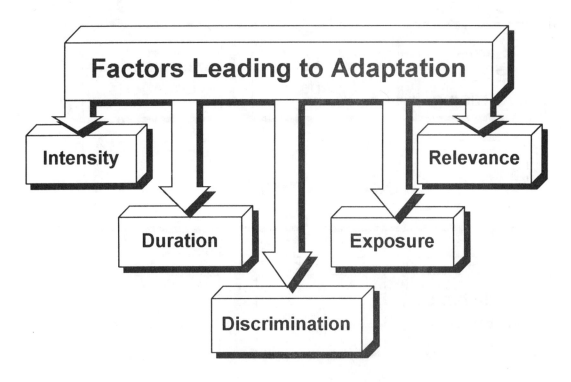

Factors Leading to Adaptation

Intensity

Duration

Discrimination

Exposure

Relevance

Attention

Attention Is The Degree To Which Consumers Focus On Stimuli Within Their Range of Exposure.

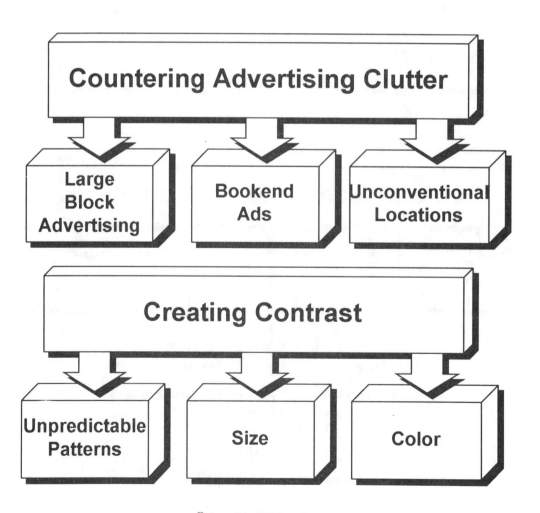

Countering Advertising Clutter

- **Large Block Advertising**
- **Bookend Ads**
- **Unconventional Locations**

Creating Contrast

- **Unpredictable Patterns**
- **Size**
- **Color**

Interpretation

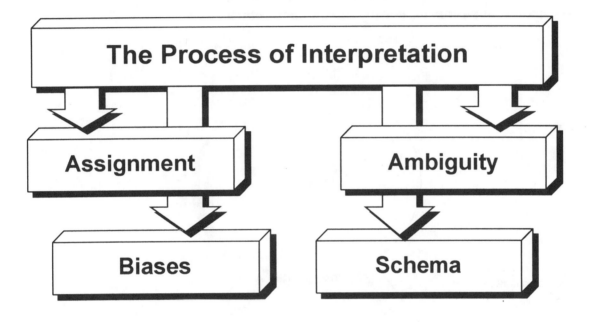

The Process of Interpretation

Assignment

Ambiguity

Biases

Schema

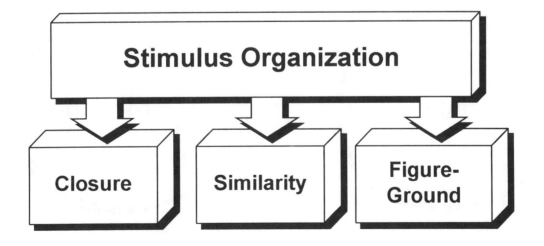

Stimulus Organization

Closure

Similarity

Figure-Ground

Symbolism in Marketing Messages

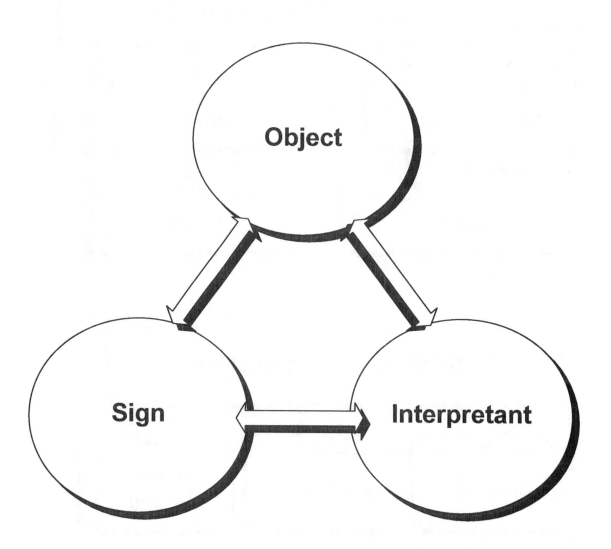

Semiotics

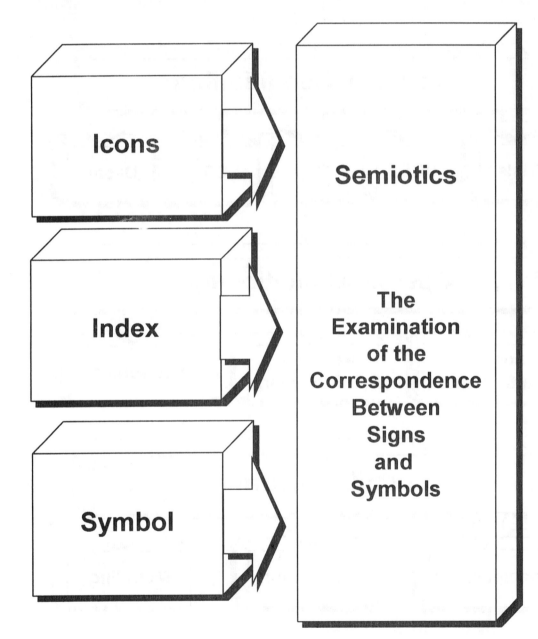

Icons

Index

Symbol

Semiotics

The Examination of the Correspondence Between Signs and Symbols

The Learning Process

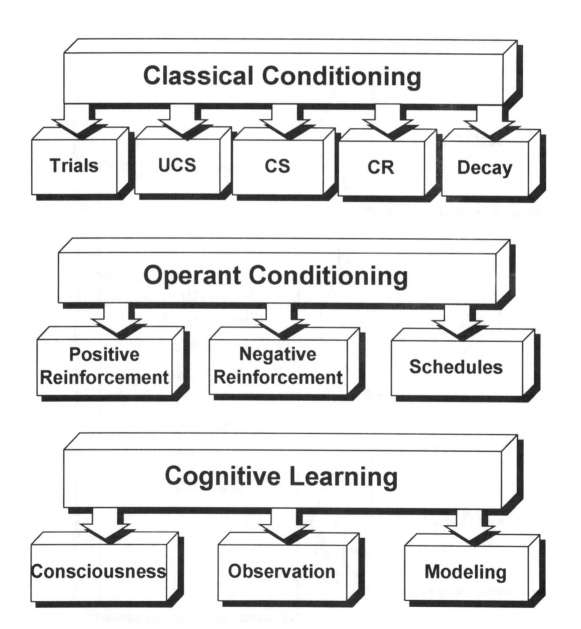

Classical Conditioning

| Trials | UCS | CS | CR | Decay |

Operant Conditioning

| Positive Reinforcement | Negative Reinforcement | Schedules |

Cognitive Learning

| Consciousness | Observation | Modeling |

Marketing Applications

Using Classical Conditioning

Repetition

Product Associations

Stimulus Generalization

| Family Branding | Line Extensions | Licensing | Look-Alike Packaging |

Stimulus Discrimination

Instrumental

Modeling

Other Areas of Learning Theory Used by Marketers

The Memory Process

External Inputs

Encoding

Information is
Placed in Memory

Storage

Information
is Retained in Memory

Retrieval

Information Stored
in Memory is Found as Needed

Memory Systems

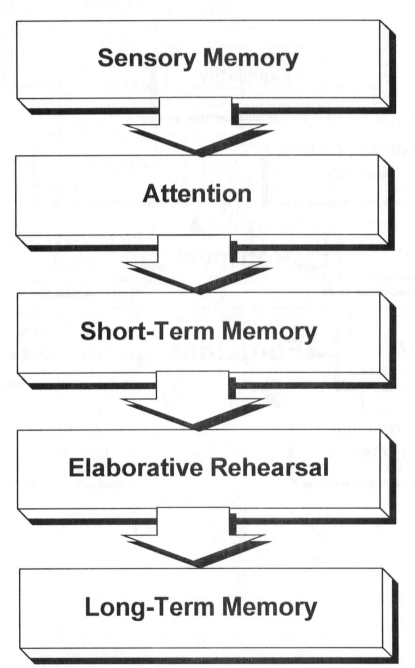

Sensory Memory

Attention

Short-Term Memory

Elaborative Rehearsal

Long-Term Memory

Retrieving Information

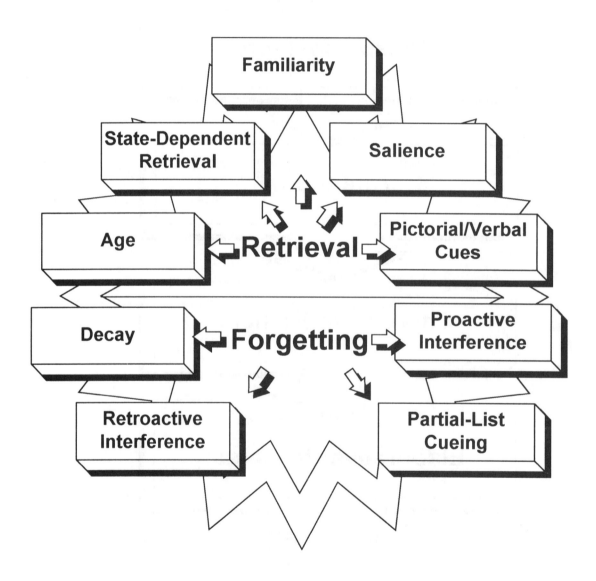

The Motivation Process

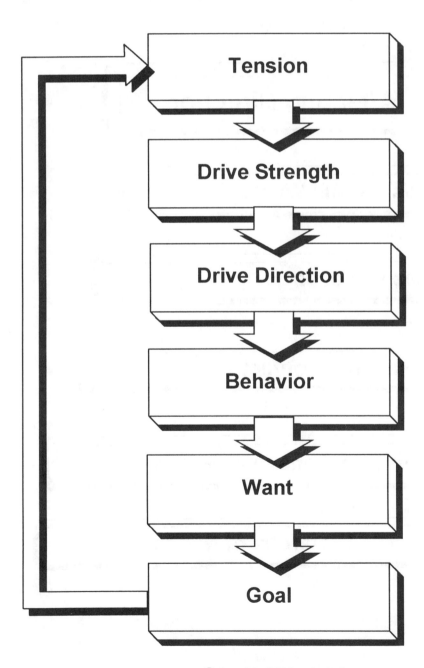

Tension → Drive Strength → Drive Direction → Behavior → Want → Goal

Motivational Direction

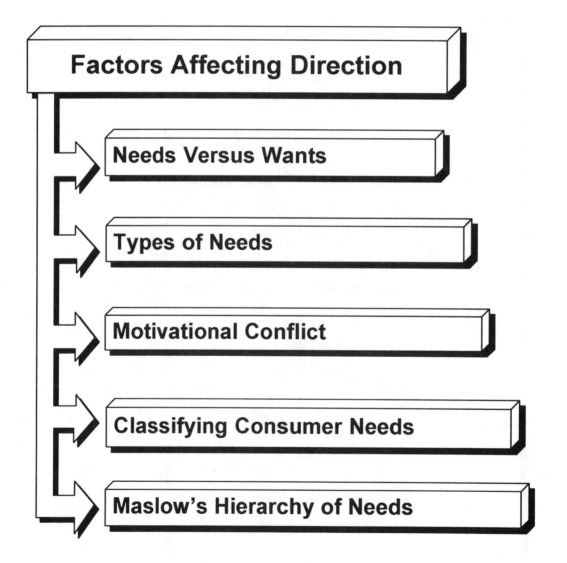

Factors Affecting Direction

- **Needs Versus Wants**
- **Types of Needs**
- **Motivational Conflict**
- **Classifying Consumer Needs**
- **Maslow's Hierarchy of Needs**

Maslow's Hierarchy

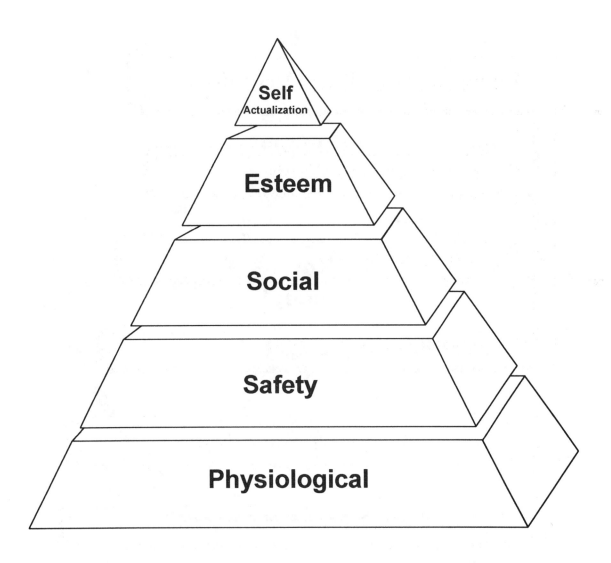

Freudian Theory

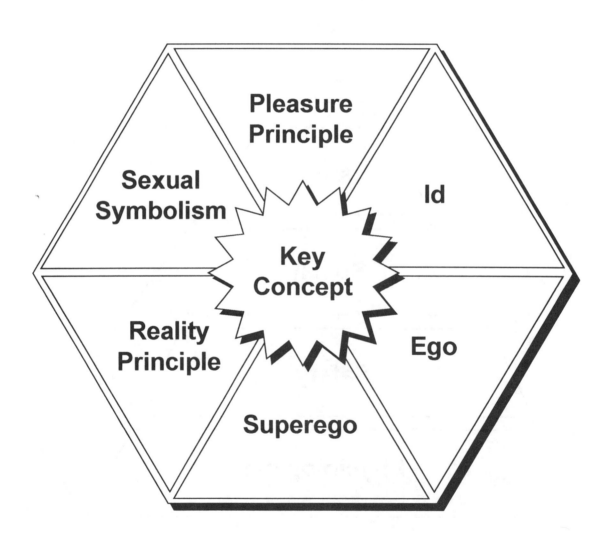

Pleasure Principle

Sexual Symbolism

Id

Key Concept

Reality Principle

Ego

Superego

Values

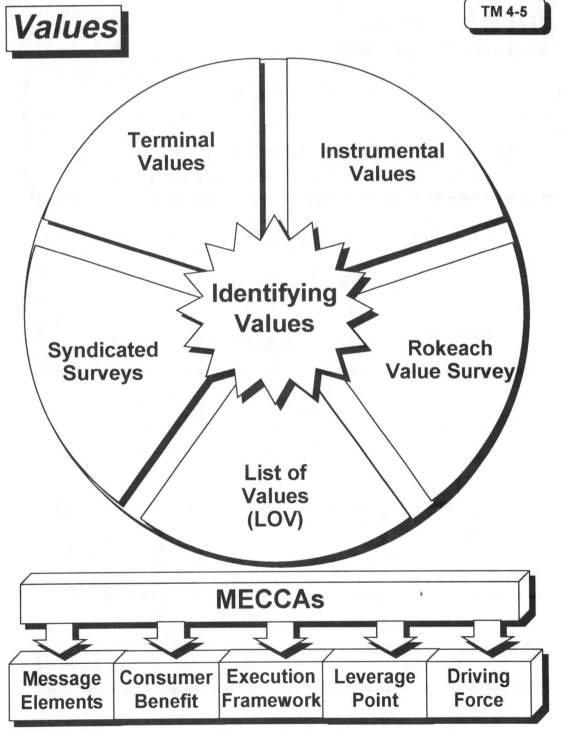

- Terminal Values
- Instrumental Values
- Identifying Values
- Syndicated Surveys
- Rokeach Value Survey
- List of Values (LOV)

MECCAs

Message Elements	Consumer Benefit	Execution Framework	Leverage Point	Driving Force

Involvement

Involvement

The Level of Perceived Personal Importance and/or Interest Evoked by a Stimulus

↓

—— **Involvement** ——

The Motivation to Process Information

↓

—— **Involvement** ——
Consumption Continuum

Simple Processing	Elaboration

Inertia	Passionate Intensity

Types of Involvement

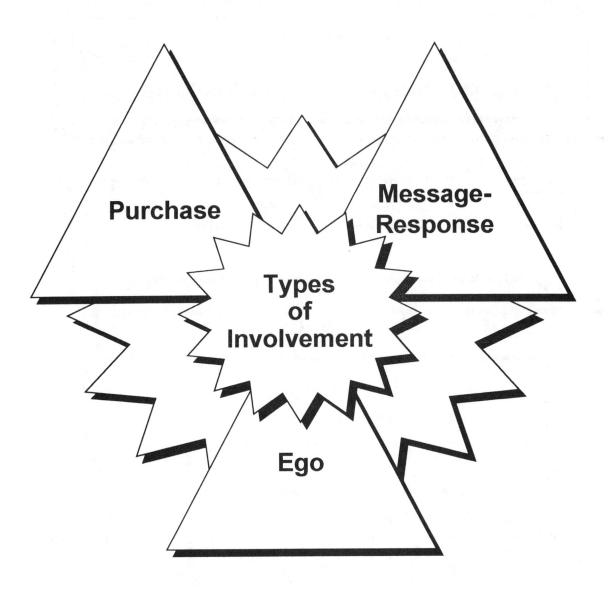

Purchase

Message-Response

Types of Involvement

Ego

Measuring Involvement

Components of Involvement

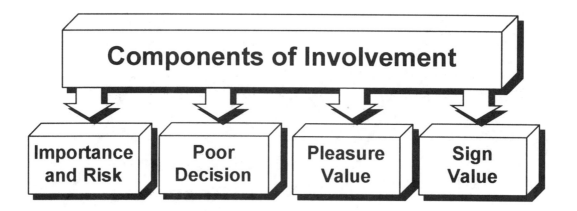

Importance and Risk	Poor Decision	Pleasure Value	Sign Value

Segmenting By Involvement

Strategies to Increase Involvement

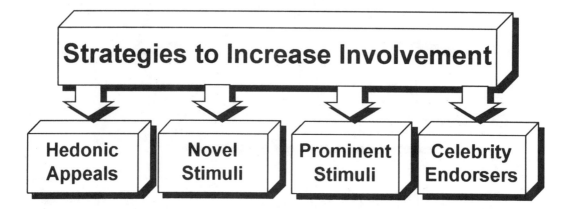

Hedonic Appeals	Novel Stimuli	Prominent Stimuli	Celebrity Endorsers

Attitudes

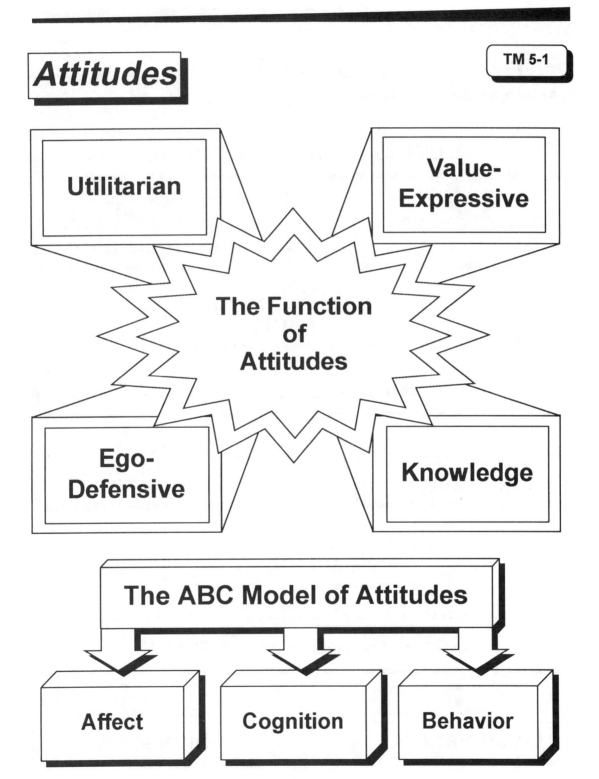

Utilitarian

Value-Expressive

The Function of Attitudes

Ego-Defensive

Knowledge

The ABC Model of Attitudes

Affect

Cognition

Behavior

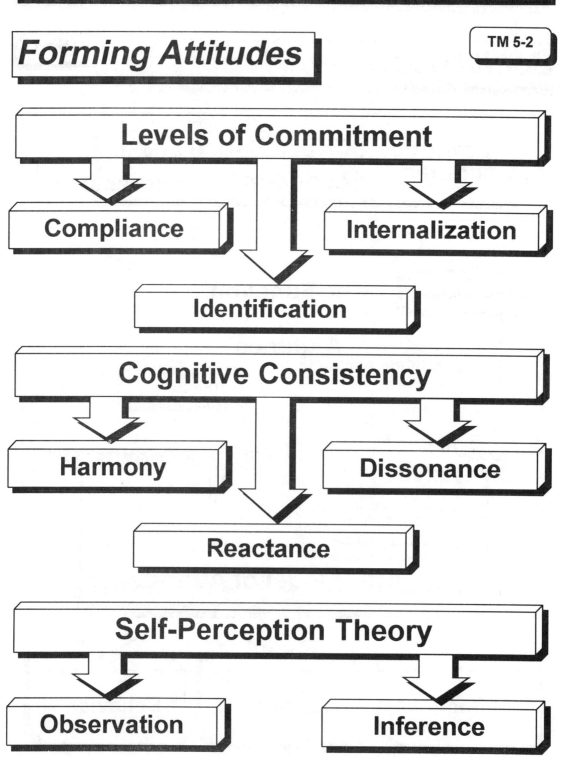

Forming Attitudes

Levels of Commitment

Compliance

Internalization

Identification

Cognitive Consistency

Harmony

Dissonance

Reactance

Self-Perception Theory

Observation

Inference

Social Judgment Theory

Latitudes of Acceptance and Rejection

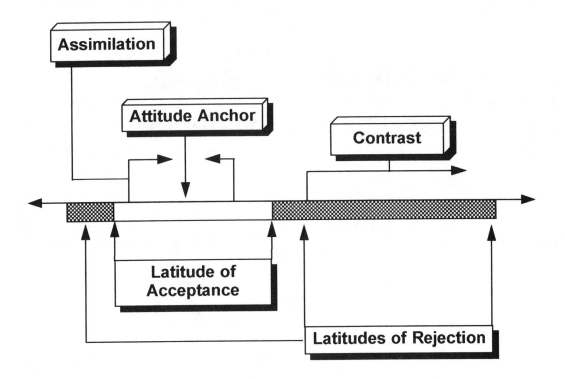

Assimilation

Attitude Anchor

Contrast

Latitude of Acceptance

Latitudes of Rejection

Multiattribute Models

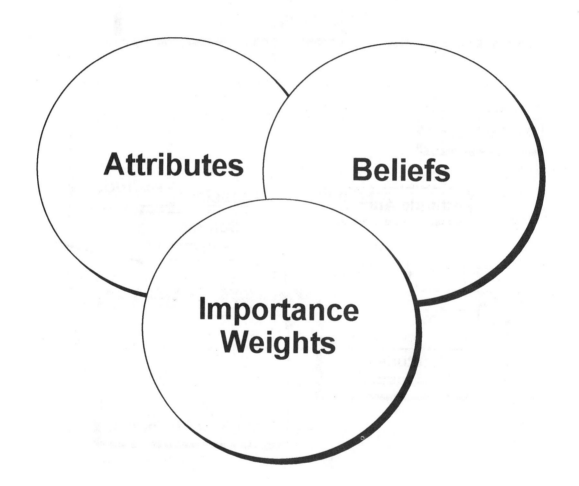

Attributes

Beliefs

Importance Weights

Predicting Behavior

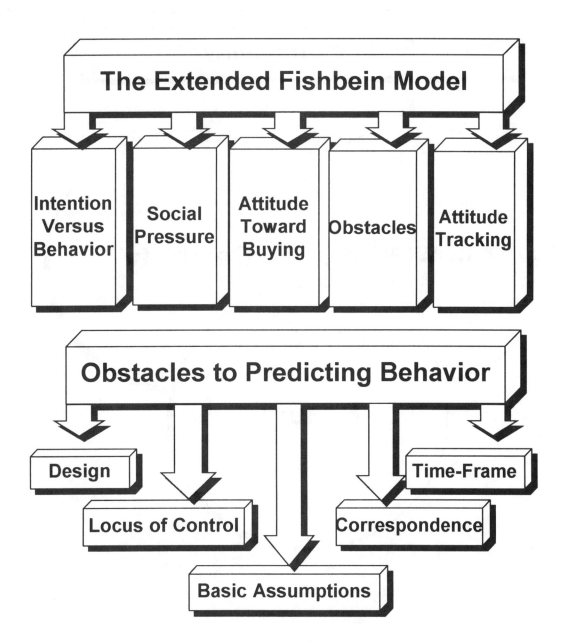

The Extended Fishbein Model

- Intention Versus Behavior
- Social Pressure
- Attitude Toward Buying
- Obstacles
- Attitude Tracking

Obstacles to Predicting Behavior

- Design
- Locus of Control
- Basic Assumptions
- Correspondence
- Time-Frame

Attitude Change

Source Credibility

Knowledge

Celebrity

Beauty

Communication Model

NO NOISE NOISE NOISE NOISE NOISE NOISE

Source

Encoding

Message

Transmission **Medium** **Feedback**

Receiver

Decoding

Feedback

NO NOISE NOISE NOISE NOISE NOISE NOISE

Message Elements

Words Versus Pictures

Message as Metaphor

Vividness

Factors Affecting Persuasiveness

Type of Appeal

Repetition

Argument

Message Appeals

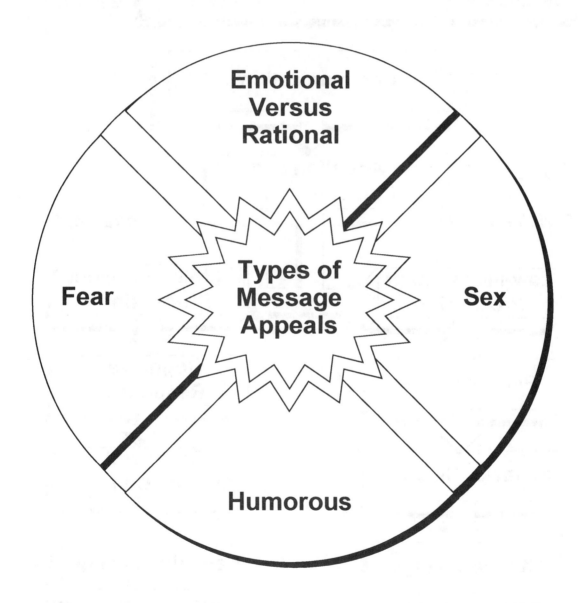

The Elaboration Likelihood Model

Communication

↓

Attention and Comprehension

Peripheral route   *Central route*

Low-Involvement Processing ⟷ **High-Involvement Processing**

↓   ↓

Belief Change   **Cognitive Response**

↓   ↓

Behavior Change   **Belief and Attitude Change**

↓   ↓

Attitude Change   **Behavior Change**

The Self Concept

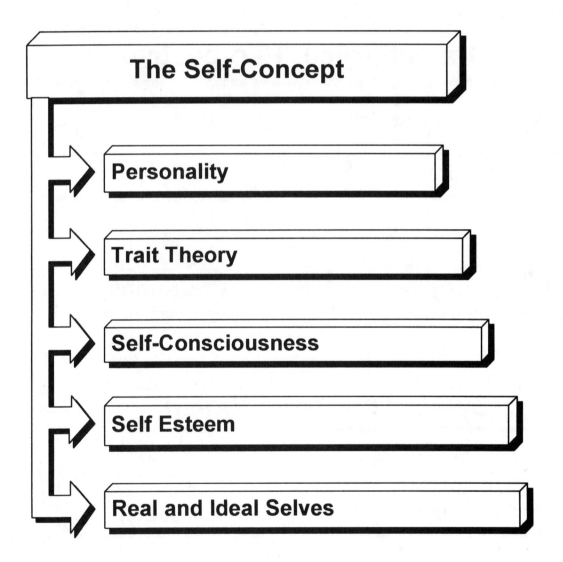

The Self-Concept

- Personality
- Trait Theory
- Self-Consciousness
- Self Esteem
- Real and Ideal Selves

Multiple Selves

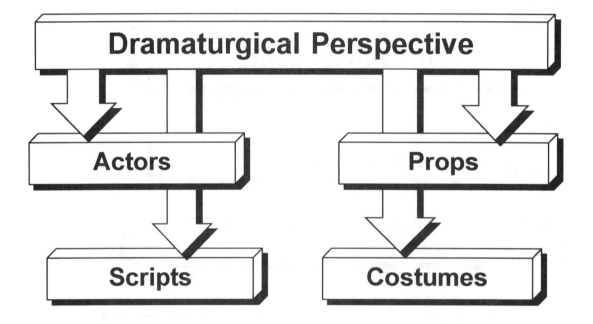

Dramaturgical Perspective

- Actors
- Props
- Scripts
- Costumes

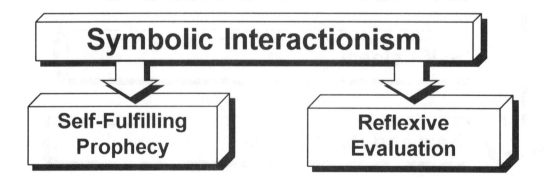

Symbolic Interactionism

- Self-Fulfilling Prophecy
- Reflexive Evaluation

Consumption and the Self-Concept

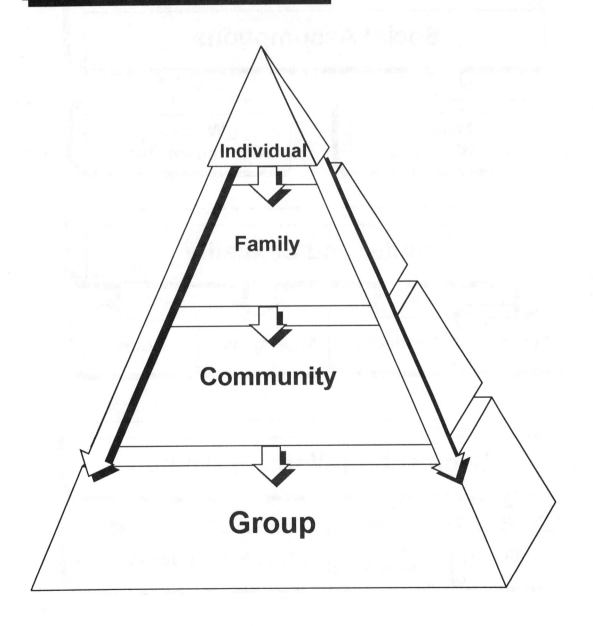

Individual

Family

Community

Group

Gender and Socialization

Social Assumptions

- Men: Agentic Goals
- Women: Communal Goals

Gender and Sexuality

- Traits
- Products
- Androgyny
- Roles

Segmenting Working Women

- Traditional
- Temporary Homemakers
- Careerists
- Just-a-Job

Body Image

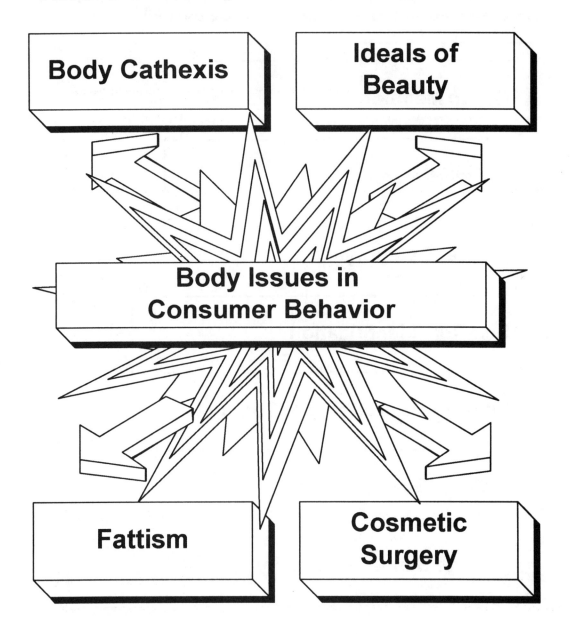

Body Cathexis

Ideals of Beauty

Body Issues in Consumer Behavior

Fattism

Cosmetic Surgery

Decoration and Mutilation

- Group Membership
- Social Hierarchy
- Gender Category
- Sex-Role Identification
- Indicate Desired Social Conduct
- Indicate Status or Rank
- Provide Sense of Security

Types of Consumer Decisions

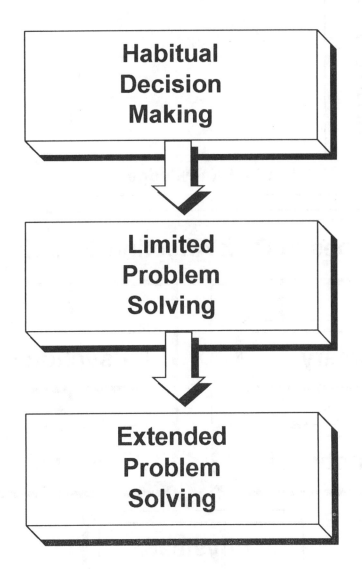

Habitual Decision Making

Limited Problem Solving

Extended Problem Solving

Information Search

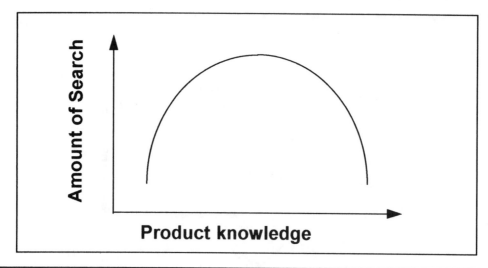

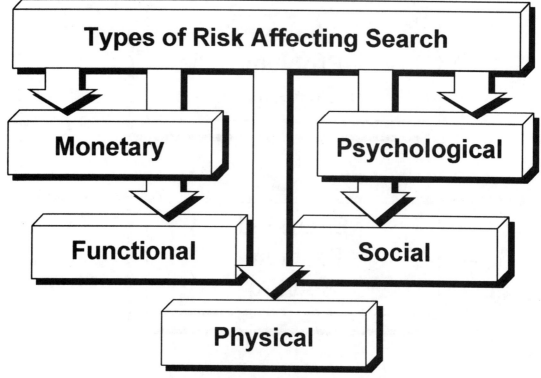

Evaluation of Alternatives

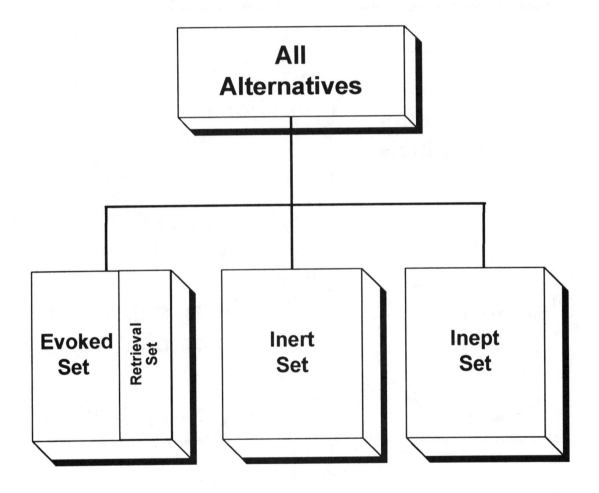

Strategic Implications of Product Categorization

- Locating Products
- Positioning and Repositioning
- Stimulating Interest
- Strategic Uses
- Defining Competitors
- Proto-typicality

Heuristics

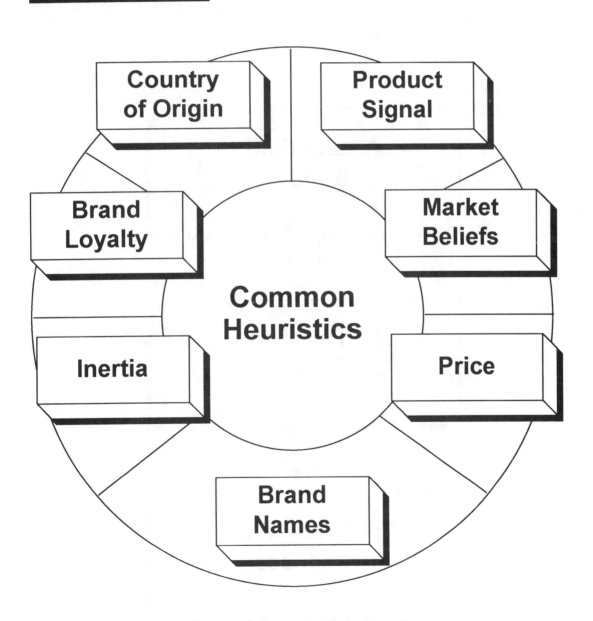

Common Heuristics

- Country of Origin
- Product Signal
- Brand Loyalty
- Market Beliefs
- Inertia
- Price
- Brand Names

Purchase Issues

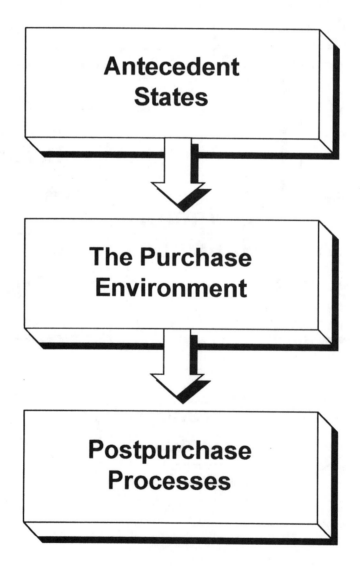

Antecedent States

The Purchase Environment

Postpurchase Processes

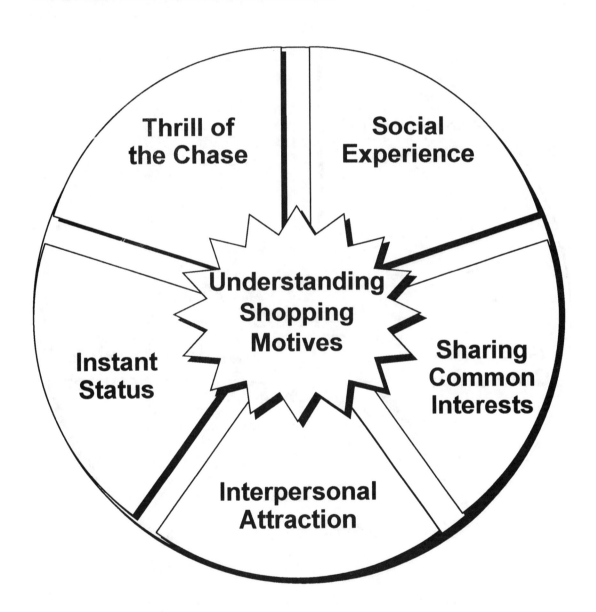

Shopping Motives

Thrill of the Chase

Social Experience

Understanding Shopping Motives

Instant Status

Sharing Common Interests

Interpersonal Attraction

Shopping Orientations

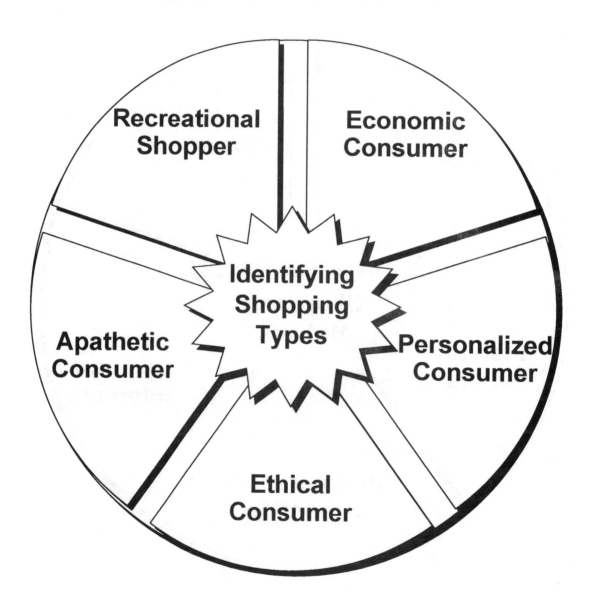

The Purchase Environment

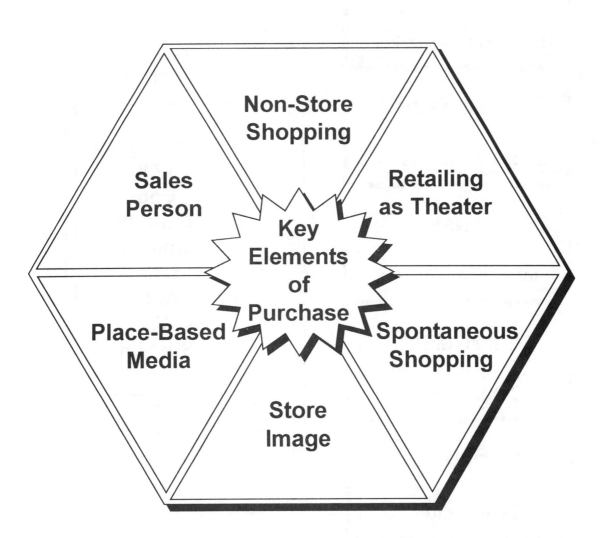

Key Elements of Purchase

- Non-Store Shopping
- Retailing as Theater
- Spontaneous Shopping
- Store Image
- Place-Based Media
- Sales Person

Relational Marketing

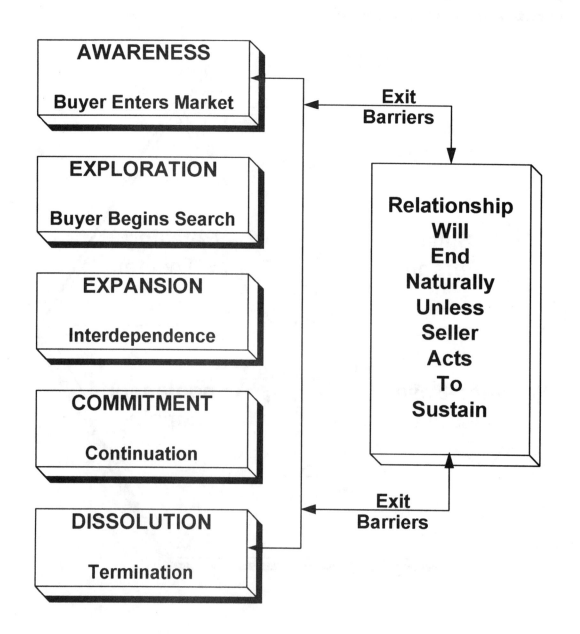

AWARENESS

Buyer Enters Market

EXPLORATION

Buyer Begins Search

EXPANSION

Interdependence

COMMITMENT

Continuation

DISSOLUTION

Termination

Exit
Barriers

Exit
Barriers

**Relationship
Will
End
Naturally
Unless
Seller
Acts
To
Sustain**

Postpurchase Satisfaction

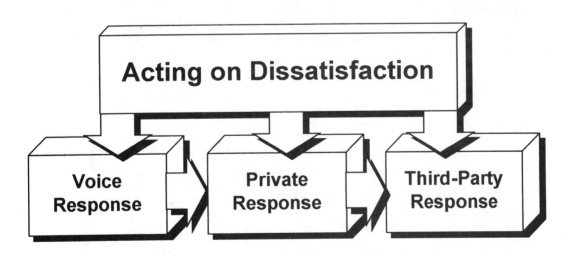

Perceptions of Product Quality

| Defining | Expectations | Importance |

Acting on Dissatisfaction

| Voice Response | Private Response | Third-Party Response |

Reference Groups

A reference group is an actual or imaginary individual or group conceived of having significant relevance upon an individual's evaluations, aspirations, or behavior.

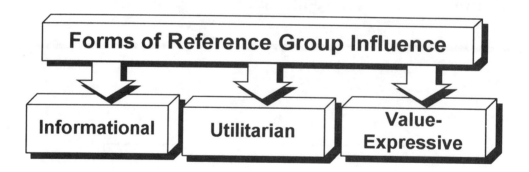

Forms of Reference Group Influence

| Informational | Utilitarian | Value-Expressive |

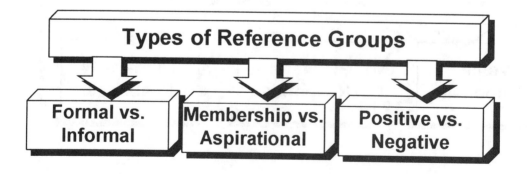

Types of Reference Groups

| Formal vs. Informal | Membership vs. Aspirational | Positive vs. Negative |

Reference Group Power

Conformity

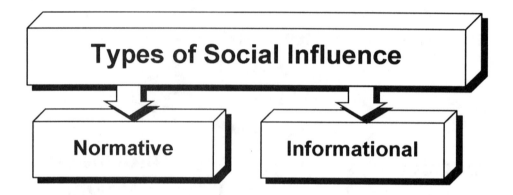

Types of Social Influence

Normative

Informational

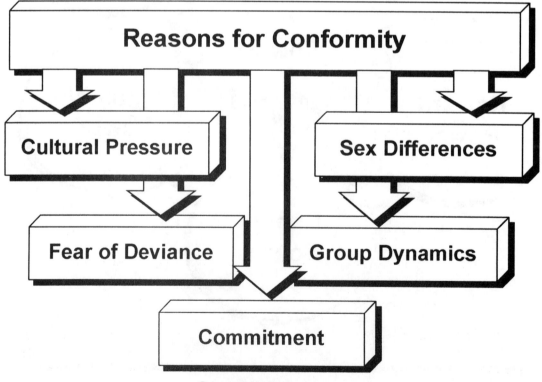

Reasons for Conformity

Cultural Pressure

Sex Differences

Fear of Deviance

Group Dynamics

Commitment

Social Influence

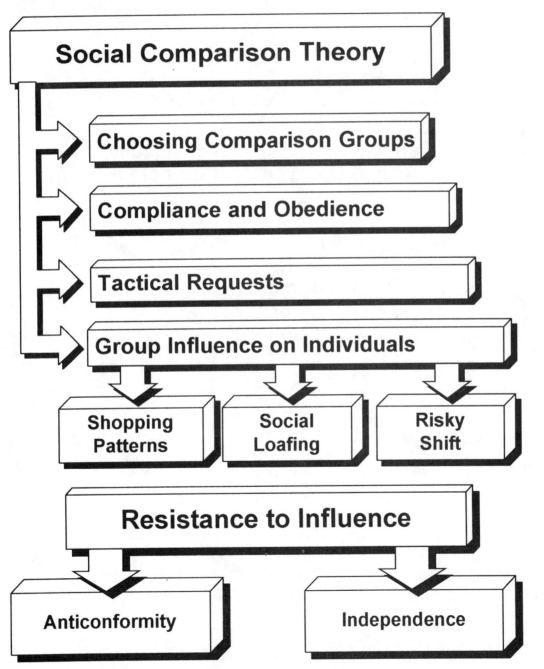

Social Comparison Theory

- **Choosing Comparison Groups**
- **Compliance and Obedience**
- **Tactical Requests**
- **Group Influence on Individuals**
  - Shopping Patterns
  - Social Loafing
  - Risky Shift

Resistance to Influence

- Anticonformity
- Independence

Opinion Leadership

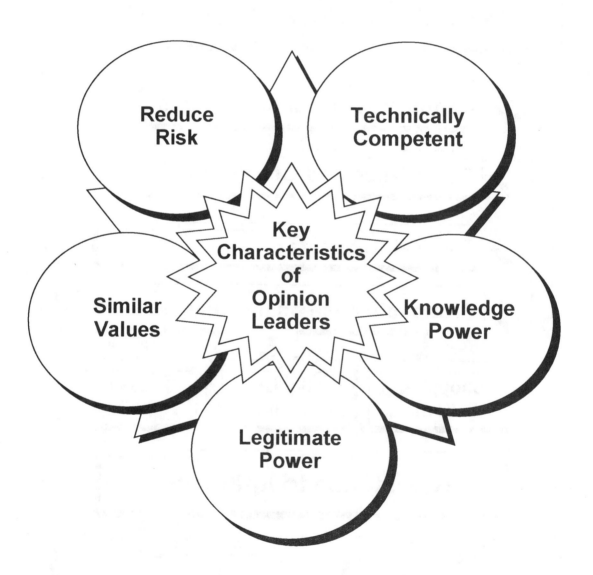

Diffusion of Innovations

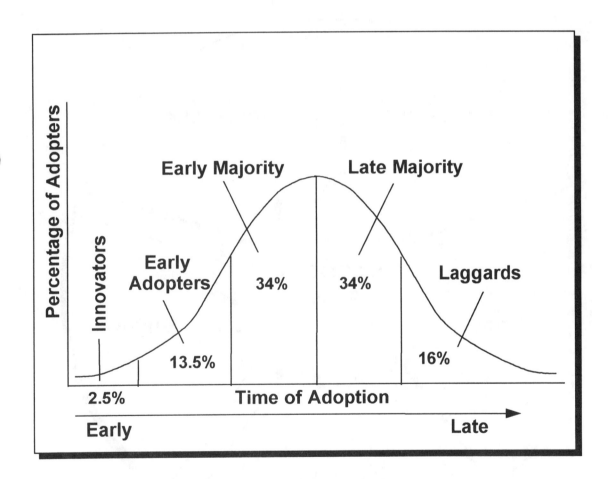

Organizational Buyer Behavior

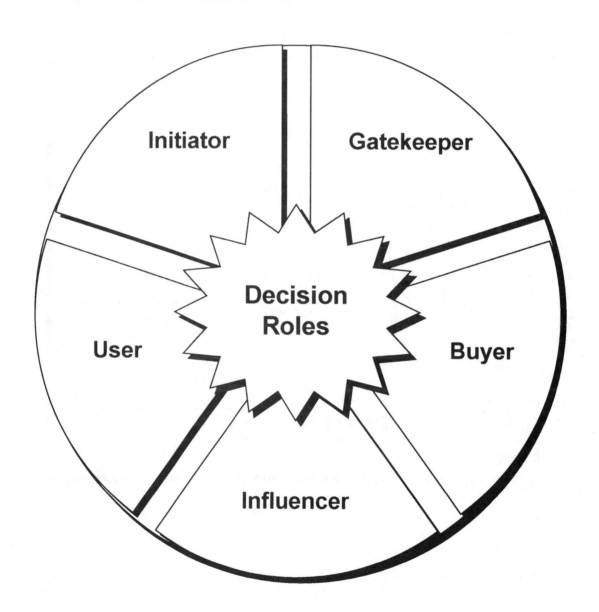

Defining the Modern Family

Describing the Family

Growth

Alternative Structure

Age

Composition

Sex

Factors Influencing Family Decisions

Sex-Roles

Socio-economic Status

Spousal Resources

Experience

Sources of Conflict

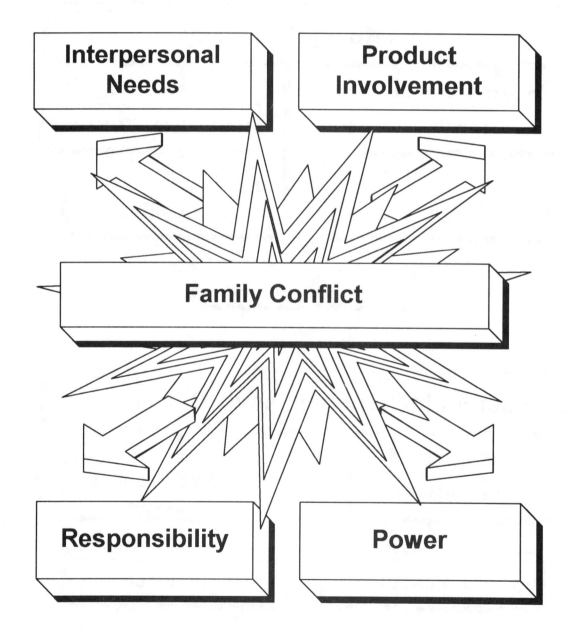

Interpersonal Needs

Product Involvement

Family Conflict

Responsibility

Power

Who Decides?

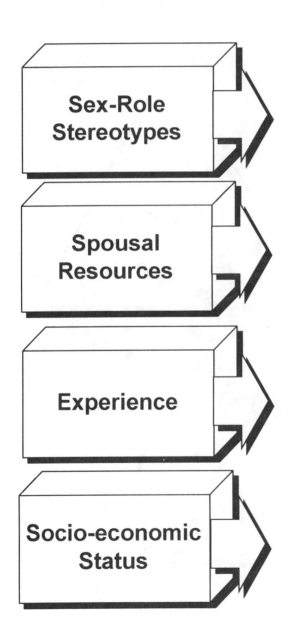

Sex-Role Stereotypes

Spousal Resources

Experience

Socio-economic Status

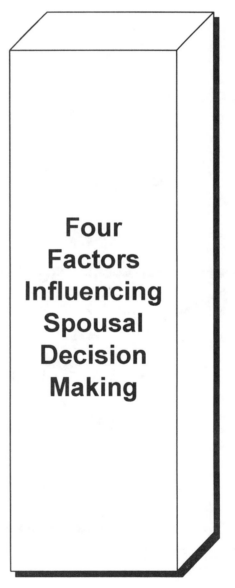

Four Factors Influencing Spousal Decision Making

Children Consumers

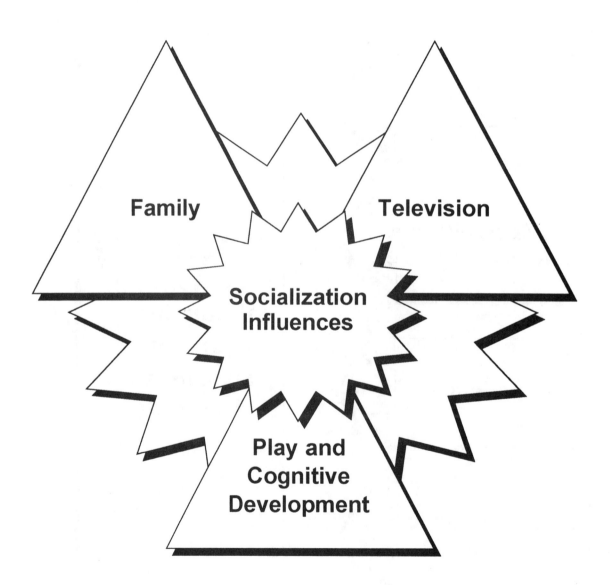

Family

Television

Socialization
Influences

Play and
Cognitive
Development

Social Class

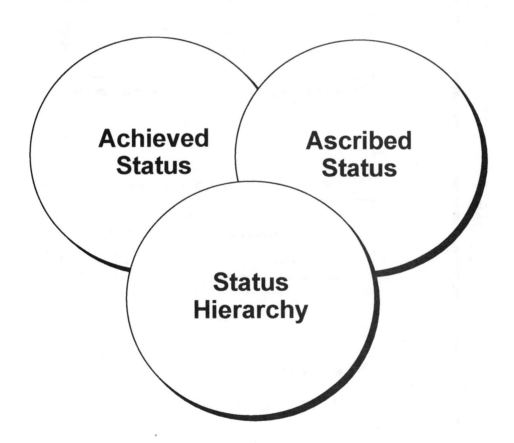

Class Structure

INCOME ↑

Upper-Upper	0.3%
Lower-Upper	1.2%
Upper-Middle	12.5%
Middle Class	32%
Working Class	38%
Lower But Not Lowest	9%
Real Lower-Lower	7%

Measurement of Social Class

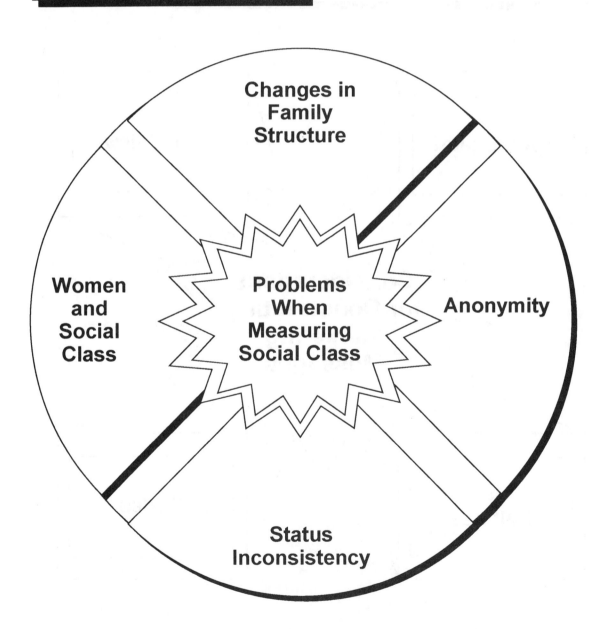

Changes in Family Structure

Women and Social Class

Problems When Measuring Social Class

Anonymity

Status Inconsistency

How Social Class Affects Purchase Decisions

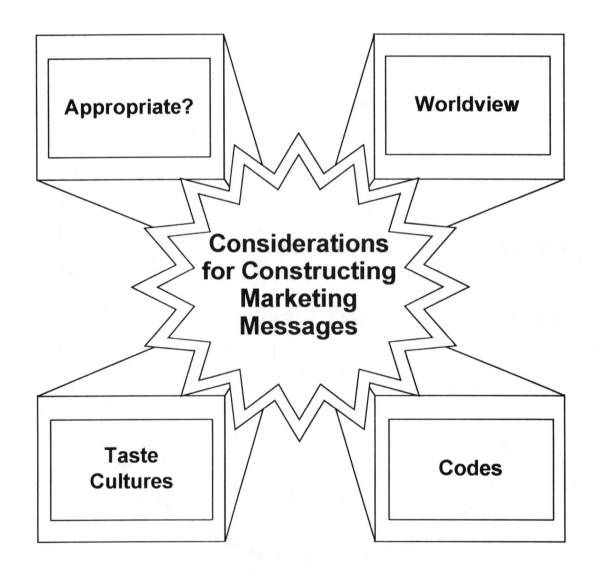

Appropriate?

Worldview

Considerations for Constructing Marketing Messages

Taste Cultures

Codes

Status Symbols

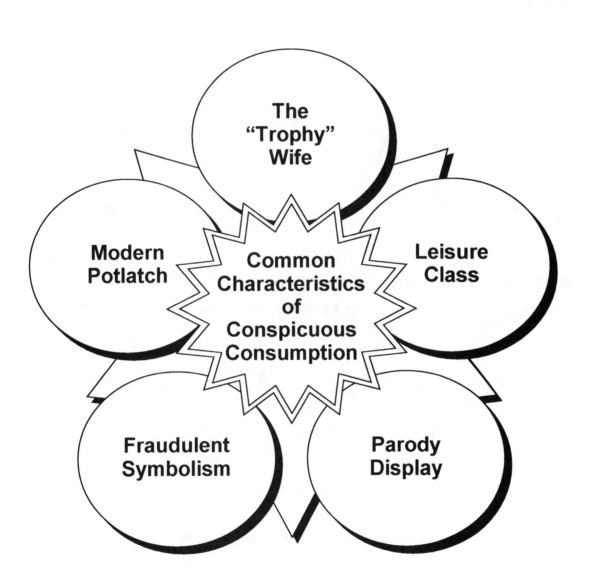

Subcultures

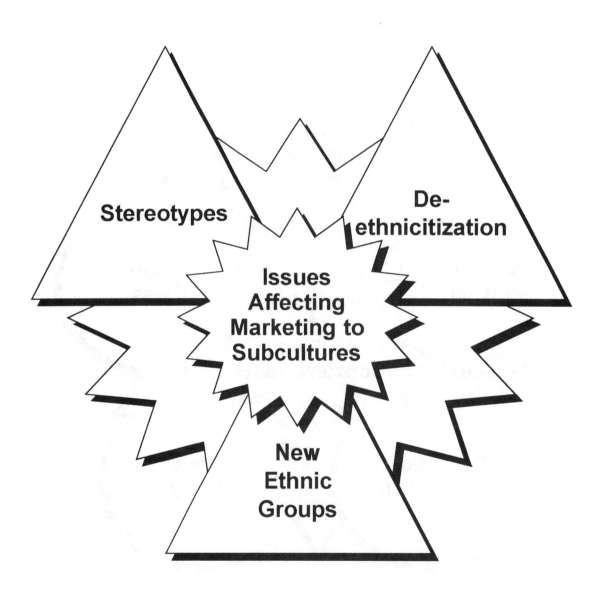

Stereotypes

De-ethnicitization

Issues Affecting Marketing to Subcultures

New Ethnic Groups

African-Americans

Mainstream Media

Black-Oriented Media

Black Celebrities

Black/White Consumption Differences

Targeted Advertising

The BUPPIE

Family Emphasis

Hispanic-Americans

Role of
the Church

Segmentation

Role of
the Family

The
Hispanic
Market

Progressive
Learning

Hispanic
Identity

Acculturation
&
Integration

Asian-Americans

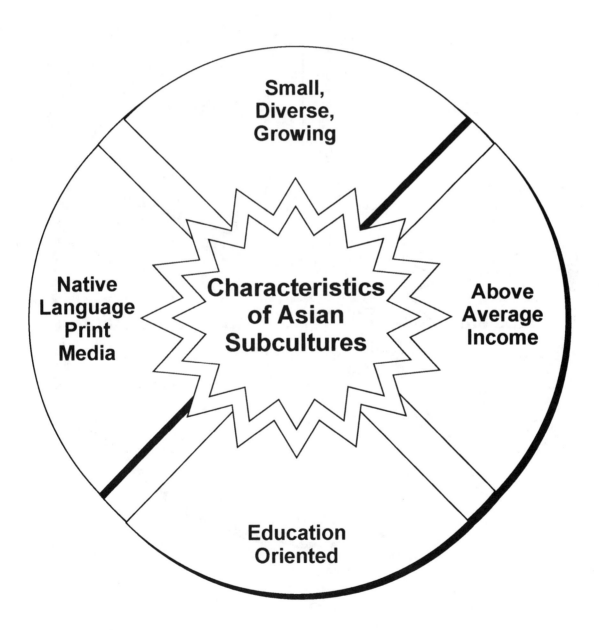

Religious Subcultures

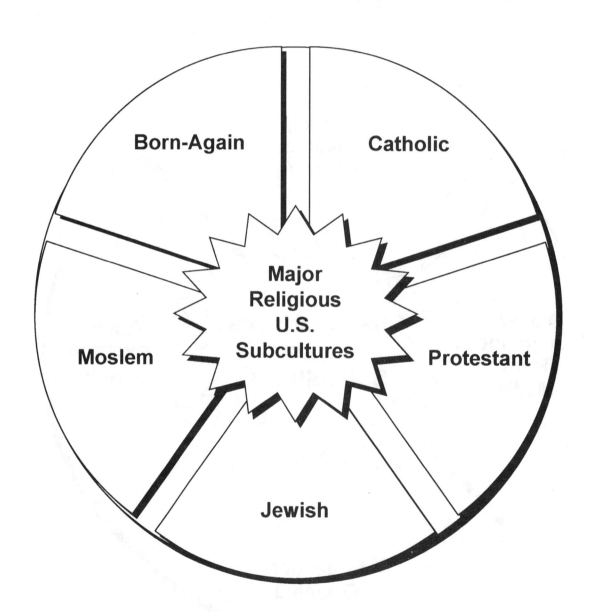

Age and Consumer Identity

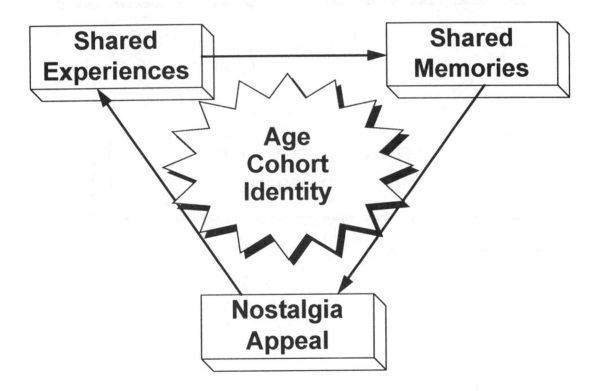

The Teen Market

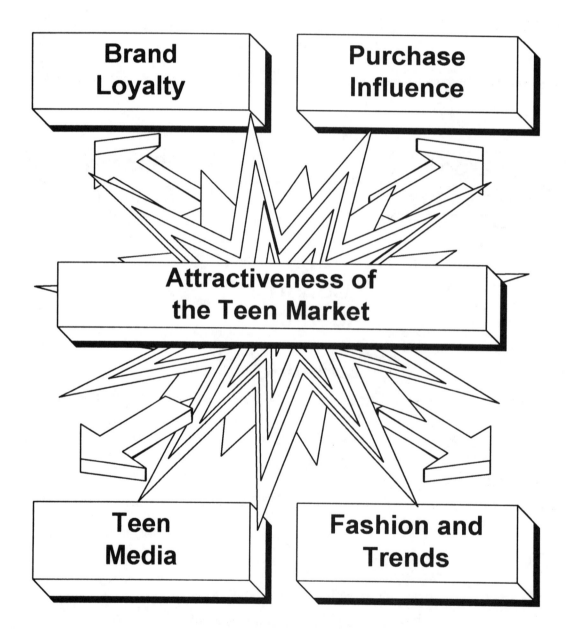

Brand Loyalty

Purchase Influence

Attractiveness of the Teen Market

Teen Media

Fashion and Trends

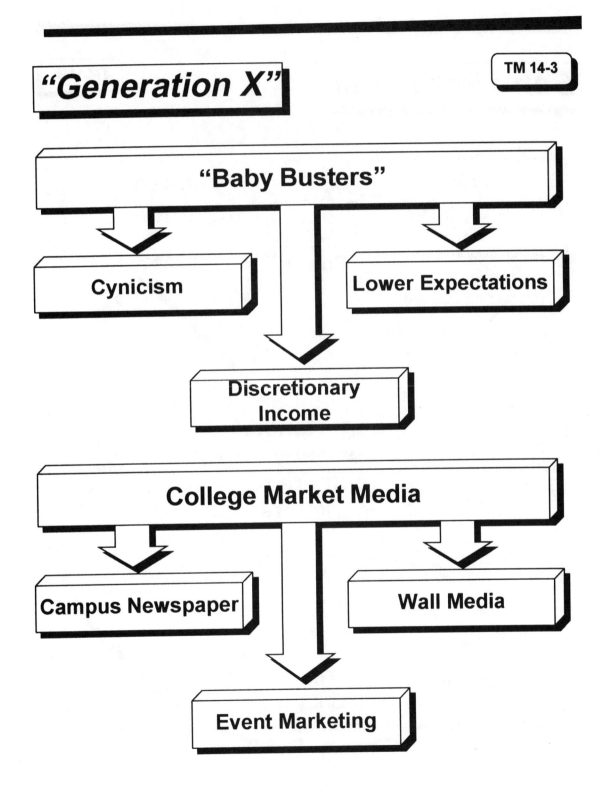

"Generation X"

"Baby Busters"

- Cynicism
- Lower Expectations

Discretionary Income

College Market Media

- Campus Newspaper
- Wall Media

Event Marketing

Baby Boomers

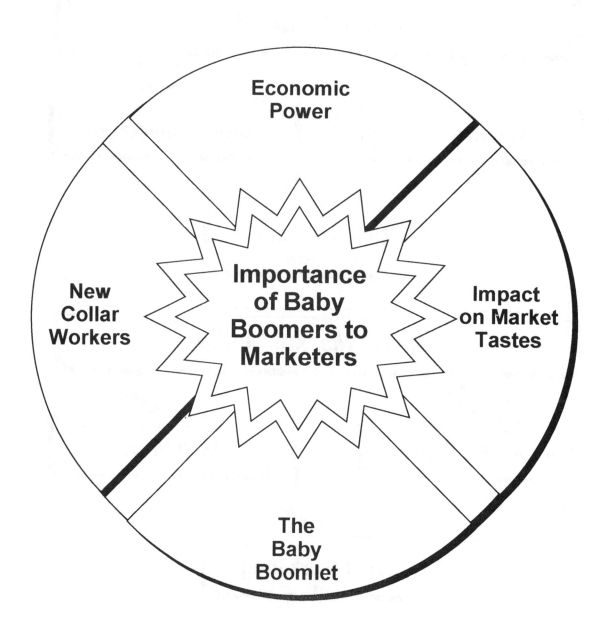

Economic Power

New Collar Workers

Importance of Baby Boomers to Marketers

Impact on Market Tastes

The Baby Boomlet

The Gray Market

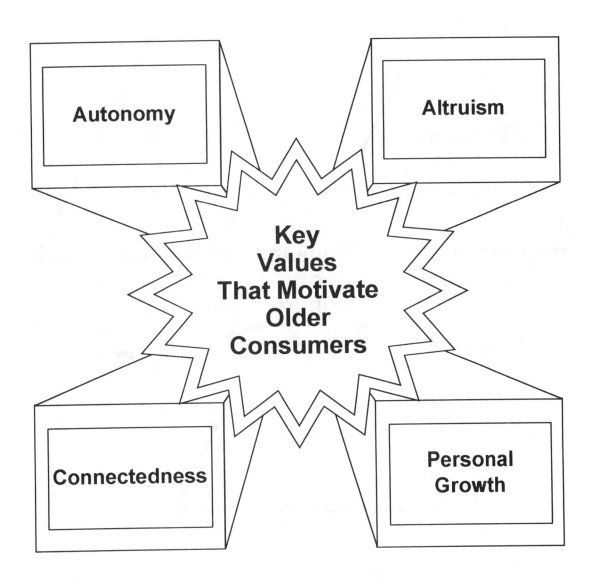

Autonomy

Altruism

Key
Values
That Motivate
Older
Consumers

Connectedness

Personal
Growth

Aspects of Culture

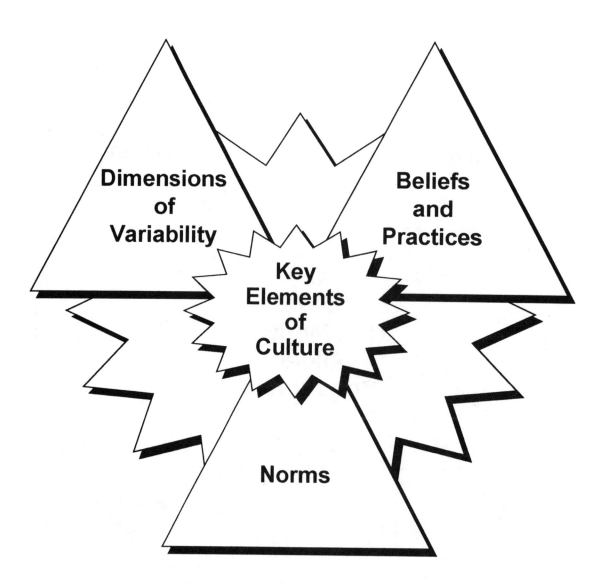

Myths

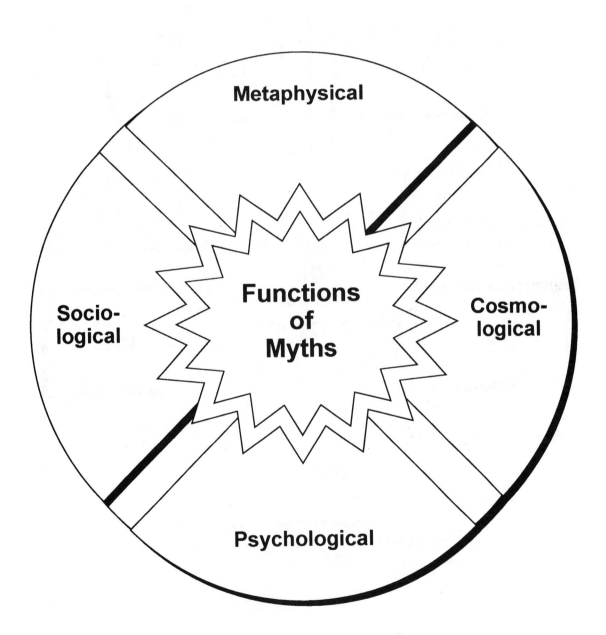

Functions of Myths
- Metaphysical
- Cosmo-logical
- Psychological
- Socio-logical

Rituals

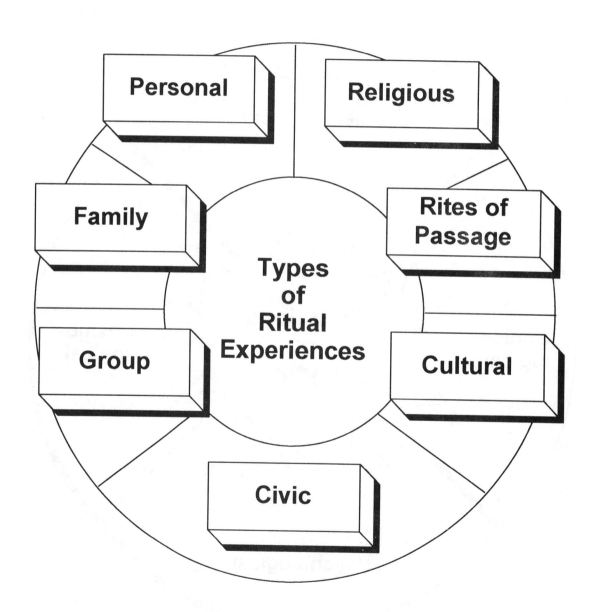

Culture Production System

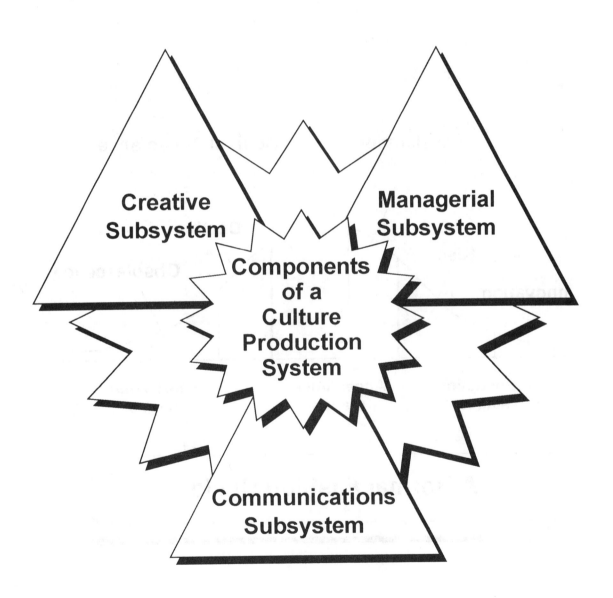

Creative Subsystem

Managerial Subsystem

Components of a Culture Production System

Communications Subsystem

The Fashion System

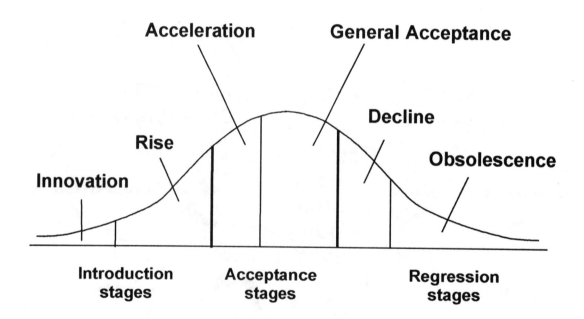

Acceleration General Acceptance

Rise Decline

Innovation Obsolescence

Introduction Acceptance Regression
stages stages stages

A Normal Fashion Cycle

Lifestyle and Consumption

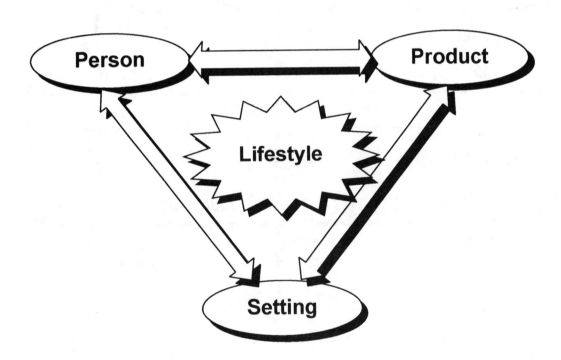

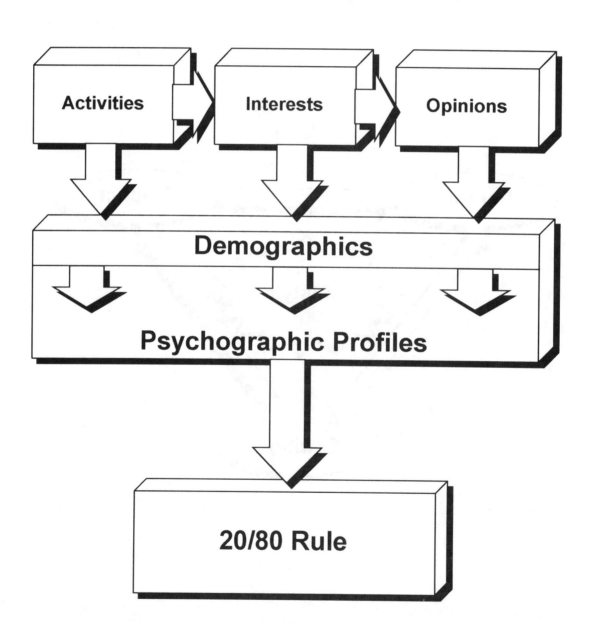

Activities → Interests → Opinions

Demographics

Psychographic Profiles

20/80 Rule

VALS 2

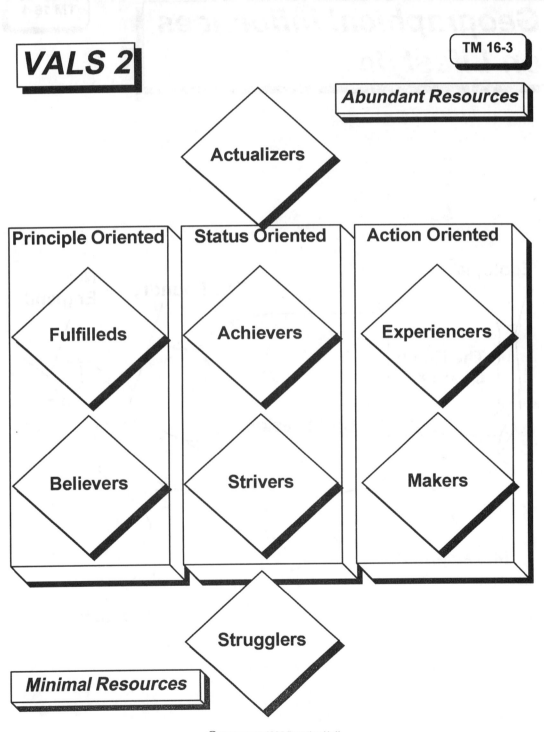

Actualizers

Principle Oriented

Status Oriented

Action Oriented

Fulfilleds

Achievers

Experiencers

Believers

Strivers

Makers

Strugglers

Minimal Resources

Geographical Influences on Lifestyle

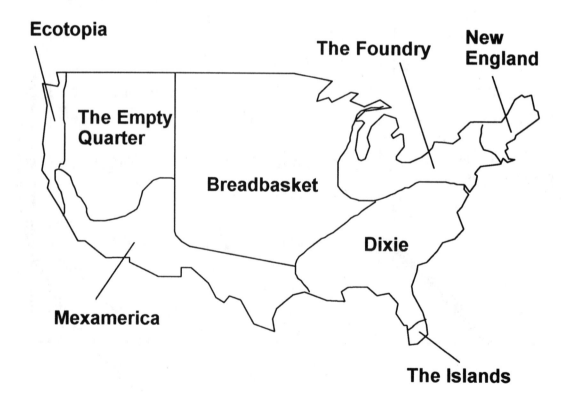

Ecotopia

The Foundry

New England

The Empty Quarter

Breadbasket

Dixie

Mexamerica

The Islands

Global Marketing and Culture

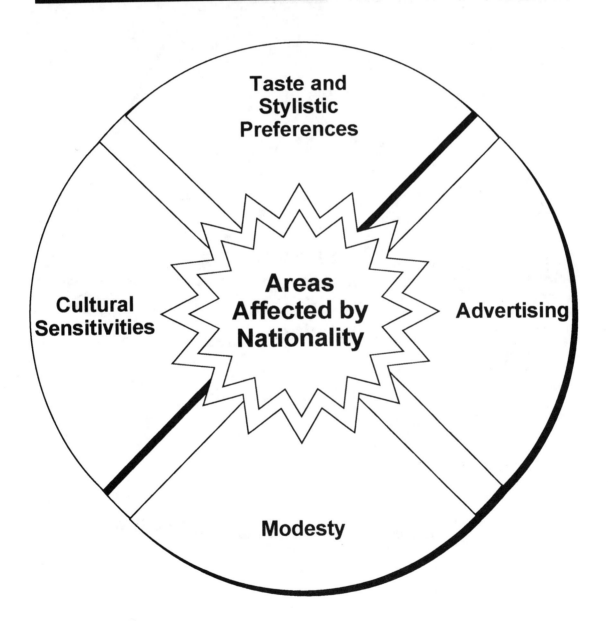

Taste and Stylistic Preferences

Cultural Sensitivities

Areas Affected by Nationality

Advertising

Modesty

The Domains of
Sacred Consumption

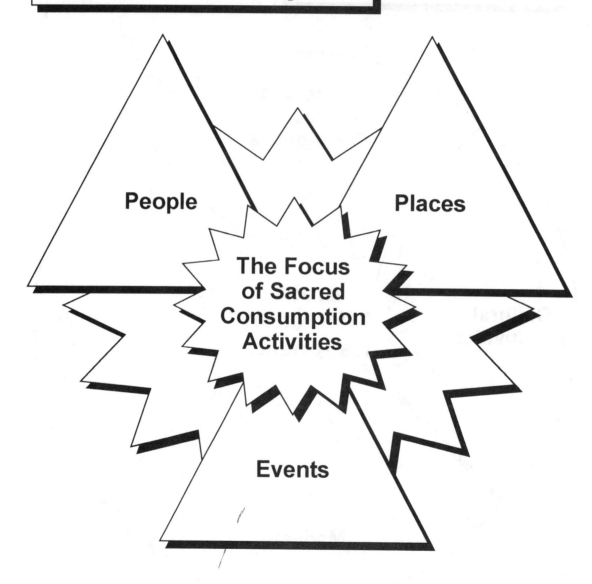

People

Places

The Focus
of Sacred
Consumption
Activities

Events

Sacred and Profane Consumption

Sacralization

The process by which ordinary objects take on sacred meaning to a culture or group.

The process by which a sacred item or symbol is removed from its special place and produced in mass quantities.

Desacralization

The Dark Side of Consumer Behavior

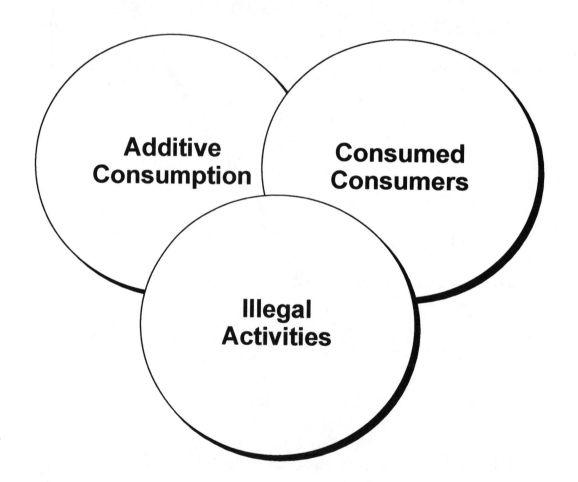

Additive Consumption

Consumed Consumers

Illegal Activities

Blurred Boundaries

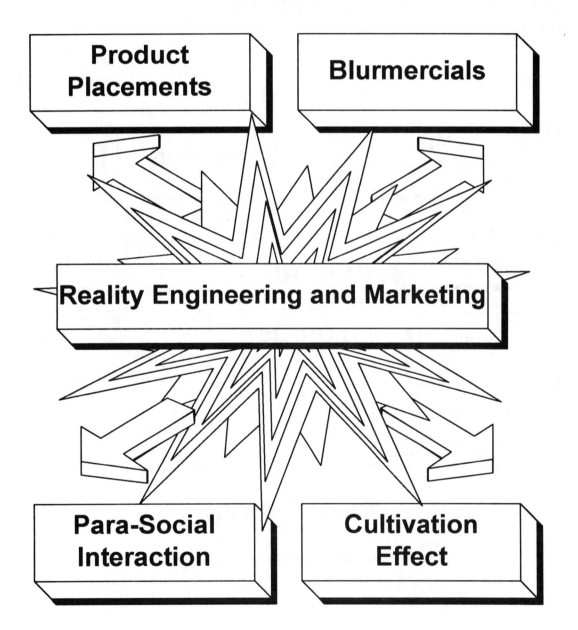

- Product Placements
- Blurmercials
- Reality Engineering and Marketing
- Para-Social Interaction
- Cultivation Effect

Major Consumer Trends

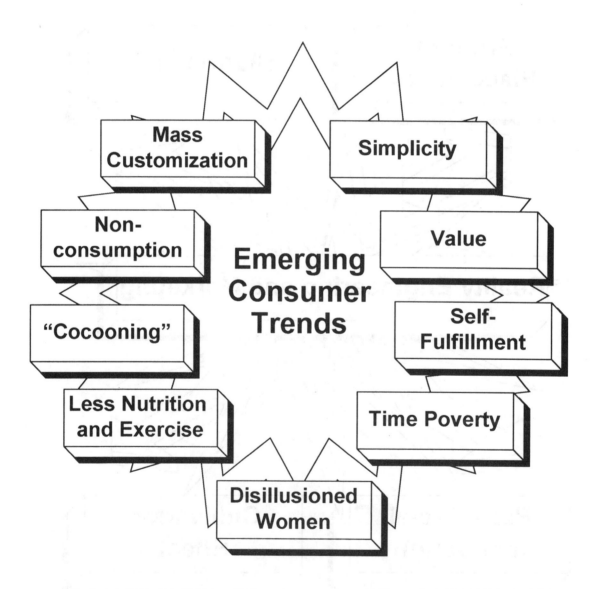